Can I Really Have a Relationship with God?

Is Anybody There?

Marion Duckworth, Fran and Jill Sciacca

Free Gifts for Everybody!

Ray Johnston and Gary Wilde

Going Against the Flow

Mike Yaconelli and John Duckworth

David C Cook

transforming lives together

CAN I REALLY HAVE A RELATIONSHIP WITH GOD?
Published by David C. Cook
4050 Lee Vance View
Colorado Springs, CO 80918 USA

David C. Cook Distribution Canada
55 Woodslee Avenue, Paris, Ontario, Canada N3L 3E5

David C. Cook U.K., Kingsway Communications
Eastbourne, East Sussex BN23 6NT, England

David C. Cook and the graphic circle C logo are registered
trademarks of Cook Communications Ministries.

Editorial Manager: Doug Schmidt
Product Developer: Karen Pickering
Series creator: John Duckworth
Series editor: Randy Southern
Designer: Bill Paetzold
Cover Designer: Granite Design
Interior Design: Becky Hawley Design, Inc.

Unit 1: Is Anybody There?
Editor: Sharon Stultz
Writers: Marion Duckworth, Fran and Jill Sciacca
Option writers: Stan Campbell, Nelson E. Copeland, Jr.,
and Ellen Larson
Inside illustrator: Al Hering

Unit 2: Free Gifts for Everybody!
Editor: Randy Southern
Writers: Gary Wilde, Ray Johnston
Option writers: Stan Campbell, Sue Reck, Randy Southern,
and Mark Syswerda
Inside illustrator: Jackie Besteman

Unit 3: Going Against the Flow
Editor: Randy Southern
Writers: John Duckworth, Mike Yaconelli
Option writers: Stan Campbell, John Duckworth, Sue
Reck, and Randy Southern
Inside illustrator: Jackie Besteman

Unless otherwise noted, Scripture quotations are from the
Holy Bible, New International Version®. Copyright © 1973,
1978, 1984 by International Bible Society. Used by permission of Zondervan. All rights reserved.

ISBN 978-0-7814-4090-5

First Printing 2003
Printed in the United States

4 5 6 7 8 9 10 11 12 13
110708

Contents

Capy Pg - 99
64 Pg - 121 Green Book
Capy Pg - 179

How to Customize Your Curriculum

We know your time is valuable. That's why we've made **Custom Curriculum** as easy as possible. Follow the three steps outlined below to create custom lessons that will meet the needs of *your* group. Let's get started!

 Read the basic lesson plan.

Every session in this book has four to six steps designed to meet five goals. It's important to understand these five goals as you choose the options for your group.

Getting Together

The goal for Getting Together is to break the ice. It may involve a fun way to introduce the lesson.

Getting Thirsty

The goal for Getting Thirsty is to earn students' interest before you dive into the Bible. Why should students care about your topic? Why should they care what the Bible has to say about it? This will motivate your students to dig deeper.

Getting the Word

The goal for Getting the Word is to find out what God has to say about the topic they care about. By exploring and discussing carefully selected passages, you'll help students find out how God's Word applies to their lives.

Getting the Point

The goal for Getting the Point is to make the leap from ideals and principles to real-world situations students are likely to face. It may involve practicing biblical principles with case studies or roleplays.

Getting Personal

The goal for Getting Personal is to help each group member respond to the lesson with a specific action. What should group members do as a result of this session? This step will help each person find a specific "next step" response that works for him or her.

2 Consider your options.

Every **Custom Curriculum** session gives you 14 different types of options. How do you choose? First, take a look at the list of option categories below. Then spend some time thinking and praying about your group. How do your students learn best? What kind of goals have you set for your group? Put a check mark by the options that you're most interested in.

 Extra Action—for groups that like physical challenges and learn better when they're moving, interacting, and experiencing the lesson.

 Media—to spice up your meeting with video, music, or other popular media.

 Heard It All Before—for fresh approaches that get past the defenses of students who are jaded by years in church.

 Little Bible Background—to use when most of your students are strangers to the Bible or haven't yet made a Christian commitment.

 Extra Fun—for longer, more "festive" youth meetings where additional emphasis is put on having fun.

 Fellowship and Worship—for building deeper relationships or enabling students to praise God together.

 Mostly Girls—to address girls' concerns and to substitute activities girls might prefer.

 Mostly Guys—to address guys' concerns and to substitute activities guys might prefer.

 Small Group—for adapting activities that might be tough with groups of fewer than eight students.

 Large Group—to alter steps for groups of more than 20 students.

 Urban—for fitting sessions to urban facilities and multiethnic (especially African-American) concerns.

 Short Meeting Time—tips for condensing the meeting. The standard meeting is designed to last 45 to 60 minutes. These include options to cut, replace, or trim time off the standard steps.

 Combined Junior High/High School—to use when you're mixing age levels but an activity or case study would be too "young" or "old" for part of the group.

 Sixth Grade—appearing only in junior high/middle school volumes, this option helps you change steps that sixth graders might find hard to understand or relate to.

 Extra Challenge—appearing only in high school volumes, this option lets you crank up the voltage for students who are ready for more Scripture or more demanding personal application.

3 *Customize your curriculum!*

Here's a simple, three-step plan to customize each session for your group:

1. Choose your options.

As you read the basic session plan, you'll see icons in the margin. Each icon represents a different type of option. When you see an icon, it means that type of option is offered for that step. The five pages of options are found after the Repro Resource student pages for each session. Turn to the option noted by the icon and you'll see that option explained.

Let's say you have a small group, mostly guys who get bored if they don't keep moving. You'll want to keep an eye out for three kinds of options: Small Group, Mostly Guys, and Extra Action. As you read the basic session, you might spot icons that tell you there are Small Group options for Step 1 and Step 3—maybe a different way to play a game so that you don't need big teams, and a way to cover several Bible passages when just a few kids are looking them up. Then you see icons telling you that there are Mostly Guys options for Step 2 and Step 4—perhaps a substitute activity that doesn't require too much self-disclosure, and a case study guys will relate to. Finally you see icons indicating Extra Action options for Step 2 and Step 3—maybe an active way to get kids' opinions instead of handing out a survey, and a way to act out some verses instead of just looking them up.

2. Use the checklist.

Once you've picked your options, keep track of them with the simple checklist at the end of the option section (just before the start of the next session plan). This little form gives you a place to write down the materials you'll need too—since they depend on the options you've chosen.

3. Get your stuff together.

Gather your materials; photocopy any Repro Resources (reproducible student sheets) you've decided to use. And…you're ready!

Unit One: Is Anybody There?

Relationship Deficiency Syndrome

by Fran and Jill Sciacca

Most teens are emotionally driven and motivated by personal experience rather than advice or education. Their feelings steer their lives. And their lives tend to migrate toward that which they feel, hear, taste, touch, and see. That translates into an obvious preference for the real world of people and events over that of the supernatural world that they cannot grasp.

So the idea of cultivating a relationship with someone (God) they cannot see, hear, or touch is foreign, impractical, and often undesirable. It involves too much effort, they believe, with too few immediate, tangible dividends.

Meaningful relationships are not an abundant commodity, particularly from the viewpoint of most young people. Many have been disillusioned by divorced parents, fractured families, fickle friends, or authority figures who have morally or ethically disappointed them. To invest in a deep relationship may seem like a sure way to get hurt, let down, or both.

As you prepare to lead these sessions in *Is Anybody There?* realize that you are working with a generation that has been shortchanged. These young people lack role models, methods, and meaning in human relationships. Though most adults agree that our young people have been pampered more than any previous generation, we fail to see that their lack of interpersonal skills is a result of broken significant relationships in their lives. On the other hand, it is also true that young people *yearn* for depth in relationships. They *fear* it, yet they *seek* it.

Failure in the realm of human relationships makes success in the world of spiritual relationships difficult to understand. This is somewhat true for all of us. Sometimes we expect God to treat us as harshly as some hurtful, significant person in our lives has done. Thus, the potential for impact as you work through *Is Anybody There?* is profound!

You have the unique opportunity to introduce teens to an abiding friend who will never fail them. You stand in a place of privilege. The Lord can use you to be His vehicle to virtually transform the way a young person sees God and learns to relate to Him. Present a relationship unlike any other he or she has ever known or believed possible—one that is permanent, dependable, deeply personal, and meaningful.

The following are some helpful "big picture" insights. They are designed to color and clarify your perception as you study the concepts of *Is Anybody There?* They will prepare you to see this curriculum from the viewpoint of the learner as well as the leader.

Half of an Orange Is __Not__ an Orange!

One morning I walked into my classroom of high-school juniors carrying half of an orange. As the pre-bell chatter began to dwindle, I held up the fruit and asked, "What do I have in my hand?"

"An orange!" said one indignant student.

"Nice try," I responded, "but not correct."

A wave of whispers rolled over the room as these astute young people tried to determine if I was merely massaging their minds or if they had really missed it.

"This is *not* an orange. It's half of an orange," I said. After some arguing, they agreed that I was right. What half of an orange is is determined by what a *whole* orange is. By now, you're probably perplexed, wondering what this has to do with cultivating a relationship with God. It has a *lot* to do with it!

Most young people in your group are probably "half orange" people. When it comes to what is real, they believe that the material world is real and the supernatural world is either less real or real in a different sense. Subconsciously they assume that the world inhabited by God, angels, and the spirits of departed people is not as real or as understandable as the world in which they live. As you work through the sessions in *Is Anybody There?* try to help your group members gain a fresh understanding of the following key concepts.

- The immaterial, spiritual world is as real as the material world.
- Being comfortable in the material world makes it seem more real to me. But my goal must be to learn how to become more at home in the spiritual world.
- As a Christian, I live in both worlds simultaneously. I do not have to go through some sort of entry procedure to connect with the world where God dwells. Both are related. What I do in one is not distinct from what happens in the other. Prayer, evangelism—all Christian living is carried out in both at the same time.
- If reality consists of both worlds, then we as Christians are the only people living in the "real world"! This is a tough concept, but a crucial one, because many teens consider the real world as the one enjoyed by nonbelievers. They feel stuck in a second-class world full of rules. Help them see that the real world is *not* the one where there are no boundaries or consequences. The *nonbeliever* actually abides in the fantasy world because he or she denies the existence of the supernatural.

Your goal is to get your group members to feel more aware of and at home in the spiritual world they are already in. God is with them at home, at school, in the lunchroom, on the sports field—even in the restroom!

Young people want to compartmentalize their lives into their "Christian life" (the way they act at church) and their "other life" (the way they act away from church). But these two worlds must be brought together in their minds because they *are* together. God is with your young people constantly. He watches them, wants to speak to them, help them, and have them obey Him.

As a high school Bible teacher, I tackle this compartmentalizing dilemma daily. Recently a student addressed a high school assembly about his summer missions trip to the former Soviet Union. Over there (in his "Christian life"), sacrifices for young believers were made easily. Several weeks into school this fall, however, this same student (in his "other life") made an underclassman and younger believer give up his bed and sleep on the floor at a weekend retreat so that he could have the whole bed! He apparently felt no tension and failed to see that his relationship with God in Kiev, which prompted his sacrifices for new Christians, should also be the driving force in *all* of his relationships *all* of the time.

In His Image, Start to Finish

A precious biblical truth in regard to cultivating a relationship with God is that we are made "in His . . . image" (Gen. 1:27). God does not have a physical body (John 4:24), so this image must have to do with that unseen part of us that really determines who we are as individuals. Simply put, God and I have something in common. I am not God, or even *a* god. But, I am "like God" in terms of who I am.

Therefore, my ability to feel, think, communicate, decide, choose, and a host of other human activities are actually abilities I share with God Himself. Young people need to know that God made us this way so that we could have a moment-by-moment relationship with Him. We can talk to Him, tell Him our feelings and fears. He understands our darkest thoughts—not because He feels the same way we do, but because He does feel, think, and choose.

Jesus Christ, God in a body, demonstrates this truth in Technicolor. We see in Christ all that humanity ought to be. Jesus took upon Himself our humanity to redeem us. But He did not sacrifice His deity in the process.

Cultivating a personal relationship with the God in whose image we were created not only makes sense, it is also the deepest cry of a person's soul, both for the young and the old. People were *made* for this relationship. We know that something is amiss without it. As you work through *Is Anybody There?* hold before your group a relationship that is attainable, permanent, and fulfilling. In fact, you can do so with confidence, knowing that it is the very thing for which you were created.

Communicate that "walking with God" is an awesome adventure in the real world. It is not simply a code of conduct that you live at church and then leave there. God loves us and deeply desires a moment-by-moment relationship with us. He wants to enter every area of our lives and reveal Himself to us. He awaits our call. To the lonely, sometimes perplexing question "Is anybody there?" we answer "Yes! Always!"

Fran and Jill Sciacca have been involved with youth ministry for nearly two decades. Fran has been teaching high school Bible since 1980 in a large Christian school serving students from over 180 local churches. Jill has a degree in journalism and sociology and is a full-time homemaker and freelance writer/editor.

The images on these two pages are designed to help you promote this course within your church and community. Feel free to photocopy anything here and adapt it to fit your publicity needs. The stuff on this page could be used as a flier that you send or hand out to kids—or as a bulletin insert. The stuff on the next page could be used to add visual interest to newsletters, calendars, bulletin boards, or other promotions. Be creative and have fun!

Is Anybody There?

How can we know if God is really there?
How close does God want us to be to Him?
If God speaks, why do we have so much trouble hearing Him?
How does the Holy Spirit "live" in us?
What does it really mean to "walk" with God?
We'll be looking at questions like these as we begin a new series called *Is Anybody There?* Come and learn how to strengthen your most important relationship.

Who:

When:

Where:

Questions? Call:

Unit One: Is Anybody There?

Can we prove that God exists?

Is anybody there?

(Write your own message in the speech balloon.)

Does God really speak to us?

How Do I Know He's Really There?

YOUR GOALS FOR THIS SESSION:

Choose one or more

☐ To help kids recognize that it makes sense to believe in God.

☐ To help kids understand that God is interested in them.

☐ To give kids an opportunity to establish or renew their relationship with God as Father.

☐ Other:_____

_____

Your Bible Base:

Isaiah 55:6-7
Acts 17:24-28
Galatians 3:26—4:7
Ephesians 1:4-5

STEP 1

What Is Real?

(Needed: Cut-apart copy of Repro Resource 1)

OPTIONS

Have group members form two teams. Instruct the teams to face each other. Distribute half of the descriptions from "Astonishing Animals" (Repro Resource 1) to Team A and half to Team B. Explain that some of the descriptions are real and some are fake. Team A is to read aloud a description as convincingly as possible and Team B is to guess whether the animal is real or fake, based on the description. Then Team B will read a description and Team A will guess. Continue until the teams run out of descriptions. The team with the most correct guesses at the end of the game wins.

Afterward, ask: **How hard was it to decide whether the animals were real or not? If it was difficult, what made it difficult?** (Some group members might say it was difficult because *all* of the animals sounded pretty weird and amazing.)

How might these animals point to the existence of a Creator? (They're so unusual, unique, and creatively formed that it seems logical to believe that only a divine Creator could have made them.)

What are some other things that seem to point to the existence of a Creator? (The human body, the stars and the universe, trees and plant life, etc.) If no one mentions it, suggest that the Bible is a piece of evidence testifying to God's existence.

Let's say that God really does exist. So what? Why should it matter to us? Get as many responses as possible.

Who Is God, Anyway?

(Needed: Chalkboard and chalk or newsprint and marker, index cards, pencils, paper)

Write the following unfinished sentences on the board.
• "Sometimes I feel as though God is . . ."
• "I wish that God . . ."

Distribute index cards and pencils. Have group members complete the sentences and return the cards to you. They should not write their names on the cards. After you've collected the cards, shuffle them and read them aloud. Use the following suggestions to supplement group members' responses.

• Sometimes I feel as though God is "mad at me"; "not interested in me"; "far away"; "frightening"; etc.

• I wish that God "was visible"; "talked to me"; "was easier to get to know"; etc.

Explain: **People often feel that God is far away, that He doesn't care about them, or that He is too important to be interested in them. If you feel that way, you're normal. But you also need to take a look at facts about God. Let's see what Scripture says about God's relationship with us.**

Write the following questions and Scripture references on the board:

1. Why should I think about God anyway? (Acts 17:24-28)

2. Where is God and how does He want me to act toward Him? (Isa. 55:6-7)

3. What kind of relationship does God want to have with me and how does it begin? (Gal. 3:26–4:7)

Have group members form three teams. Assign each team one of the questions on the board. Instruct each team to look up its assigned passage and answer the question, using personal pronouns like "I" and "me" in their responses. Distribute paper and pencils to each team so team members can record their answers.

Give the teams several minutes to work. When they're finished, have each team share its response. Use the following suggestions to supplement the teams' answers.

(1) I should think about God because He is my Creator and decides when and where people should live. He wants me to think about Him and reach out to Him. He is the source of my life.

O P T I O N S

HEARD IT ALL BEFORE

LITTLE BIBLE BACKGROUND

MOSTLY GIRLS

SHORT MEETING TIME

JR. HIGH / HIGH SCHOOL COMBINED

EXTRA CHALLENGE

(2) He is not far from me and wants me to reach out to Him, seek Him, pray, turn from sin, and turn to Him for forgiveness.

(3) God wants to be my Father and wants me to be His son or daughter. He wants to make me an heir of all He owns. I can become His son or daughter when I place my personal faith in Jesus Christ as Savior.

Say: **If you were drowning in a lake or hanging from a cliff and a hand reached out to save you, you would really want to have a relationship with that hand. A relationship with that hand—and its owner—would be of prime importance to you at that moment. So why do you think God wants to have a relationship with people, even though we're not critical to His survival?**

If your group members have trouble coming up with answers, give them the following Scripture passages to look up. Or even if they have some ideas, they may not be able to come up with evidence from Scripture. In that case, you can write their ideas on the board, give them the references to look up, and have them match their statements with the appropriate references.

Here are some reasons why God wants to have a relationship with us:

- We were chosen according to His will (Eph. 1:11).
- It gives Him pleasure (Eph. 1:5).
- The result of not having a relationship with Him now is separation from Him forever. God does not want anyone to suffer that fate (2 Pet. 3:9).
- He loves us (Eph. 2:4-7).

Tell about repair on or hell - away from God.

A Special Relationship

Have your group members sit in a circle on the floor for a brain-storming game. The object of the game is to list as many "famous pairs" as possible. Each person will have five seconds to name a famous pair. If he or she cannot name one or names a pair that has already been used, he or she is out. Continue the game until only one person remains.

Write group members' responses on the board as they are named. Use the following suggestions to supplement their ideas.

- Bert and Ernie (from *Sesame Street*)
- Peanut butter and jelly
- Batman and Robin
- Road Runner and Wile E. Coyote
- Abbott and Costello
- Burgers and fries
- Chip and Dale
- DeGarmo and Key (Christian recording artists)
- Mickey Mouse and Minnie Mouse
- Wayne and Garth (from *Wayne's World*)
- David and Goliath

Briefly discuss the relationship that the members of each pair have with each other. For example, you could point out that the Road Runner and Wile E. Coyote have an antagonistic relationship, to say the least, because one is always trying to eat the other.

After you've had some fun with this activity, get group members thinking about their relationships with God by adding "God and I" to the list on the board. Have group members think about which pair relationship listed on the board is most similar to their relationship with God. For example, some group members may think that their relationship with God is antagonistic, like the relationship between David and Goliath. Others may think their relationship with God is more like that of Bert and Ernie—a friendship. Invite volunteers to explain their ideas, but don't pressure anyone.

Afterward, say: **God wants to have a relationship with all of us. But His relationship with each one of us is unique because we are so different from one another. Nobody else has your DNA. Nobody else has your fingerprints. Nobody else has your exact personality. So nobody else can have the exact relationship with God that you can have.**

OPTIONS

EXTRA ACTION

LARGE GROUP

LITTLE BIBLE BACKGROUND

MOSTLY GUYS

EXTRA FUN

MEDIA

URBAN

Let's take a look at how different we are. Then we'll be able to better understand why our relationships with God are unique.

Label one side of the room "A" and the other side "B." Explain that you will be reading several pairs of opposite personality characteristics ("A" and "B"). After you read each pair, group members will move to the "A" side of the room if Characteristic A best describes them. They will move to the "B" side of the room if Characteristic B best describes them. Group members will move from one side of the room to the other as often as necessary as you go through the list. If some kids say that neither statement applies, tell them to choose the one that they identify with most or stand somewhere between the two points.

(1) **Characteristic A—I can yak it up with the best of them.**
Characteristic B—I'm pretty quiet.

(2) **Characteristic A—I like to read.**
Characteristic B—If it weren't for the TV listings, I probably wouldn't read at all.

(3) **Characteristic A—I laugh easily.**
Characteristic B—I don't laugh very often.

(4) **Characteristic A—I flip through TV channels a lot.**
Characteristic B—I can't stand it when people flip through TV channels.

(5) **Characteristic A—I'm pretty trusting of other people.**
Characteristic B—I'm pretty suspicious of other people.

(6) **Characteristic A—I am neat and tidy.**
Characteristic B—I usually just drop my things wherever I happen to be.

(7) **Characteristic A—I enjoy watching sports on TV.**
Characteristic B—I think watching sports on TV is a boring waste of time.

(8) **Characteristic A—I'm patient enough to untie a tangled knot in my shoelace.**
Characteristic B—I usually let knots stay knotted.

(9) **Characteristic A—I'm pretty good about controlling my temper.**
Characteristic B—I have a low boiling point and can "explode" easily.

(10) **Characteristic A—I'm most alert late at night.**
Characteristic B—I'm most alert early in the morning.

Afterward, say: **Most likely, no one else moved in the same pattern that you did from wall to wall. And even if someone did move the same as you, he or she still didn't have the same feelings about each statement as you did. For instance, concerning the first two statements, you may talk a lot more than a friend, yet you may have both leaned against the "yak it up" wall. The point is that we are all very different. So God deals with us differently.**

STEP
4

Coming Close

(Needed: Copies of Repro Resource 2)

Say: **Even though none of us can remember being born, there is one thing about it that you can know for sure: Not only was it tough on your mom, it was also probably tough on you. You probably were squeezed and pushed and twisted every which way. No doubt about it, being born was not easy!**

By the same token, you may feel that being born into God's family isn't easy either. You may feel as if God is a far-away stranger, despite what the Bible says. Let's take a look at a true story that might shed some light on what it takes to begin a relationship with God.

Distribute copies of "Jillian's Journey" (Repro Resource 2). After group members have had time to read the sheet, ask: **What similarity do you see between the way Jillian's relationship with her parents began and the way our relationship with God begins?** (Both begin with adoption.) Have someone read aloud Ephesians 1:4-5.

Then say: **Jillian was abused by foster parents so she was afraid to trust the Ryans. While God hasn't abused us, some kids might feel nervous about trusting Him. What might be some reasons?** (They might have some wrong ideas about God and don't know what He's really like. They might have had some bad things happen to them and blame God for it. People may have been mean to them, causing them to think that God acts the same way.)

What did Jillian's new parents do to change her mind? (They remained patient and kept showing their love for her.)

Point out that because God loves us, He waits for us to reach out to Him. If you think some of your group members need to accept Christ as Savior, read aloud John 1:12 and explain that they can receive Him into their lives today. Invite those who are interested to see you after the session is over.

Say: **Receiving Christ as Savior is only the beginning of your relationship. Once God is your Father, you'll spend the rest of your life getting to know Him better.**

As you wrap up the session, remind group members that the three principles in Acts 17:27 are always true. You may want to write them on the board:

1. God wants us to reach out to Him.
2. If we do, we will find Him.
3. He isn't far from each one of us.

Close the session in prayer, thanking God for choosing to reach out to us.

NOTES

Do

A̶ ...shing Animals

1. The m........................ful that it can break a person's b........

2. Some ba........................tons. (True)

3. Each year,........................ngs to sing to attract female........................(True)

4. The male crab........................om he chooses to mate.

5. Koko, a gorilla, w.......... its ...te .... .uman language. Koko also had a puppy for a pet. (Fals. Kok .art..... ...guage and had a kitten for a pet.)

6. When a female lobster sheds her shell, the male lobster eats it. (True)

7. The Japanese goldfish contains a poison so powerful that one drop can kill a human. (True)

- -

8. The cicada, an insect, lays its eggs in twigs. The young hatch and burrow into the ground where they stay 4-20 years, before emerging. (True)

9.The "sloth" is rightly named because it's lazy and dull-witted. (False. The sloth, whose name means "lazy," was thought to be that kind of animal. Now we know that it was designed to use as little energy as possible so it can survive on a diet of leaves.)

10. The tilapia macrocephala fish carries its fertilized eggs in its mouth and doesn't eat until the little ones are born. (True)

11. The guiana termite has a "squirt gun"-like appendage on its head, which it uses to "shoot" invaders. (True)

12. The mudskipper fish can climb trees. (True)

13. Cowbirds, appropriately named because they follow cattle and eat the grain the cattle leave, are among the best parents in the bird kingdom. (False. Cowbirds do follow cattle and eat grain, but they lay their eggs in the nests of other birds, hoping that the unsuspecting "foster parents" will raise their young.)

14. The necrophorus beetle is the "undertaker" of the insect world because it buries dead animals. (True)

Jillian's Journey

Jillian was adopted when she was eight years old. The Ryans, her new parents, were excited to have her as their daughter. One way they showed their excitement was by preparing a beautiful bedroom for her. In it, there were lots of toys and a desk of her own—complete with crayons, pencils, and paper.

"But my years of misery couldn't be erased by an adoption ceremony," Jillian recalls. "Hurt and anger still boiled inside me.

"I found that it is one thing to need love…

to want it desperately…

to cry for it…

but quite another thing to *accept* love when it is offered."

That's because, before age eight, Jillian had been rejected, humiliated, neglected, and abused by a series of foster parents. Once she was locked out of the house overnight to stay in the dark with "monsters."

Because of her bad experiences, it took Jillian years to be able to feel close to her parents and to accept their love. Now, though, she is able to do that.

Today, Jillian is a successful Christian recording artist who travels around the world telling others to let God love them. (From *Please, Somebody, Love Me!* by Jillian and Joseph A. Ryan, Baker Book House, Grand Rapids, MI, 1991.)

STEP 1

As soon as you finish the "Astonishing Animals" quiz on Repro Resource 1, ask: **What is something you can do that, if someone happened to see you do it, might qualify you for his or her list of astonishing animals?** Give group members a few minutes to think of an unusual talent or to find nearby props that might be needed. Make sure everyone knows that you're not expecting anything complicated. Most young people, however, have perfected particular sound effects, facial expressions, or goofy mannerisms—perhaps something handed down from parents. If time permits, let each person demonstrate his or her talent individually. If not, give a signal for everyone to *simultaneously* begin. (Try to position group members so that they can see everyone else while performing their own talents.)

STEP 3

Rather than have group members brainstorm the famous pairs, write the pairs down ahead of time on individual slips of paper (adding others of your own) and let group members play charades. Before you begin, pair up students and let them know in what order they are to participate. Each pair of students should quickly draw a slip from the "Famous Pairs" stack and assume the roles of the pair listed there. As soon as someone else guesses the famous pair, those two students should rejoin the group as the next two students *immediately* draw another slip from the pile. Try to maintain an intensity to the pace of this activity. Charades can drag if you allow it to, but it can generate a lot of activity if you keep the action going and make sure everyone stays involved.

STEP 1

Small groups often feel they cannot do things large groups do, so try to capitalize on opportunities you have that large groups *don't*. Since one of the themes running throughout this session is being aware that God is definitely nearer than we sometimes realize, consider going "on the road" to look for indications of His presence. If possible, borrow a van and hold your meeting as you drive along some back roads, parks, or other scenic areas. Your discussions and Bible study can be done as usual, but you will have the added opportunity to observe the wonders of creation as you drive around. Even the "A" and "B" sides of the room in Step 3 can be adapted to "Front" and "Back" of the van. (If you are the only adult, it is probably too much of a challenge to drive and teach at the same time, but you could still drive to a more remote spot, park, and then teach.)

STEP 4

Even if you don't choose to hold the meeting in a moving vehicle (see the "Small Group" option for Step 1), consider ending it by retiring to a small and confining space (a closet, the pastor's office, or some other tight area). Discuss how we sometimes take for granted the amount of "space" we have. (In some countries, the sidewalks, trains, buses, and so forth are almost always overcrowded.) But sometimes we begin to feel too removed from other people. As you stay packed closely together, the discussion of the discomfort of being born will likely take on a new reality. And as you end the session by reminding everyone that God isn't far from each one of us, the closeness will be an object lesson. End with a challenge: **The next time you feel isolated and alone, try to remember this feeling. God is always just this close. If we are willing to reach out, we discover that He is already right there.**

STEP 1

In a large group, don't use Repro Resource 1 as a handout. Rather, read one example at a time and let group members respond individually. To ensure complete honesty, have group members write down their answers. If your group is competitive, you could even make this an elimination game. Begin with everyone standing as you read the first description; then have each person record his or her answer. Those who answer correctly remain standing while the others sit down. Anyone standing at the end is certainly an unusual animal in his or her own right. And if everyone is sitting before the end of the list, start over again and give everyone another chance.

STEP 3

Pair up your group members before you get ready to brainstorm famous couples. Then, rather than have them name the couples, have the members of each pair strike a pose (simultaneously) to represent a famous couple they have thought of. As they hold the pose, go around the room and let the members of each pair say who they are portraying. The first time through, you will probably get some of the basic, expected couples. But with a large group, you can do this several times and create a long list of famous pairs in a short amount of time. The more times you do this, the more creative your students will be in coming up with pairs of people or things.

STEP 2

If your group members are well acquainted with the basics of God's love and availability, you might want to cover the same material by having them role-play a situation in which they are forced to share what they know—or think they know. Ask two volunteers to pretend that they are shipwrecked on an island where the natives have never heard about God. The natives, rather than being ignorant savages, should be very intelligent and sophisticated. The rest of the group members should play the natives, who observe the shipwrecked people thanking God for safety in reaching land and then begin to quiz the people about this "God" they were speaking to.

STEP 4

It is common for young people to think they know all about God—until their knowledge is questioned. Given time to prepare, they may come up with the right answers. But an unanticipated question might catch them off guard. If possible, try to arrange a "plant" to sit through the session—someone your group members think is a first-time visitor, but who actually is a young, mature Christian from another church. The person should absorb what is discussed throughout the session. Then as the meeting draws to a close, he or she should ask these questions:
• "How can you guys be so sure that God exists when you can't see Him?"
• "Do you really believe that just thinking about God brings Him closer?"
• "Even if God exists, do you expect me to believe that He cares about a regular person like me?"
• "Are you telling me that my life is going to change drastically if I just decide today that I'm going to believe in God and follow Christ? Just how does that work?"

When the questions begin, quickly toss them to the group to handle. When you ask the questions, your kids probably feel pretty sure about the answers. But see how well they do when the questions are being asked by a total stranger.

STEP 2

Even though each portion of Scripture in this section is short, there are quite a few references for group members who don't know their way around the Bible very well. To make this step a bit less intimidating for such students, you might consider simply talking your way through the questions and answers, focusing on just one or two of the passages you feel are most important to your group members. Then, at the end of the session, provide lists of the Bible passages you used during the session. (Or provide a single list and let everyone copy down the passages.) Challenge students to use these verses/passages as texts for personal devotions during the week as they continue to think about the things you have discussed. (Appropriately, there are seven separate Bible references given in this section.) As inexperienced group members begin to explore the Bible on their own—at their own pace—they will become more comfortable with Bible study.

STEP 3

If your group members don't know much about God, it may be difficult for them to think in terms of a close relationship with someone they cannot see, hear, or feel. You might want to deal with the concept of God by having kids try to think in terms of a perfect parent. Could they relate to a parent who loved them no matter what they did wrong? One who could discipline them without yelling or making them feel worthless? One who cared about their innermost hopes, dreams, and fears? Tie this concept into a challenge for increased Bible involvement. Say: **We aren't given instruction manuals to know how we need to relate to our parents. But we do have a wonderful manual to show us how we can have the best possible relationship with our perfect heavenly parent.** If group members see the personal benefit, rather than the obligation of Bible study, they may be willing to become more involved.

STEP 1

Before you ask group members to list things that seem to point to the existence of a Creator, lay out a large piece of newsprint and have them create a "reminder mural." Rather than *naming* things, have group members *draw* them instead. It should be fairly simple to illustrate the stars and universe on one portion of the mural as well as the earthly reminders in another portion. Keep your mural in view as you go through this session (and any other sessions in this series) as a reminder of things to be thankful for. Your students can continue to add items to the mural as they continue their study of God's presence in their lives.

STEP 4

After you read Jillian's story on Repro Resource 2, keep the discussion on a personal level rather than a spiritual one as you deal with the concept of adoption. Ask: **If you were being adopted, what do you think would be your main fears or concerns?** Record group members' answers. *Then* move on to the spiritual significance of adoption. It should quickly become clear that God would never be abusive to His adopted children. God would not play favorites by giving some people privileges that others don't have. God wouldn't lose interest in the ones He adopts. With all the negative publicity concerning adoption and foster homes, adoption may have bad connotations. Yet when God is the adopting parent, we have great cause for celebration. You might want to use a red marker to put a dot on each person's hand to remind him or her that even though we are adopted individually, we become "blood brothers" as we serve the same Father in Christian fellowship.

All about Match's coach.

MOSTLY GUYS

EXTRA FUN

THURSDAY

JAN FEB MAR APR MAY JUN JUL AUG SEP OCT NOV DEC

...eir
...em
...de

...ey
...e
...ho
...h

it ...ve t ...he ...ers of t roo .
... ...g in
position, ask volunteers on each side to
explain why they responded as they did.

STEP 4

After discussing "Jillian's Journey" (Repro
Resource 2), ask your group members to
think about their own response to God's
love. Distribute paper and pencils. Instruct
each person to write a personal journal
entry in response to one of these statements: **"God doesn't really love me
all that much," "I know God loves
me enough to die for me, but I
don't want His love,"** or **"I know
God loves me enough to die for me
and my response is . . ."** Have group
members write for three to five minutes.
Then ask for volunteers to share what
they've written. Afterward, suggest that
group members take their entries home
and add to them as they learn more
about the nature of God and His love.

STEP 3

When you begin to describe each individual's relationship with God, try to
incorporate the concept of God as a
coach. Let guys who have been on sports
teams describe the characteristics of a
good coach: motivating the team to work
together; helping individuals identify and
strengthen weaknesses, expecting the
best possible performance from everyone involved, providing instruction and
assurance throughout the game, challenging everyone to maintain a daily regimen
of personal development, and so forth.
Be forewarned that some people may
have had negative experiences with poor
coaches; but some of the strongest
bonds young people form with adults are
with coaches who help them realize (to
some degree) what their inner potential
might be. Help your group members
realize that God can provide the leadership and support of the best coach they
can ever imagine.

STEP 4

Rather than handing out copies of Repro
Resource 2, simply read it and let your
group members know that Jillian's story is
true. But before you begin to discuss it,
adapt the circumstances to a masculine
point of view. Rather than a beautiful bedroom with toys, desk, crayons, pencils, and
paper, let them envision a large yard with
a tree house and baseball diamond. The
feelings that are evoked are likely to be
the same, but male group members will
be more likely to relate to specifics from
their own childhoods. Be sensitive to their
feelings. We sometimes tend to assume
that young boys are not as sensitive to
emotions of fear, distrust, suspicion, etc. as
young girls are. But at such an early age,
there is little difference in the way people
respond to such things. Teenage boys
might be more reluctant than teenage girls
to express how they feel now (or at age
eight), but their feelings are just as strong.

STEP 1

Before you hand out Repro Response 1,
play "Barnyard." Divide into two teams of
equal size. Put the teams at opposite ends
of a large room. Assign everyone at one
end of the room the name of a barnyard
animal. Then assign the same animal names
to the group members at the other end.
Blindfold everyone (or have group members keep their eyes closed) and explain
that the goal is to find the other animal
of one's own species by making the noise
of that animal. (Cows should moo, ducks
should quack, etc.) With everyone making
noise at the same time and unable to see,
this isn't as easy as it sounds. Afterward,
move right into the "Astonishing Animals"
segment of the meeting.

STEP 3 *add from previous photos*

When you get to the section in which you
are discussing each person's uniqueness
through DNA, fingerprints, and so forth,
let students create a more tangible reflec-
tion of their own individuality. Pull out a
stamp pad and squares of paper and ask
group members to create "thumbprint
people." They should ink their thumbs,
make a clear print on the paper, and then
create a person from the print. The dress,
expression, surrounding, and possessions
of the thumbprint person should reflect
the group member's own personality
and interests. Football players might want
to draw helmets and shoulder pads, and
surround the figure with goal posts and
cheerleaders. Musicians might want to
draw the appropriate instrument for the
thumbprint person to play. Any number of
creative, individual, and unique applications
can be made from each person's unique
and individual thumbprint.

STEP 3

After you brainstorm the famous pairs, help kids think about the "God and me" relationship by having them create a TV pilot for a new series called "God and Me." Have them consider these questions:

- **Who will be the main character?**
- **What is the setting of the show?**
- **Since a good show has good conflict, what will be the conflict of this series?**
- **What are some silly things the main character does to resolve the conflict?**
- **How would God be represented in this show? If visually, who would be the actor? If just a voice is used, whose voice would it be?**

Try not to let the discussion get too flippant where God is involved, but challenge kids to think creatively. If they truly believe that God is a major influence in their lives, they may need to consider new and better ways to relate to Him.

Very good

STEP 4

As you invite people to consider beginning a relationship with God, have kids think in terms of joining a fan club. Ask:

- **If new Christians could join a "New Kids in the Flock Fan Club," what would be the requirements for membership?**
- **What would be the primary benefits of being members?**
- **What do people do to show support when they really like a rock star or other hero?** (Read material about him or her, listen closely to song lyrics, go to concerts, talk about the person with friends, etc.)
- **Why do you think we can get so excited about a sports hero or rock group, while at the same time we may find church stuff so "boring"?**
- **Do you think anyone deserves our support and enthusiasm more than God does?**
- **How do you think we can get more excited about our faith?**

STEP 1

This step (and most of the others) can be abbreviated so you can teach the whole session without eliminating any entire activities. You can choose a couple of animals from Repro Resource 1 rather than dividing into teams and doing them all. In Step 2, rather than having kids write out their responses to the two unfinished sentences, ask for verbal responses. Also deal with the Bible portions as a single group rather than dividing into teams. In Step 3, the "A" or "B" choices can be determined by show of hands rather than moving around the room. By revising these few things, you can save a great deal of time overall.

STEP 2

If you still feel you need to shave a few minutes, you as leader can summarize the content of this step as a mini-lecture. Otherwise, kids usually take quite a bit of time dividing into groups, looking up several verses, answering predetermined questions, and so forth. You can regulate their pace by "walking them through" what you want them to know and asking just enough questions to ensure that they're staying with you. That should also give them time to participate in most of the other activities and experiences.

STEP 1

Here are some urban additions to "Astonishing Animals" (Repro Resource 1):

(1) Many city pigeons sleep in crevices on buildings. (Correct.)

(2) All alley cats live in alleys. (Wrong.)

(3) Some rats are as big as cats. (Correct.)

(4) A trained dog will never turn against its owner. (Wrong.)

STEP 3

Another option for this activity is to name the first person of a famous pair and see if group members can name the other. You could make the activity competitive by having group members form two teams and awarding a point to the first team that responds correctly. You might want to use some of the following suggestions for an urban audience.

- **Ike Turner** (Tina Turner)
- **Kid** (Play)
- **Lone Ranger** (Tonto)
- **Salt** (Peppa)
- **Bullwinkle** (Rocky)

Point out that when we hear the name of one member of these pairs, we automatically think of the other.

Ask: **When people think of you, do they automatically think of someone else too?** (Some teens form friendship duos so tight that one person is never seen without the other.)

Say: **If you are really living the Christian life to the fullest, people will always see that you are in a relationship with God.**

STEP 1

Junior highers are a lot more motivated when it comes to "doing" than they are with "thinking." Therefore, let them do Repro Resource 1 as written. But as you make the transition into discussing other things that seem to point to the existence of a Creator, make this a doing exercise. Have everyone go outside and find something to bring back and show as an evidence of God's creative skill. (Be sure to set a time limit.) Most junior highers won't mind turning over a few rocks, climbing trees, or getting a little dirty to come up with just the right artifact for their presentation. In addition, it allows them to get rid of a little restless energy at the beginning of the session.

STEP 2

High schoolers should have no problem with the session as is, but junior highers might have a bit of difficulty finding the right words in this step to describe their thoughts and feelings about God. For many of them, it will be much easier (and more natural) to draw out their mental images of God. So rather than using the unfinished sentences, you might instruct them to draw God as they perceive Him. Or you might ask them to draw pictures to demonstrate the relationships they have with God. As with the unfinished sentences, you are likely to discover a variety of responses: fear, distance, protection, confusion, etc.

STEP 2

The analogies of drowning or hanging from a cliff are only mentioned in passing, yet they offer a strong mental image. Divide your students into two teams. Ask each team to quickly create a skit—one with a drowning person and the other with a person dangling from the top of a cliff. Each skit should deal with the possible "hands" that reach out to the person and how the desperate person would respond to each one. (One hand might belong to a small child, unable to help. One might belong to a beautiful girl—someone half the size of the victim. One hand might belong to a very rich person who doesn't want to get his expensive clothes dirty. Or what if the victim is a white racist and the helping hand is black?) Through the skits, group members should see that the desire to be rescued is only one issue. Equally important is the ability of the other person to provide any real help.

STEP 4

To emphasize the issue of adoption, ask your group members to consider sponsoring a child through a reliable organization that seeks aid for starving children. Most such organizations will provide pictures of the children and the exchange of cards and letters. The monthly cost is not usually high; yet this is not something your group members should commit to unless they are absolutely certain that the money will continue for the prescribed time. If your kids are interested in becoming "adoptive parents," you might check with one or both of the following organizations:

Compassion International
P. O. Box 7000
Colorado Springs, CO 80933
1-800-336-7676

World Vision
Childcare Sponsorship
P. O. Box 1131
Pasadena, CA 91131
1-800-777-5777

DATE USED:

Approx. Time

STEP 1: *What Is Real?* _____
- ❏ Extra Action
- ❏ Small Group
- ❏ Large Group
- ❏ Fellowship & Worship
- ❏ Extra Fun
- ❏ Short Meeting Time
- ❏ Urban
- ❏ Combined Junior High/High School

Things needed:

STEP 2: *Who Is God, Anyway?* _____
- ❏ Heard It All Before
- ❏ Little Bible Background
- ❏ Mostly Girls
- ❏ Short Meeting Time
- ❏ Combined Junior High/High School
- ❏ Extra Challenge

Things needed:

STEP 3: *A Special Relationship* _____
- ❏ Extra Action
- ❏ Large Group
- ❏ Little Bible Background
- ❏ Mostly Guys
- ❏ Extra Fun
- ❏ Media
- ❏ Urban

Things needed:

STEP 4: *Coming Close* _____
- ❏ Small Group
- ❏ Heard It All Before
- ❏ Fellowship & Worship
- ❏ Mostly Girls
- ❏ Mostly Guys
- ❏ Media
- ❏ Extra Challenge

Things needed:

How Close Does God Want to Be to Me?

READ

Choose one or more

☐ To help kids recognize the kind of closeness God wants to have with them.

☐ To help kids understand that their friendships with God can be real.

☐ To help kids develop an intimate relationship with God.

☐ Other: _____
_____

Your Bible Base:

Genesis 1:26-27; 2:18;
   3:8-9, 21
John 15:1-8
Romans 8:35-39
James 2:23

Do

Too Close for Comfort

Have group members form pairs. Explain that the members of each pair should try to follow your instructions while they stand nose to nose. Read each of the following instructions one at a time, giving the pairs a chance to complete it before moving on to the next one.

- **Touch your toes.**
- **Walk in a circle.**
- **Sit down.**
- **Each of you take off one shoe.**
- **Shake hands with the members of another pair.**
- **Nod yes.**
- **Stand back to back.**
- **Pretend to wash your face.**
- **Hop on one foot.**

Afterward, ask: **Why did you have trouble following some of the instructions?** (Because we were "attached," we didn't have much freedom to move.)

Which instruction was impossible? (Standing back to back.)

What do you think it be like to be a Siamese twin joined at the nose? Get a few responses.

Say: **It's nice to be close to people, but not that close. But what about God? How close can we get to Him? How close do you want to get to Him?** Encourage most of your group members to offer their opinions.

STEP 2

Voices from the Past

(Needed: Bibles, chalk and chalkboard, copies of Repro Resource 3)

Ask: **Do you think people in Bible times had closer relationships with God than people today have with Him?** Explain. Get several group members' opinions.

Then say: **Let's take a look at the relationships between God and some famous Bible characters. And let's start with the first two people on earth.**

Have someone read aloud Genesis 1:26-27; 2:18; 3:8-9, 21. Then say: **Describe the roles God played in His relationship with Adam and Eve.** (God was their Creator [1:26-27; 2:18]. He was an accessible friend who talked with them in the garden [3:8-9]. He was a concerned friend who took care of their needs [3:21].)

Does God fill similar roles in His relationship with us? If so, how? (Yes. God created us; He is accessible to us through prayer; and He meets our needs.) Ask volunteers to give specific examples of how God has taken care of their needs. You may want to be prepared with an example of your own.

Then say: **Now take a look at the relationship between God and Abraham.** Have someone read aloud James 2:23.

Ask: **What one word in this characterizes Abraham's relationship with God?** (Friend.)

What do you think it means to be God's friend? Encourage most of your group members to offer their opinions.

Distribute copies of "God Came Through" (Repro Resource 3). Choose three actors to read the script. While the actors are getting ready, have the rest of the group members review the script because they'll be creating the sound effects (which are indicated by parentheses). You might want to recruit a sound-effects coordinator to stand in front of the group and lead each effect.

After group members have performed the skit once or twice, ask: **How can we tell that God was close to each of these Bible characters?** (He knew what was going on in their lives. He took action to help them.)

What specific actions did He take to help these characters? (He protected Moses when he was a baby, and protected the Israelites from the Egyptians. He helped Joshua and the children of Israel

OPTIONS

LARGE GROUP

HEARD IT ALL BEFORE

LITTLE BIBLE BACKGROUND

FELLOWSHIP & WORSHIP

MOSTLY GIRLS

MEDIA

URBAN

EXTRA CHALLENGE

destroy the walls of Jericho. He freed Paul and the others from prison, and He protected Paul and his shipmates during the shipwreck.)

Is God someone we should be scared of? (No. His power is awesome, but He always has people's good at heart.)

Which of the "God Came Through" situations impressed you most, and why? Get several responses.

The Bible is filled with examples of God being close to people. He walked with Adam and Eve in the garden of Eden. He talked to Abraham and even called him "friend." God even came to earth in a human body and lived among people.

Get your group members thinking about how close *they* feel to God. Draw a horizontal line on the board. Instruct group members to mentally draw two short vertical lines that intersect it. One line should represent themselves and the other line should represent God. Tell kids to place the two lines close together or far apart based on how close they feel to God.

STEP 3

The King and I

Say: **Maybe you want to get close to God, but not so close that He controls everything you do. You probably don't want to feel confined by God the way that you felt confined when you were nose to nose with your partner at the beginning of this session.**

On the other hand, maybe you feel that God is so powerful, so important, and so holy that people like you and I couldn't possibly be His friends, let alone have any kind of relationship with Him.

Have group members form pairs. Explain that one person in each pair should assume the identity of a famous person from TV, movies, the music industry, the sports world, politics, etc. The other person will be himself or herself. Give the partners a few minutes to come up with common interests or abilities on which they could build a friendship. If they don't know much about the interests of the celebrities they've selected, they can make some up. For example, the partners might both collect baseball cards or enjoy mountain climbing. After the partners have identified common interests, have them discuss how those interests might bring them closer together.

As time permits, find out what interests the members of each pair had in common and how the two could build a friendship.

Ask: **Could you be friends with your partner even though he or she is more famous than you?** (Some group members might agree that common interests could make a friendship possible. Others might feel that they have little grounds for a friendship with a famous person.)

How might a friendship with a famous person be different from a friendship with someone "ordinary," like a friend at school? (You might be more willing to "give" more in a friendship with a famous person because you're in awe of that person. Maybe you would be more respectful to a famous person. You might not act as much like yourself around a famous person as you would around an ordinary friend.)

What similarities do you see between a friendship with God and a friendship with an important person? If someone suggests that a friendship with God might be imbalanced (like a friendship with a famous person) because of the "awe" factor, help him or her see the matter from a different perspective.

Ask: **What do you have in common with God that can bring you close to Him?** (Some of your group members may feel that they have very little in common with God—that they don't understand Him at all or aren't even sure if He exists. Others who are confident in their faith might recognize that they have been made in the likeness of God; that they have the same interests, such as the welfare of loved ones; they both care about the earth; and that they have some of the same characteristics—like the ability to love.)

Explain to your group members that you will be taking a look at Scripture to see how we can be friends with God even though He is infinitely more important and powerful than we are. Acknowledge the "awe" factor and the need to respect God because of His position; but emphasize that God can be a friend and that He is not unreachable, withdrawn, or unknowable.

STEP 4

A Branch in the Vine

(Needed: Bibles, pencils, paper, chalkboard and chalk or newsprint and marker, a plant)

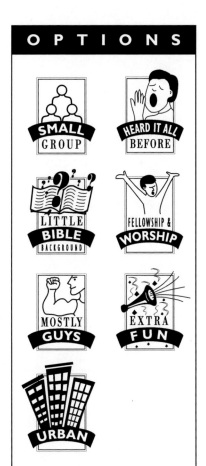

OPTIONS

SMALL GROUP

HEARD IT ALL BEFORE

LITTLE BIBLE BACKGROUND

FELLOWSHIP & WORSHIP

MOSTLY GUYS

EXTRA FUN

URBAN

Say: **Just before Jesus' trial and crucifixion, He described to His disciples the kind of close relationship God wants to have with believers.** Have someone read aloud John 15:1-8.

Then ask: **Who is the vine in this illustration?** (The Lord.) **What is our relationship to the vine?** (We are branches.)

Distribute paper and pencils. Give group members two minutes to write down as many similarities as they can think of between a branch's relationship with a vine and gardener and our relationship with God. Afterward, have volunteers share their responses. Use the following suggestions to supplement your discussion.

• A vine and its branches usually has a gardener; God is our gardener. He cares for us and looks after us.

• Dead branches must be pruned so that a vine can grow stronger and produce more; God prunes Christians so that we can grow stronger and become more fruitful.

• The branch depends on the vine for life and nourishment so it can bear fruit; we depend on Christ for hope, strength, peace, love, etc.

Ask: **How are we different from a branch?** (We have brains and emotions, so we can be tempted to stop depending on Christ and go off on our own.)

Ask two volunteers to act out the differences between branches and Christians. One should use his or her imagination to play the part of a branch. This person might hug the wall or gently stretch as if in a soft breeze. Encourage the "branch" to ham it up.

The other volunteer should pretend that he or she is involved in a powerful physical struggle against a temptation to sin. This person will demonstrate common spiritual struggles in physical ways.

The rest of the group members should try to tempt both the "branch" and the Christian to sin by saying things like "We're going to a crazy party tonight. Wanna come?" or "Wait until you see the magazines my cousin has!" or other things that may be tempting to Christian teens.

The volunteer portraying the struggling Christian should mime a wrestling match against these invisible temptations and then get on his or her knees and pray. Meanwhile, the branch should wave gently in the breeze (or do whatever branches do), not tempted by anything that is being said. Afterward, thank your volunteers and have them sit down.

STEP 5

Inseparable

(Needed: Bibles)

Introduce the topic of "separation" to your group members. Ask if any of them have ever experienced any kind of separation. If so, ask them to describe how it felt. You may want to use the following questions to focus your discussion.

How did you feel when . . .
- **one of your friends moved out of state?** *Tell about Ken*
- **an older brother or sister left you behind to start college?**
- **a friend started going out with someone who didn't like you?**
- **someone you loved died?**
- **you got lost at a mall or amusement park when you were little?**
- **you made the team but your best friend didn't?**
- **the subway door separated you from your family?**
- **a friend got involved in illegal activities that you didn't participate in?**

Let group members share for a while about their experiences. Then acknowledge that separation can be painful and cause us to feel fearful. Separation hurts.

Say: **The good news is that God promises that believers in Christ will never be separated from the love of Christ. Nothing in life or in death can separate us from Christ because of His sacrificial death on the cross, His resurrection, His ascension into heaven, and His constant intercession for us.**

Have someone read aloud Romans 8:35-39. As the person is reading, have the rest of your group members call out things the passage says will never separate us from the love of Christ.

Depending on the spiritual maturity of your group members, you may want to read the passage from the Living Bible: "When we have trouble or calamity, when we are hunted down or destroyed . . . if we are hungry, or penniless, or in danger, or threatened with death. . . . For I am convinced that nothing can ever separate us from his love. Death can't, and life can't. The angels won't, and all the powers of hell itself cannot keep God's love away. Our fears for today, our worries about tomorrow, or where we are—high above the sky, or in the deepest ocean—nothing will ever be able to separate us from the love of God demonstrated by our Lord Jesus Christ when he died for us."

As you wrap up the session, distribute balloons to your group members. Have your group members blow up the balloons and tie them.

Then say: **These balloons can remind you of your relationship with God. Think of yourself as the balloon and God as the air inside the balloon. This is how close God wants to be to you. God gives us every breath we take. Job 33:4 says, "The Spirit of God has made me; the breath of the Almighty gives me life." God is as close as your breath—even closer.**

Close the session in prayer, asking God to remind your group members that He wants to have a very close relationship with each of them.

GOD CAME THROUGH

M O S E S : The king was killing all baby boys, so my mother hid me on a riverbank *(splash, splash, splash)*. God saw to it that the king's daughter found me and hired my mother to be my nurse *(waah, waah, waah)*. When I grew up, I led the Israelites out of Egypt. The Egyptians followed us with horses *(sound of hoof-beats)*. If they caught us, they were either going to take us back to Egypt *(cries of "No! No!")* or kill us *(sounds of people dying)*. When we came to the Red Sea and had nowhere else to go, things looked hopeless *(dejected cries of "awww")*. But God parted the waters so we could escape *(cheer)*.

J O S H U A : I was chosen to lead Israel *(tramping of feet)* into the Promised Land. God told us to take a fortified city by marching around it for seven days *(tramping of feet)*. On the seventh day, the priests blew trumpets *(ta-dah)* and the walls fell flat *(crash)*.

P A U L : Silas and I were in prison when an earthquake *(rumble, rumble)* freed us. Another time, I was a prisoner being transported by ship when a violent storm came up *(roaring winds, crashing waves)*. The ship was wrecked *(crash, bang)*, but God saved our lives as He promised *(sigh of relief)*.

STEP 1

To infuse a bit more action at the beginning of the session, expand the nose-to-nose activity. Depending on your meeting area, you might want to divide into teams and attempt a number of relays (or even race around the outside of the building). Of course, increased activity will likely lead to occasional cheating by not being *completely* nose to nose. To avoid having pairs take too many liberties, you might want to supply lengths of string (or perhaps even Twizzlers) that are about six inches long. Have each member of the pair hold one end in his or her mouth. If either person lets go, or if the string breaks, the pair is disqualified. If you're really brave, let your group members put some creative thought into the possibilities of additional nose-to-nose competitions. They may surprise you with some truly exciting options.

STEP 5

Before beginning this step, reacquaint your group with the childhood game "Red Rover." Divide into two teams. The members of one team stand side by side, interlock arms, and challenge one person from the other team to try to break through between any two team members. (You can do away with the chant ["Red rover, red rover, let Billy come over"] if you wish. After all, this is going to be *American Gladiator*-level competition.) Set up a scoring system that provides more points for breaking through between two senior football players as opposed to two junior-high girls. It shouldn't take long playing this game before you're ready to move into the subject of the pain of separation.

STEP 4

Sometimes small groups adapt a "second-class citizen" attitude as they compare themselves to large groups who are able to do more things because of significantly larger financial budgets. So to accompany your discussion of the vine and the branches, bring a small clipping from a healthy plant and a pot of dirt to plant it in. Let the clipping serve as on ongoing object lesson. As it grows and flourishes, compare it to your own group. As long as it's from a strong and healthy parent plant, its size is no limitation. It can grow to be just as large and productive as any of its kind. And as group members discover the plant's need for water, fertilizer, proper sunlight, and other nourishment, perhaps they will make the obvious connection to their own growth needs.

STEP 5

Another option to help your kids feel better about being a small group is to let them talk about it. Instead of dealing with the individual feelings of separation in this step, let kids discuss how they feel *as a group* about being separated from the large numbers of other Christian kids who go to other churches. The application will be the same: nothing will ever separate them from love of God. He cares every single bit as much for them as for big and glitzy church groups. But if you detect any serious feelings of isolation or regret about not being bigger or able to do everything other groups can do, you might want to spend some time here brainstorming exactly what your group members are looking for. You could even have volunteers contact other church groups in your community or denomination to try to plan some activities that would include several youth groups.

STEP 2

In a large group, a lot of people would be left out of the skit on Repro Resource 3 (except for sound effects). So as you hand out copies, ask some of your more biblically knowledgeable people to create additional paragraphs based on other Bible characters for whom "God Came Through" (Daniel, Jonah, Peter walking on water, etc.) Be sure as they write their paragraphs that they also create fun sound effects for the others to do. You'll probably discover that some people have more fun creating their own versions than performing what is already written.

STEP 3

The topic of friendship with God can be understood on a cognitive level without actually being felt at a level that changes the behavior of group members. You might want to spend some time explaining that a person's love for God is accurately reflected by his or her love for other people. One common problem with big groups is that shy or somewhat unusual kids can get lost amid all the others without anyone realizing it. Even those who attend every week can come and go without truly being noticed or appreciated. To see if this is happening in your group, give a dollar bill (before the session) to several people you feel may be overlooked. Instruct one person to give the dollar to anyone who asks about his or her school or family life. Another person should give the dollar to anyone who does a favor for him or her. Another might give the dollar to the first person who smiles at him or her. At this point, or perhaps even later in the session, let your volunteers report on whether or not they have given away their dollar bills. Emphasize that we cannot truly consider ourselves friends with God if we are ignoring the needs of the people around us (1 John 4:20-21).

STEP 2

Even before you mention God in this session, move from the nose-to-nose activity in Step 1 to a discussion of friendship. Ask: **What characteristics do you look for in a friend? What attracted you to the person who is your best friend? Why are friendships important?** Try to get beyond all the usual answers to things like friends share secrets, friends tell the truth even when it might hurt, friends accept each other as they really are, and so forth. Your "heard it all before" group will expect a follow-up Bible study on relationships or the importance of being a good friend. But you can then resume the session as written and emphasize the privilege of being able to have God as a friend.

STEP 4

If your group has a good knowledge of the basic Bible stories and analogies, the vine-and-branches concept might be something they think they fully understand. But you can study the same concept in a different way. Explain that this was written before people knew the secrets of cloning. Ask: **How might a person's spiritual development be compared to becoming a clone?** (We start with a small degree of understanding of who Jesus is and what He has done for us. From there, we attempt to conform ourselves to that image. The more like Him we become, and the less we allow ourselves to be shaped according to our sinful human nature, the more successful we will be.) Ask: **What major "operation(s)" would you need before you could become as good a clone as you know you should be? What else do you need to know about Jesus before you know enough to become a good clone?**

STEP 2

This step refers to several different Bible characters, but doesn't go into much detail about any of them. Rather than try to study so many, focus on just one. The "friend of God" concept is a strong one, so you might want to delve into the life of Abraham. Start by letting kids tell you everything they know about Abraham; then fill in other important events of his life from Genesis 12–22: his faithful response to God's call, his association with Lot, the incident with Hagar and Ishmael, the eventual birth of Isaac, and his willingness to offer Isaac back to God. Explain that because of Abraham's long and faithful relationship with God, and the fact that he and God were "friends," Abraham was able to trust God to deliver Isaac on the mountain (Gen. 22). Explain that as we become able to trust God as a friend, He will do great things for each of us as well.

STEP 4

The vine-and-branches passage is not easy to understand if it is being read for the first time. Therefore, spend some time discussing it at this point rather than moving directly into the skit. Kids new to this passage need to be able to ask questions about the pruning concept, the emphasis on bearing fruit, and the necessity of an ongoing relationship between the vine and the branches. More importantly, they need to be given a sensitive interpretation of all of the "threatening" portions of this passage: being "cut off" by the gardener (God), being thrown into the fire and burned, etc. At first reading, this passage can sound more scary than encouraging, so don't rush through it. Explain that Jesus' words are strong because He is speaking to His closest friends the day before He is to die. You can then continue the "friends with God" theme to show that His disciples certainly saw themselves as the branches attached to the vine—not the "deadwood" who rejected Jesus. We can be just as confident that Jesus considers us His friends.

STEP 2

After you do the "God Came Through" activity on Repro Resource 3, ask group members to complete this sentence: **When I want to draw closer to God, I . . .** You might suggest that Moses went up on Mount Sinai and Daniel prayed three times a day at his window. As your students respond, listen for geographic locations, activities, feelings, and so forth. Later, point out that even though we might feel distant from God, He is always nearby. Rather than seek after a feeling, we need to focus on obeying Him. This is an ideal time to learn to celebrate the friendship between ourselves and God—a bond that Jesus has made possible for us. If you stop to give thanks at this point, it may well be something that your group members will remember sometime in the future when they really *need* a spiritual boost.

STEP 4

By this time in the session, you've made passing references to God as friend, king, creator, and vine. Spend some time brainstorming other roles He fills (Father, protector, provider, fair judge, shepherd, etc.). On the board, list all of these roles and what each should mean to us in our ongoing relationship with Him. From time to time, we need to stop and let the importance of these things sink in. You might want to take some time for discussion and sentence prayer at this point to express thanks that we serve a God who is able and willing to attend to our every need. It should not be enough to *know* what God has done. We need to stop and worship Him as well.

STEP 2

After reading and discussing "God Came Through" (Repro Resource 3), have group members form teams. Assign each team one or more of the following names of a woman in the Bible and the accompanying references: Hannah (I Sam. 1:26-28); the Shunammite woman (2 Kings 4:8-22, 32, 37); Mary, mother of Jesus (Luke 1:28-31); Mary, sister of Lazarus (John 11:32-35, 41-44); Lydia (Acts 16:14-15); Tabitha (Acts 9:36-42). Ask the teams to read the Bible verses and discuss at least one way we know that God was close to that person. After a few minutes, have each team present its findings to the entire group.

STEP 3

At the end of your discussion in this step, ask group members to think about their friendship with God from God's point of view. Ask: **If you were God, more powerful than anyone or anything, how would you feel about being a close friend with a mere human? Since, as God, you would know everything there is to know about your friend, what might you do to improve the friendship?**

STEP 3

Most guys can spend the entire meeting time talking about their sports heroes. So when you get to this step, encourage them to cut loose. Ask: **Who are your favorite sports heroes and why? In what ways would you like to be more like the people you admire? How are you most different from those people? Do you think your hero(es) would like to spend a lot of time with you? Do you think you will ever have the same talent, skills, and character of your heroes?** Then shift the discussion to the approachability of God. Ask the same questions in terms of developing a better relationship with Him. Point out that even though the distance between ourselves and God may seem infinitely greater than between ourselves and Michael Jordan, we can spend unlimited time with God and become more like Him every day of our lives.

STEP 4

Skip the mime exercise, but try to develop the wrestling concept contained in it. For a group of mostly guys, an actual wrestling match is likely to teach a more lasting lesson. (If space is a problem, settle for arm-wrestling.) Select one of your stronger guys and label him the "potential victim." Let others in the group represent temptations of various strengths. Have the "potential victim" take on the first temptation. As soon as that match is over, bring on the next temptation. Don't allow the potential victim much opportunity to rest or regain his strength. If he proves strong enough to master all of the individual temptations, let the temptations begin to attack two at a time. After a while, stop the activity and discuss the vine-and-branches concept again—this time in terms of remaining connected to the Vine for a continual source of strength. Otherwise, our temptations may prove too much for even the strongest of us to master.

STEP 1

This session contains passing references to several well-known Bible characters, so you might want to "preview" these characters by singing some favorite songs that pay tribute to these people. For example, you could sing "Father Abraham," "Joshua Fought the Battle of Jericho," "Children, Go Where I Send Thee," "Pharaoh, Pharaoh" (to the tune of "Louie, Louie"), or any other familiar songs about the people mentioned in this session. Or, if your group members are particularly creative, have them write a song that includes all of the characters you mention. (You might be surprised at what your group members can turn out on short notice.)

STEP 4

Convert the vine-and-branches analogy into a game. Play by the rules of the pool game "Sharks and Minnows." Designate one person (the vine) to stand in the center of the room. The other group members (useless deadwood) should gather at one end of the room. At your signal, they should run past the vine to the other end of the room. Anyone who is tagged is "grafted," and becomes part of the vine. (They must remain connected.) At your next signal, the deadwood group runs back across the room while the vine members try to tag (graft) more of them. See how long it takes to incorporate all of the people into the vine. If you wish, you can also deal with the real-life applications of this exercise (the powerful effect of evangelism).

STEP 2

Rather than leading the group through Repro Resource 3 yourself, pretend to be a movie mogul who is bringing a script to Youth Group Pictures International to be produced. Assign one of the group members to be the director of the picture; then sit back to wait for the "screening." Your director should take responsibility for seeing that all of the functions of filming are taken care of. He or she should find the best actors, see that the lighting is taken care of, and find a good sound-effects crew that will not be content to make the sounds themselves, but will find the right props to create the needed noises. If possible, find a video camera and record the results of your group's "rough cut" of the script.

STEP 3 *good*

When you begin to discuss the relationships that your young people have with God, give the discussion a media "spin." One option is to ask each person to think of a title of a TV show or movie that best describes his or her relationship with God ("Who's the Boss?" *Gone with the Wind, Nothing in Common, Bound for Glory,* "Quantum Leap," *Home Alone,* "Three's Company," etc.). Another option is to have group members act out a classic scene that could be applied to their relationship with God (for example, the famous line at the end of *Casablanca:* "I think this is the beginning of a beautiful friendship," or some other meaningful scene from film or television). You're likely to get more quotes from *Revenge of the Nerds* or *Batman Returns* than *The Ten Commandments,* but if kids are honest in their responses, this will be a productive time for them.

STEP 1

This session contains many short activities within most of the steps, so you can choose at will. One way to save time is to eliminate Step 2, which is somewhat supplemental to the theme of the session. You can go directly from the questions at the end of Step 1 to the introduction of Step 3. Another shortcut is to emphasize the Bible texts in Steps 4 and 5, and make your own applications. Both the vine-and-branches passage and the "What shall separate us from the love of God?" passage are fairly straightforward. Most group members should be able to find applications to both teachings on their own.

STEP 5

If time is extremely tight for you, jump straight from Step 1 to Step 5. The nose-to-nose activity will work well as a lead-in to the reminder that nothing can separate true believers from God's love (Rom. 8:35-39). If you then have time for the balloon activity, have kids write down some of the passages on their balloons that they didn't have time to cover during the session (John 15:1-8; Jas. 2:23; etc.). Or challenge them to create slogans to write on their balloons that would help remind them that God is never far away from them.

STEP 2

Point out that not only is God an accessible friend today, Jesus (when He lived on earth) *chose* people to be His friends and to give Him support during the tough times of His ministry. These friends included many types of people. Help your group members recognize the diversity among the disciples, Jesus' closest friends.

(1) Peter—Bold, trustworthy, hot-tempered.

(2) Andrew—Helpful, eager.

(3) James (of Zebedee)—Active, strong personality.

(4) John—Zealous, strong personality.

(5) James (of Alphaeus)—Faithful to Scripture, Jesus' brother.

(6) Philip—Organizer.

(7) Bartholomew (or Nathanael)—Very intelligent, true Israelite.

(8) Thomas—Investigator, risk-taker.

(9) Matthew—Detailed, picky, tax collector.

(10) Simon (the Zealot)—Committed to a cause, wanted little to do with the government.

(11) Judas Iscariot—Untrustworthy, betrayed Jesus.

(12) Thaddaeus (or James)—Quiet.

Have group members decide which disciple's personality is similar to their own. Then read aloud John 15:13-16. Encourage group members to choose Jesus as their personal friend as Jesus chooses them as His personal friends.

STEP 4

Rather than having volunteers mime the branch and the person facing temptation, you might want to have them simulate a boxing match in which a fighter "battles" various temptations.

STEP 3

Junior highers are usually better able to deal with tangible things than with conceptual ideas. Many of them are also enthusiastic about science and nature subjects. So as you discuss topics such as closeness to God and the development of a friendship with Him, here's a way to do it in both a tangible and "scientific" way. Set up a solar system in your room, with the sun at one end and the planets (Mercury, Venus, Earth, Mars, Jupiter, Saturn, Uranus, Neptune, and Pluto) at intervals out from the sun. Also designate a far corner of the room as "the other side of the galaxy." Explain that God's presence is represented by the sun. Then instruct kids to stand in the appropriate places in response to these questions:

• **Where would you say you are now in your relationship with God?**
• **Where would you say most people your age are?**
• **Where do you think the most comfortable place for you would be?**
• **Where do you think God wants you to be?**
• **What's the closest you've ever been to God?**
• **What's the farthest away you've ever been?**

Discuss why kids are more distant than they want to be, what causes them to draw near or move away from God, etc.

STEP 5

Rather than discussing how nothing can separate us from God's love, junior highers might be more inclined to need some motivation to *start* a personal relationship with Him. If possible, bring in some samples of good devotional materials. If group members find something that seems promising, encourage them to invest in the book as a first step in their ongoing spiritual development. Later, after they've dealt with the basics of their relationship with God, they will be more prepared to deal with the assurance that nothing can separate them from God's love.

STEP 2

A group that is ready for a deeper-than-average level of study might appreciate a different twist on the "God Came Through" activity on Repro Resource 3. Have group members form teams. Instruct the teams to study ways that God comes through even when He chooses not to deliver His people right away. For example, one team might look at Job (Job 1–2; 42). Another might study Jesus' trial and crucifixion (Matt. 27; Luke 23; John 19). Yet another might examine the ongoing sufferings of Paul (2 Cor. 11). Have all of the teams discuss how personal suffering may indeed be one way that God "comes through," even though we may not realize it at the time. Conclude by looking as a group at Romans 5:3-5 to see how our ultimate hope in God is rooted in our sufferings.

STEP 5

Ask group members to write their own, personalized versions of Romans 8:35-39. They may not be able to relate well to persecution, famine, nakedness, danger, or sword; but most of them are well aware of other threats such as sexual temptation, intense pressures to excel, financial shortcomings, and so forth. Each person should insert his or her own spiritual struggles into the passage. Let volunteers read what they've written, but don't force anyone to do so. Encourage group members to hang on to these paraphrases and pull them out during times when they feel as if no one understands what they're going through.

DATE USED:

Approx. Time

STEP 1: *Too Close for Comfort* _____
❑ Extra Action
❑ Extra Fun
❑ Short Meeting Time
Things needed:

STEP 2: *Voices from the Past* _____
❑ Large Group
❑ Heard It All Before
❑ Little Bible Background
❑ Fellowship & Worship
❑ Mostly Girls
❑ Media
❑ Urban
❑ Extra Challenge
Things needed:

STEP 3: *The King and I* _____
❑ Large Group
❑ Mostly Girls
❑ Mostly Guys
❑ Media
❑ Combined Junior High/High School
Things needed:

STEP 4: *A Branch in the Vine* _____
❑ Small Group
❑ Heard It All Before
❑ Little Bible Background
❑ Fellowship & Worship
❑ Mostly Guys
❑ Extra Fun
❑ Urban
Things needed:

STEP 5: *Inseparable* _____
❑ Extra Action
❑ Small Group
❑ Short Meeting Time
❑ Combined Junior High/High School
❑ Extra Challenge
Things needed:

If God Speaks, Why Can't I Hear Him?

YOUR GOALS FOR THIS SESSION:
Choose one or more

☐ To help kids recognize the different ways God communicates with them.

☐ To help kids understand reasons why they may not "hear" God.

☐ To help kids make changes in their lives so that they can hear God better.

☐ Other:_____
_____

Your Bible Base:

1 Kings 9:11-13
John 4:24; 10:1-5
1 Thessalonians 5:23

Speak to Me!

OPTIONS

Have group members form pairs. Then have each pair choose another pair to compete with. The members of each pair will stand back to back, with the backs of their heads touching. Each set of competing pairs will stand next to each other.

Designate one person in each pair to be the "sender," and the other to be the "receiver." The object of the game is for the sender to communicate a message to his or her partner (the receiver) without being heard by the members of the competing pair. Group members may not move or even turn their heads during the activity.

The first pair to successfully communicate its message without being heard by its opponent wins.

Afterward, ask: **Which is harder, communicating back to back or face to face? Explain.** (Communicating back to back is harder because we often depend on sight to communicate. Making gestures and facial expressions is an important part of the communication process.)

Explain: **Some people find it hard to talk to God because they can't see Him. Other people say they find it hard to talk to God because they can't hear God speak to them. Have you ever felt this way?** Encourage several group members to respond honestly.

Imagine asking someone all kinds of questions or telling that person all kinds of personal secrets and never getting any kind of response. It would be very frustrating. Yet some people feel this is what it's like when they talk to God. They feel as if they never get a response. So they give up. If you've ever felt this way, today's session is for you.

STEP 2

I Can't Understand You

(Needed: Three index cards prepared according to instructions, large marsh-mallows, dinner roll, banana, paper, pencils)

Have group members form three teams. Instruct each team to choose a representative (preferably someone who is hungry). Give the representatives what you think are equal amounts of food. You should give each representative enough food to fill up his or her mouth. You might give one person three large marshmallows; you might give another a small dinner roll; and you might give the other half of a banana.

Also give each representative an index card with the following message written on it: *Isn't it frustrating when your mom calls to you from another room and tells you something important, but you can't quite hear what she said? So you yell, "What?" And she says it again, but you still can't hear her. The best way to solve this problem is to <u>move closer to each other</u>. Then you'll be able to communicate better.*

Distribute paper and pencils to the rest of the team members. Explain to the representatives that they are to stuff the food in their mouths (no chewing allowed) and read aloud from the cards you gave them. [NOTE: Emphasize caution on the part of your representatives. Don't have them put so much food in their mouths that they run a risk of choking.]

The first team to figure out and write down exactly what its representative is saying wins. When a team has figured out the message, the representative may swallow or spit out the food.

Afterward, focus on the message communicated by the representatives—particularly on the idea of "moving closer" to facilitate communication.

Say: **The same solution applies to people who are having trouble hearing what God is saying to them. In a sense, they've got <u>to move closer to God</u>. Then they will be able to hear Him better.**

STEP 3

More Than One Way

(Needed: Bibles, Repro Resource 4, paper, pencils)

Say: **Let's take a look at some ways God spoke to people in the past.** Distribute copies of "How God Spoke" (Repro Resource 4) and pencils. Have kids work in pairs to unscramble the words on the sheet.

The answers are as follows:

(1) ANGEL in a VISION—An angel interpreted a vision for Zechariah. Zechariah found out that God would bless His people (Zech. 1:8-17).

(2) THREE MEN appeared to Abraham to announce that his wife would have a son (Gen. 18:1-2, 10).

(3) BURNING BUSH—God's voice came from a fiery bush to tell Moses that God would rescue the Israelites from slavery (Exod. 3:1-8).

(4) WRITING on the WALL—God sent a hand that wrote a message on a wall telling King Belshazzar that he would die (Dan. 5).

(5) DONKEY—God let Balaam's donkey speak, which helped save a disobedient Balaam from being destroyed by God (Num. 22:1, 4-6, 21-33).

(6) ANOTHER MAN—Gad was told by God to tell David to build an altar (2 Sam. 24:18-19).

(7) God told Paul through HIS SPIRIT that people will abandon the faith (1 Tim. 4:1).

(8) God spoke to our forefathers through the PROPHETS (Heb. 1:1).

(9) In these last days, God has spoken to us through HIS SON (Heb. 1:2).

After you go through the answers, discuss which methods of communication were most bizarre, which might have been frightening, which messages brought good news, which ones brought bad news, whether the people who received the messages were obedient or not, etc.

Have group members remain in their pairs. Give each pair a pencil and paper. Then say: **Imagine that one of you needs directions from the other on how to get to the new video store. But the person giving direction has laryngitis, and can't talk. List as many different ways as you can think of for communicating the directions without talking.** After a minute or two, ask volunteers to share their ideas. Answers might include writing out directions, using sign language, miming the answer, finding someone else to help, taking the person to the store yourself, etc.

Say: **As you've discovered, there are other ways to communicate besides using audible words.** Talk about how God communicates with us today and if His methods are anything like ours. (For instance, we write directions for each other; God wrote directions for us in the Bible. God doesn't use sign language, but He does "show" us things about Himself through His creation. God also communicates to us through pastors and other Christians.)

Have you ever heard someone say, "God told me," or "God spoke to me"? What you think people mean by these phrases? Point out that while God *can* use an audible voice to speak to us, more often than not He communicates in other ways. Most often, He speaks to us through the Bible.

Say: **There is one other unique way in which God can communicate to us.** Have someone read aloud John 4:24.

Then ask: **What does "God is spirit" mean?** (He is invisible and without a flesh-and-blood body like ours.)

Have someone read aloud I Thessalonians 5:23. Ask: **What three aspects of a human are mentioned here?** (Spirit, soul, and body.)

Explain: **God is a spirit. When He created us, He gave us a spirit so we would be like Him and, therefore, could communicate with Him. So, one of the important ways God talks to us is silently, in our spirit, in an inaudible voice.**

If your group members seem confused by this, or want further clarification, have them look up Romans 8:16, which says, "The [Holy] Spirit . . . testifies with our spirit that we are God's children." In ways we can't put into words, God can assure us inwardly that we belong to Him.

STEP 4

Listen Up!

(Bibles, tape recording of familiar voices, tape player)

Have someone read aloud I Kings 19:11-13. Then ask: **What does this passage say about the way the Lord speaks to us?** (Rather than using some dramatic and powerful wind, earthquake, or fire, God speaks to us in a "gentle whisper.")

To demonstrate this, have a volunteer stand in front of the group and read aloud Psalm 23 while several other volunteers talk loudly.

[handwritten note: See about God dealing with me about teens!]

[handwritten note: Good]

OPTIONS

Afterward, ask: **How well could you hear God's Word being spoken to you amidst all the noise and talking?** (Probably not very well.)

That's one reason why Christians are not always able to hear God's silent inner voice: There's too much going on. We get too busy; our lives are too noisy to hear God's voice.

Have group members sit for one minute in complete silence and ask them to listen for as many background sounds as they can hear.

Afterward, ask: **What sounds could you hear when it was silent?** (The sounds of traffic, the heater or air conditioner, a dog barking, breathing, etc.)

In which situation would it be easier to hear God's inner voice—the first situation or the second? Most group members will probably agree on the second.

What percent of your waking day would you describe as very noisy? Somewhat noisy? Somewhat quiet? Very quiet?

Have someone read aloud John 10:1-5. Explain that in this illustration Jesus compares us to sheep and Himself to the Shepherd. He speaks to His own—that's us Christians. He knows us personally and communicates personally to us. We can hear Him because we're listening (vs. 3). We know His voice and can tell it from a stranger's (vs. 4, 5).

Play a tape recording of voices familiar to your group members. Have your group members try to identify the voices.

Then ask: **Why were you able to identify the voices?** (We know the people or have heard them a lot. The voices are distinctive from everyone else's.)

Have a volunteer reread John 10:4. Explain: **It's pretty easy to recognize the voice of someone you know well or someone you've watched a lot. The same applies to hearing God's voice. The more that we get to know God, the better we will recognize His voice. His silent inner voice will become familiar to us when He communicates to us through a Scripture passage, through another Christian, through a life experience, or silently in our spirit.**

What are some ways God speaks to us.
Why don't we always hear Him

STEP 5

Seeing Me

(Needed: Copies of Repro Resource 5)

Distribute copies of "Hearing God" (Repro Resource 5). Give group members a few minutes to complete the sheet. For #6, have them draw their own pictures. When they're finished, ask volunteers to share their responses.

Answers might include the following: (1) It's too noisy. (2) She doesn't have enough time. (3) She's too busy. (4) They're not listening. (5) He's not paying attention.

Briefly discuss each scenario, asking your group members how big of a problem they think each one is in most kids' relationships with God.

Then say: **Look at the scenarios again. Write a "1" next to the one that you need to work on first. Then write a "2" next to the one you need to work on next, etc.**

Before you close the session in prayer, give group members a minute of silence so they can ask God to help them work on their #1 priority so they'll be better able to hear Him. Also, challenge your kids to spend more time reading God's Word. As they do, they will be more likely to really hear Him.

O P T I O N S

LARGE GROUP

FELLOWSHIP & WORSHIP

MOSTLY GIRLS

MEDIA

URBAN

EXTRA CHALLENGE

How GOD Spoke

Unscramble the following words to find out how God spoke to people in the past. Then look up the passage to see who He was speaking to and what He said.

1. **GALNE in a SIVNIO** (Zechariah 1:8-17)

2. **RETEH ENM** (Genesis 18:1, 2, 10)

3. **UBNIGNR HUSB** (Exodus 3:1-8)

4. **TGNWIRI on the LWLA** (Daniel 5)

5. **KDEOYN** (Numbers 22:1, 4-6, 21-33)

6. **RETOHNA NMA** (II Samuel 24:18, 19)

7. **HSI IITPSR** (I Timothy 4:1)

8. **OHSTPPRE** (Hebrews 1:1)

9. **SHI SNO** (Hebrews 1:2)

Hearing God

1. Reason he may not be able to hear God:

_____

_____

_____

2. Reason she may not be able to hear God:

_____

_____

_____

SO THEN WE'LL GO TO THE MALL, AND THEN GO SWIMMING, AND THEN BIKE RIDING. TOMORROW WE CAN GO TO THE BEACH AND THEN...

3. Reason she may not be able to hear God:

_____

_____

_____

4. Reason they may not be able to hear God:

_____

_____

_____

THIS PLACE IS SOOO BORING!

5. Reason he may not be able to hear God:

_____

_____

_____

6. Reason this person may not be able to hear God:

_____

_____

_____

STEP 3

When you get ready for Repro Resource 4, don't hand out copies as instructed. Instead, use the various methods God uses to communicate with us as clues for a Pictionary-type drawing activity. Divide group members into teams. Have one person from each team come to the front of the room and look at the clue (angel, vision, burning bush, writing on the wall, donkey, etc.) he or she is to draw. Then the players should return to their teams and, at your signal, begin to draw. Drawers are not allowed to write words, numbers, or symbols. They must simply attempt to draw the image they are assigned. Don't tell them what the common theme is, but let them try to figure it out after they've done a few drawings. Some of the methods on the sheet may need to be adapted for this type of activity. (For example, you might want to have kids draw *companion* rather than *another man*.) But at the end of the exercise you can clarify how each drawing represents a different means of God's communication to us.

STEP 4

As a variation of discussing how we are like sheep and Jesus is like a shepherd, have someone lead a quick game of Simon Says. The leader should begin with simple commands, and then increase the pace and the difficulty. (Go from "Simon says raise your hands" to "Simon says don't refuse to keep your hands up.") After many people have been eliminated, discuss why they messed up when they were intentionally listening so closely. (Didn't understand the instruction? Didn't pay attention for a moment? Imitated the movement of someone else?) Then move into the sheep-shepherd relationship discussion as you explain that sheep are also easily confused and must listen very closely to the voice of the shepherd or they stand to get in a lot of trouble.

STEP 1

Members of a small group might know each other too well to need to guess partners or find out additional information about others. So take a different approach to show the benefits of face-to-face communication. Ask one person to volunteer to tell about his or her day at school. The others should listen; but before they do, give each person a slip of paper that contains an imaginary situation that would influence the level of interest he or she has in the speaker. Situations might include the following:
• Your dad just had a heart attack this morning and his condition is still unstable.
• You have a massive crush on the person who is speaking.
• The speaker's father owns a company that needs a summer worker. You want the job because it's easy, and pays better than anything in town.
• You've stayed up the past two nights cramming for exams—and you still failed.

The speaker should get quite a variety of nonverbal responses based on facial expressions of the listeners. Afterward, have him or her describe the speaking experience. Was he or she annoyed by any of the audience's responses? Did he or she think some of the listeners cared more than others about what he or she had to say? Explain that sometimes the situations we face may prevent us from *hearing* God when He communicates to us.

STEP 2

With a small group, you have the ability to give *everybody* a mouthful of food, rather than just choosing three volunteers. And instead of using a "script," have group members try to carry on a regular conversation. Try to keep the conversation light and humorous, because the more you can get them laughing, the more effective the food will be as a distortion device. If you want to add an additional challenge, put more distance between the kids. It may be a challenge to see which they project farther: their voices or food particles.

STEP 4

Sometimes the more people who get involved in the communication process, the less effective their efforts become. Divide your large group into three or four teams. Blindfold one person per team. Hide a small item somewhere in the room where everyone (except the blindfolded people) can see it. Then spin the blindfolded people enough for them to lose their bearings and give a signal to begin. Each team should try to direct its blindfolded member to the hidden item by giving *only the following directions*: "left," "right," "forward," "behind you," "up," or "down." When everyone begins this process at once, it will cause quite a commotion—one that isn't likely to be helpful to the blindfolded people. Smart teams will discover that they should appoint only one person to give directions, but see how long it takes them to find this out.

STEP 5

Since you have a lot of people on hand, let them adapt Repro Resource 5 into roleplays rather than just still art. Challenge everyone to make the situations "come alive" by providing personal experiences wherever possible. Feel free to adapt them if you want to, or let kids come up with additional situations of their own. You should still discuss the reasons the people may be unable to hear God in each case. You should also have kids follow up the roleplays with a priority list of which situations they most need to work on.

HEARD IT ALL BEFORE

LITTLE BIBLE BACKGROUND

FELLOWSHIP & WORSHIP

STEP 3

Instruct group members to sit in a circle. Have each person in turn mention a method that God uses to communicate with people. Make an elimination game of it. When one person is unable to answer, he or she is "out"; continue until you get down to a single person. Before beginning, make sure kids understand that any biblical example is OK to use. So while God rarely uses burning bushes today, it's still a valid example because He used one with Moses. But don't provide *too much* leeway. All answers must be valid historic or current means of communication. While God *could* certainly choose to manipulate clouds into spelling out "I want you to become a missionary," this answer would not count unless it had actually happened to someone. When everyone is out, see how well your group members did by having them complete Repro Resource 4.

STEP 4

The image of Jesus as shepherd and Christians as sheep is quite common. Your heard-it-all-before group might be quick to write it off as just another Bible cliché. If they don't appreciate it, have them come up with something better. Tell them you understand the difficulty of cool kids like them relating to anti-quated agricultural images like the one in John 10:1-5. Then ask each person to come up with a "new and improved" analogy that would make the same point. It needs to be something that most people can relate to in their own relationship with Jesus—simple and universal. Group members are likely to discover that it's harder than it seems to create effective analogies. They might come up with things like CEO/employees, coach/team members, day-care leader/little kids, etc.

STEP 3

Repro Resource 4 could be intimidating to people who don't know much about Scripture. While the unscrambling should go fine, looking up the verses and trying to understand what's going on in each case might be much more confusing. Dismembered hands writing on walls, talking donkeys, angels, and visions are all amazing and mysterious events that may become overwhelming when combined into a single activity. It will probably be far more helpful if you lead a group discussion about one or two of the main stories instead. The story of Balaam is a tough one for people new to the Bible to understand, so you could help them understand the events of the story that led to the talking donkey. The burning bush, on the other hand, is a story that most kids can deal with on their own because the events are clear and easy to understand. You know your group better than anyone else, so cover the stories you think would be most beneficial to them.

STEP 4

In contrast with the earlier references to burning bushes, talking donkeys, and other miraculous signs, you might expect a bit of confusion when you get to the passage in I Kings 19:11-13. A logical question might arise at this point, especially from someone not well versed in Bible teaching. If not, you should ask it yourself: **Since God is able to perform any powerful and wonderful sign He wishes, why in the world does He ever choose to speak in a "gentle whisper"?** Let kids offer answers. They should eventually come to the conclusion that God almost always provides us with a choice of whether or not we hear and/or obey. His preference is usually two-way communication (like father to child or friend to friend) rather than dictatorial shows of force. We need to remember that He is always able to express Himself in powerful and perhaps frightening ways, but He shouldn't always *need* to in order to capture our attention.

STEP 4

As a group, create a "covenant to listen." We may not think in terms of listening as being a worship activity, yet it is an important part of any person's relationship with God. So try to think of a number of things your group members will agree to do individually as they strive for spiritual maturity. Structure your covenant any way you wish. One option, however, would be to begin with a section of *confession*. ("We talk too much and don't listen enough." "Our quiet times are not usually quiet enough.") Then write a section of *appreciation* for God's patience with us and all He has done and continues to do. Finally, conclude with a section of *intention*—what your members will agree to change in the future to improve their relationships with God.

STEP 5

Too often, closing prayers are taken for granted. Some young people tend not to give them adequate thought or attention. In this case, if time permits, make your closing prayer more of a worship activity. First, challenge each group member to mentally complete this sentence: **Because God speaks _____, I will _____ .** Give some examples. ("Because God speaks softly, I will make more of an effort to have a regular quiet time to listen for Him." "Because God speaks clearly, I will do whatever He tells me to do.") Then close with sentence prayers. Encourage each person to participate. The listening covenant (from the "Fellowship & Worship" option for Step 4) is a group commitment, but when it comes to listening for God's voice, the responsibility must be up to each individual.

MOSTLY **GIRLS**

MOSTLY **GUYS**

EXTRA **FUN**

STEP 4

After you discuss I Kings 19:11-13, ask your group members if they know someone who is hearing impaired. Discuss any experiences they've had. Talk about the adjustments a hearing-impaired person must make and what things might help to aid in communication with such a person.

Tell about neighbor

STEP 5

After completing "Hearing God" (Repro Resource 5), ask your group members to use the back of the resource sheet to write a brief schedule of one day in the previous week. Then have them consider how important it is to them to hear God's voice. Ask: **What can you shorten or eliminate in your daily schedule in order to have time that is quiet enough for you to listen to God?** Ask some volunteers to discuss possible **options**.

*Write down
your daily
schedule*

STEP 2

Guys are usually pretty competitive, so make more of a contest out of the food exercise. Keep the three volunteers who cram food in their mouths, but assign each of these people a team and a list of instructions to call out to their team members (who should be standing a far distance away). The instructions you hand to one person might read: "Your team members are Bill, John, Chad, Taj, and Simon. You are to instruct Bill to hop up and down on his right foot. John should stand with his hand on his head. Chad should sit on the floor. Taj should 'assume the position' against the wall as if he were being arrested. And Simon should turn toward the wall and look at you over his shoulder." The list of team members and their assigned commands should be different for each of the three volunteers. When the exercise begins, no one should know which of the three people is on his team. At your signal, the three volunteers will simultaneously try to outshout each other and be the first to have all of his team members acting according to instructions.

STEP 3

Have guys pair up. Ask each pair to demonstrate one way that guys indicate that they like or admire each other. It's no easy task to appear manly and expressive at the same time, and many guys have quite a system worked out. Pairs should be able to think of a number of ways: high fives, special handshakes, a pat on the back, a thumbs-up signal, a punch on the arm, and so forth. Tie this exercise in with the session's discussion of how, since God is spirit, we have a special way of relating to Him as well. You might also want to point out that guys who are good friends tend to be able to be in each other's presence for hours at a time without necessarily feeling the need to say anything. This observation can tie in to the need for periods of quiet in the time we spend with God.

STEP 3

A good game to accompany the introduction to nonverbal communication is "Peep, Peep." Have everyone sit in a circle except for one blindfolded person who sits in the center of the circle. Spin the center person around and have him or her walk until he or she bumps into one of the seated people. He or she should then sit in the lap of (or stand next to) the person and say, "Peep, peep." The person should respond in the same manner, though may change his or her voice to try to prevent being recognized. The blindfolded person can say "Peep, peep" up to three times and have the other person respond. Then he or she must guess who the person is. If he or she is correct, the other person goes to the center. If not, the blindfolded person returns to the center and tries again. You can use this activity to point out that as we begin to deal with unusual forms of communication, they may be hard to get used to at first. It may be difficult to understand God's "inaudible voice" if we aren't accustomed to listening for it.

STEP 4

When you deal with familiar voices during this step, an additional observation to make is that sometimes familiar voices cannot be trusted. Call for volunteers, four at a time. One should be blindfolded. One should have a prize of some kind (dollar bill, candy bar, etc.). One should have some kind of penalty (squirt gun, water balloon, etc.). The last person has neither prize nor penalty. At your signal, all three people try to convince the blindfolded person to choose them. They can promise, lie, threaten, or do whatever they wish to sway the person's decision. When the person chooses, he or she gets whatever the person is holding. Explain that this demonstrates why it is so important to learn to hear God's gentle voice. We hear a lot of advice and promises; sometimes the number of voices confuses us. God, however, will never lie to or mislead us.

OPTIONS

STEP 3

Rather than using Repro Resource 4 as an unscrambling exercise, use it as a basis for news reports instead. Let kids form news teams and choose one of the examples to research and report on. In each case, the teams should lead off with, "Our top story tonight—God speaks!" Encourage them to "ham it up." For example, one or two people could be seated at the anchor desk and "go live to the scene" where other kids give on-the-spot reports. They might simply report the facts, or they might interview the character(s) involved. Afterward, you can do a "recap" that includes all of the methods the teams chose as well as the others on the sheet.

STEP 5

After you finish Repro Resource 5, say: **Suppose you had a message you wanted to take to all of the other people your age and an unlimited budget to spend. How would you go about reaching the most people? What types of media would you use? Within those categories of media, what specific ones would you target?** (If television, which shows? If magazine advertising, which magazines?) Have kids share their plans with each other. Then ask: **With all of these possibilities, why does God still use a gentle whisper to speak to the hearts of individuals?** Wait for students to respond. Some may comment on the frequent misrepresentations of a few TV preachers. Some might realize that what is basically an entertainment medium is not an effective channel for deep spiritual truth or personal development. Others are sure to have their own unique observations. But all should appreciate the easy (and perpetual) accessibility of God in our lives. We never have to worry about having "the cable go out" or having our "subscription canceled."

STEP 3

Begin the session with the Repro Resource 4 activity, but focus only on the ways God has used to communicate with people. Let kids take their sheets home to look up the verses and see who God spoke to and what He said. The tape-recorded exercise in Step 4 can be eliminated. And you can plan on making Repro Resource 5 optional. If time permits, the sheet is a good way to end the session. If not, however, you can close in Step 4 after reading John 10:1-5. Challenge your young people to learn to identify the voice of God in their lives and to trust whatever He has to say. Otherwise, they are liable to follow some voices that don't have their best interests in mind.

STEP 4

If your time is very limited for this session, your kids shouldn't have a problem drawing applications directly from the two main Bible passages. Divide into two teams. Have the first team read and discuss I Kings 19:11-13. Have the second team read and discuss John 10:1-5. Have the teams prepare to report what they discover about hearing and responding to God's voice. Challenge them to "read between the lines" and deal with inferences and applications in addition to the obvious answers that are contained there. Since these passages are short, the teams should have time to "spin off" into several related areas and ideas. Close by having everyone complete Repro Resource 5 and determine which of the areas he or she needs to work on first.

STEP 1

Try another activity to help young people put the noise of their lives in perspective. Have group members form pairs. Give one person in each pair a slip of paper that reads, "The lively liver of London lies lonely in the laboratory." Give the other person a piece of paper and a pencil. Instruct the first person in each pair to read his or her message once. The object of the activity is for the second person to write down what he or she hears the first person say. Sounds easy, huh? It's not. Bring in a large tape player or radio and play some extremely loud music. Also, the pairs should stand back to back for the activity. Give the pairs a minute to complete the assignment; then see how well some of them do. Try a second round, with the members of the pairs standing face to face, and with no music at all. The pairs will probably find the second round to be much easier than the first one. If you wish, repeat the activity using another phrase. Afterward, point out that "noise" in our lives can lessen our ability to understand God's "gentle whisper" in our hearts and minds.

STEP 5

Integrate into the activity this question: **What words would the people in this city hear from God if they took time to listen?**

STEP 3

The instructions in this step are to "imagine" a problem that involves the inability to communicate verbally. But junior highers will get more involved if they can act out situations rather than imagining them. So give a few volunteers some instructions to try to communicate to other people in nonverbal ways. Here are a few for starters:

- "You're in danger. Come with me."

- "I think you're cuter than anyone else in this room."

- "Do you want to go to your house for a Coke and to study math?"

This activity should lead right into the discussion on God's use of nonaudible communication.

STEP 4

The value of silence may best be appreciated by going to the other extreme. Junior highers usually don't have a problem being loud, so challenge them to see just how good they are at it. Divide into four teams (or two, for smaller groups) and conduct a shouting contest. Start with two of the teams competing for volume as well as sustained noise. Determine a winner and then let the other two teams compete. Determine the winner there and have the finals between the two winning teams. You may not accomplish a lot with this activity, but it's a lot of fun. And in addition, many of the members will welcome the opportunity to sit quietly and listen to you for a while after going all-out in this kind of competition.

Have everyone be quiet!

STEP 3

The fact that God doesn't always try to overpower us with His "voice" lends itself to some creative discussions. Ask: **Does this mean that we have the choice and/or the ability to overpower God?** Let kids comment. They should eventually reach the conclusion that, in fact, we can block out God's voice if we don't attempt to "tune in" to what He wants to tell us. However, that doesn't mean He won't continue with His plans. It simply means we're in the dark about what's going on—and we could face potentially dangerous situations—if we don't listen for His leading. Have volunteers read aloud Ephesians 4:30 and 1 Thessalonians 5:19. Based on these verses, it seems clear that we are able to both "grieve" the Spirit of God and quench the Spirit (or, "put out the Spirit's fire," according to NIV.) But in both cases, we are instructed to avoid these things. While we may be able to ignore what God is trying to tell us, it is never wise to do so.

STEP 5

As an alternative to Repro Resource 5, ask your group members to construct "Daily Noise Pie Charts." Using a circle to represent a day's worth of conscious time (not including time asleep), they should determine an average of how much time they spend listening to various things. Some of these things might include "forced listening" (such as classes at school or similar settings), conversations, TV, radio/Walkmans, music on their stereos, and so forth. As they fill out their charts, they should also determine what percentage of each day involves pure, complete silence. Some of your members might discover that if hearing God's voice requires a totally quiet and isolated setting, maybe He's not getting through because He rarely has a good opportunity. If so, let each person determine how he or she might rearrange the percentages and leave more time devoted to listening for God's voice.

DATE USED:

APPROX. TIME

STEP 1: *Speak to Me!* _____
- ❏ Small Group
- ❏ Urban
Things needed:

STEP 2: *I Can't Understand You* _____
- ❏ Small Group
- ❏ Mostly Guys
Things needed:

STEP 3: *More Than One Way* _____
- ❏ Extra Action
- ❏ Heard It All Before
- ❏ Little Bible Background
- ❏ Mostly Guys
- ❏ Extra Fun
- ❏ Media
- ❏ Short Meeting Time
- ❏ Combined Junior High/High School
- ❏ Extra Challenge
Things needed:

STEP 4: *Listen Up!* _____
- ❏ Extra Action
- ❏ Large Group
- ❏ Heard It All Before
- ❏ Little Bible Background
- ❏ Fellowship & Worship
- ❏ Mostly Girls
- ❏ Extra Fun
- ❏ Short Meeting Time
- ❏ Combined Junior High/High School
Things needed:

STEP 5: *Seeing Me* _____
- ❏ Large Group
- ❏ Fellowship & Worship
- ❏ Mostly Girls
- ❏ Media
- ❏ Urban
- ❏ Extra Challenge
Things needed:

How Does the Holy Spirit "Live" in Me?

YOUR GOALS FOR THIS SESSION:
Choose one or more

☐ To help kids recognize that the Holy Spirit lives in them if they're Christians.

☐ To help kids understand the roles the Holy Spirit wants to fill in their lives.

☐ To help kids discover what the Holy Spirit will and will not do for them and how to allow Him to work in them.

☐ Other:_____
_____

Your Bible Base:

John 14:15-27
1 Corinthians 6:19

STEP 1

Tricked!

(Needed: Coin, paper of various sizes)

O P T I O N S

Begin the session by having your group members try to perform a few impossible stunts. However, don't tell them that the stunts are impossible until after they've attempted them.

First, ask a volunteer to stand with his or her heels against the wall. Set a coin on the floor in front of the person about two feet away. Have the person reach for the coin, keeping his or her heels against the wall. He or she may not hold on to anyone or anything in reaching for the coin. When he or she fails, ask for other volunteers to attempt it.

Next, hand a sheet of paper to one of your group members. Instruct him or her to fold the paper in half 10 times. When he or she fails, ask for other volunteers to attempt it. Give them various sizes of paper to try to fold. Folding any size sheet of paper 10 times is impossible.

Next, walk up to one of your group members (preferably one who is the same sex you are) and say: **I'm the leader; you're the follower. I can find a place to sit in this room that you can't sit in.** Sit down on the floor. Then get up, and invite the follower to sit on the floor too. Then sit on a chair in the room, get up, and invite the follower to sit on the chair too. Before the follower has a chance to stand up again, quickly sit on his or her lap. This proves the point of the activity: The follower can't sit on his or her own lap. (The ideas for these stunts came from *I Bet I Can: I Bet You Can't* by E. Richard Churchill [Sterling Publications Co., 1982].)

Ask group members if they know any similar tricks. If they do, let them demonstrate—if the tricks are appropriate for your group.

Afterward, say: **OK, I admit it, these were simple stunts. But were some of these outcomes easier to predict than others? What's the most baffling magic trick you've ever seen?** Get a few responses.

Besides stunts and magic tricks, what are some other things in life that are hard to figure out? (Group members may list things like algebra, science, how to stay out of trouble, the opposite sex, the Bible, parents or siblings, evil, etc.) List group members' responses on the board as they are named.

If group members didn't mention "the Bible" on their list, add it yourself. Then say: **Many people think the Bible is difficult to** understand. They say there are doctrines, events, and people in it that are hard to figure out. One of these hard-to-understand teachings is the concept of the Holy Spirit living inside of Christians. It's no stunt, illusion, or trick; it's a fact.

Try to remember back to the first time you heard this teaching about the Holy Spirit living in believers. Did you find it hard to believe or understand? How did you feel about it? Some group members may say that it was hard to imagine that God Himself would come to live inside someone once he or she became a Christian. Perhaps it was hard for them to think of a holy God in contact with a sinner.

Say: **It's important to understand and believe the teaching of God living in us, so we're going to investigate this biblical truth in this session.**

STEP 2

An Awesome Fact

Ask: **Which is easier to believe: that God would live in a building or in a person?** Get several responses, if possible.

Then explain that God actually *did* choose to focus His manifested presence in a building at one time. It was the temple that the Israelites built. But after Jesus died on the cross and was resurrected from the dead, God sent the Holy Spirit to live in every person who received Jesus as Savior (Rom. 8:9).

Have someone read aloud I Corinthians 6:19. Then ask: **How are we like the building the Israelites built?** (We are temples too, because God lives in us.)

Explain: **Whether we feel God or not, the fact is that when we genuinely invite Jesus to be our Savior, the Holy Spirit does come to live in us. The Holy Spirit's presence can bring about great changes in our lives. In other words, the One who *resides* in our lives wants to preside over our lives.**

OPTIONS

EXTRA ACTION

LARGE GROUP

EXTRA FUN

MEDIA

URBAN

EXTRA CHALLENGE

Meet the Holy Spirit

(Needed: Bibles, copies of Repro Resource 6, pencils)

Distribute copies of "The Spirit of the Spirit" (Repro Resource 6) and pencils. Have group members work on the sheets individually or in small groups. Assign each person or group to work on only one of the "committees" mentioned in question 3.

Give your group members a few minutes to work. When they're finished, ask volunteers to share their responses. Use the following information to supplement group members' answers.

(1) Jesus promised to ask God to send the Holy Spirit (vs. 16). The Holy Spirit will stay forever (vs. 16). Jesus wouldn't leave us as orphans, but came to us through the Holy Spirit (vs. 18). The Holy Spirit is God because He replaces Jesus on earth (vss. 16-18). The Holy Spirit will make His home with us (vs. 23). The Holy Spirit will teach us and remind us of Jesus' words (vs. 26).

(2) Counselor—One who gives aid and comfort; Spirit of Truth—One who shows what's right in all areas; Guide—One who shows the way; Teacher—One who instructs.

(3) *Committee #1: Most Helpful Person of the Year*—One who is always there for you; one who offers help, but doesn't take over or force his or her way on you; one who is willing to do hard things if necessary.

Committee #2: Most Truthful Person of the Year—One who always tells you the truth, even if he or she knows it might be painful to hear; one whose words are based on accurate information, not inaccurate; one who doesn't change what he or she says so you'll like him or her better.

Committee #3: Best Teacher of the Year—One who is interested in you as a person; one who knows how to teach so you'll learn; one who challenges you to be the best person you can be.

Committee #4: Best Wilderness Guide of the Year—One who knows the area well and helps you through the dangerous places; one who stays with you all the way; one who cultivates courage in you.

(4) The Holy Spirit has all of the qualities mentioned in question #3. Because He is God, He's the perfect helper; He's perfectly truthful; He's the best teacher available; and He's the best guide for our lives.

Summarize: **The Holy Spirit sounds like someone who is pretty wonderful to have around.**

O P T I O N S

SMALL GROUP

LARGE GROUP

HEARD IT ALL BEFORE

LITTLE BIBLE BACKGROUND

MOSTLY GIRLS

MOSTLY GUYS

MEDIA

SHORT MEETING TIME

JR. HIGH / HIGH SCHOOL COMBINED

EXTRA CHALLENGE

STEP 4

Expectations

(Needed: Chalkboard and chalk or newsprint and markers)

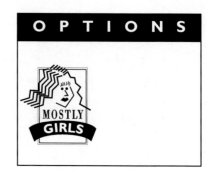
Explain: **The Holy Spirit is more than our helper, truth giver, teacher, and guide. The Holy Spirit is God Himself who gives us wisdom and shows us things we need to know about Jesus. He also lets us know when we're heading in the wrong direction.**

Write on the board key words from the following statements.

What can we expect the Holy Spirit to do for us in each of the following situations? What can we not expect Him to do?

1. I have to take a hard test in math. (The Holy Spirit will help you stay calm so you can do your best. He will not put answers in your mind if you didn't study.)

2. I'm going to be late getting home and don't know what to tell my parents. (The Holy Spirit can give you the courage to tell the truth. He will not excuse you for lying so you don't get in trouble.)

3. I want to know more about God. (The Holy Spirit will help you understand the Bible when you study it. He will not just put information about God in your mind so you don't have to study.)

4. My friend has the key to his parents' liquor cabinet and wants me to come over and drink with him. (The Holy Spirit will help you say no by reminding you of what's right and giving you the desire to do so. He won't "look the other way" if you disobey.)

5. Someone I like wants me to have sex with him or her. (The Holy Spirit will help you say no by reminding you of what's right and giving you the desire to do so. He won't "look the other way" if you disobey.)

6. My best friend wants me to lie for him so he won't get in trouble. (The Holy Spirit will help you say no by reminding you of what's right and giving you the desire to do so. He won't help you make up lies or "look the other way" if you disobey.)

Say: **Because God is merciful and kind, the Holy Spirit helps us even when we don't have a chance to ask for His help, such as in an emergency. But God does want us to ask for His help when we have the opportunity to do so. When you get involved in situations like the ones we just mentioned, the Holy Spirit is ready and willing to help. So it's**

important to reme~
board in big letters. **Pr**
teach you, and sho
in you.

STEP 5

A Look

(Needed: Unshelle~ p~

Give each group member an unshelled peanut ~, **this is the first time you've seen a peanut. Someone cracks it open, shows you the nut inside, and tells you that it's good to eat.**

Have group members crack open and eat their peanuts. Then say: **You find that you like it and you want more. The next time you see a peanut, you remember that there is something good inside and you want one.**

Every time you open something and see something good that you like, let it remind you of the Holy Spirit. When you open a present or a door, crack a peanut, peel a banana, or something like that, remember the Holy Spirit and the fact that if you're a Christian, He is living inside of you and is ready to help you.

Even if you're not a Christian, I challenge you to think about the Holy Spirit every time you open something this week. God is more than willing to forgive your sin when you receive Jesus Christ as your Savior. Then He'll send the Holy Spirit to be your counselor, comforter, guide, and teacher.

Distribute paper and pencils. Instruct your group members to draw a picture of something they open often that will remind them of the Holy Spirit from now on.

You may want to take this opportunity to invite kids who are not Christians to stay after the session and talk with you about how to receive Christ as their Savior.

Close the session in prayer, thanking God for the miracle of the indwelling Holy Spirit. Ask God to help you and your group members depend on Him more and more.

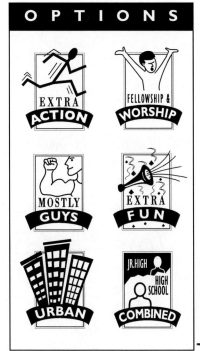

O P T I O N S

EXTRA ACTION

FELLOWSHIP & WORSHIP

MOSTLY GUYS

EXTRA FUN

URBAN

JR.HIGH HIGH SCHOOL COMBINED

1. John 14
might help

pirit of THE Spirit

:15-27 is full of good news! What statements about the Holy Spirit in John 14:15-27
you feel peaceful and confident?

_____

_____

2. Jesus uses four words or phrases to describe the Holy Spirit. Here are their definitions. Draw
lines connecting the words and phrases to their correct definitions.

COUNSELOR	One who shows what's right in all areas
SPIRIT OF TRUTH	One who shows the way
GUIDE	One who instructs
TEACHER	One who gives aid and comfort

3. Imagine that you're on a committee for a nationwide contest in search of people who qualify
to be given one of the following awards. Before you begin your search, you have to define what
kind of people you're looking for. Write down the qualifications a person needs in order to receive
these awards:

COMMITTEE #1 Most Helpful Person of the Year	**COMMITTEE #2** Most Truthful Person of the Year	**COMMITTEE #3** Best Teacher of the Year	**COMMITTEE #4** Best Wilderness Guide of the Year

4. Would you say the Holy Spirit has the qualifications you listed for question #3?
Why or why not?

_____

_____

STEP 2

As you begin to compare Christians to temples of the Holy Spirit, hand out paper and pencils. Ask each person to take a few minutes to draw the "temple" that best reflects his or her character. Most kids probably are much more familiar with churches than actual temples, which is fine. You should help them see that no matter what they look like on the outside, the important thing is that the Holy Spirit is inside. One person might illustrate a chapel in the woods; another might feel more like a big downtown church; another might even perceive himself or herself as a classic European architectural work of genius. Encourage honesty and creative expression. No "residence" is too humble or too big if the Holy Spirit is truly welcomed there.

STEP 5

Rather than simply handing each person a peanut, make a game of it. Provide a bag of peanuts for the group and, at a distance, set up open paper bags with the names of group members boldly written across the front. Set a time limit and see who can toss the most peanuts into his or her bag. At the end of the time limit, have everyone pick up his or her bag and count the peanuts inside. (Also have group members pick up all the "strays" scattered across the floor.) Then proceed with Step 5 as written.

STEP 1

With a small group, you have the opportunity to start with what group members know about a topic and adapt the session to their specific needs. So as soon as you move from the opening exercises to the introduction of what the session is about, say: **Tell me everything you know about the Holy Spirit. You should suppose I don't know anything about it. Can you help me out?** (One of the first things they should do is correct your choice of pronouns, since the Holy Spirit is a "Him" rather than an "it.") This exercise should not only bring up student questions, but clue you to any misconceptions they have as well.

STEP 3

In the intimate setting of a small group, when you get ready to read John 14:15-27, ask one person to assume the role of Jesus and the others to imagine they are His disciples hearing these words for the first time. As the passage is read, the "disciples" should make mental notes of any questions that come to mind. One question is noted within the text, but your group members are likely to have others. After the entire passage has been read, let them express their questions. Many of the questions will be answered as students move on to Repro Resource 6. But if they ask something that will not be covered there, deal with those concerns before passing out copies of the handout.

STEP 2

This step concludes with the statement, "The Holy Spirit's presence can bring about great changes in our lives." You might want to take a few minutes at this point to put to work the collective brain power of your many group members. Divide into several teams of four to six people. Ask each team to put together a skit to show a "before-and-after" comparison of a person who has been influenced by the Holy Spirit. Give as few directions as possible so the skits will be varied. Teams might focus on the dramatic differences in wisdom, power, moral concern, relationships, or any number of other changes the Holy Spirit can make. As you continue through the session, you should be able to refer back to several of these skits to emphasize key points you want to make.

STEP 3

Another way to get your large group more involved is to let group members act out the "award presentations" listed on Repro Resource 6. Divide into four teams and let each team create an award. The teams should list the qualifications for the award (as instructed on the sheet); but rather than simply read off the awards, they should work them into a presentation speech delivered by one of its members. Then another member could step up to receive the award and give a short acceptance speech. While the two speech-givers are working on what they want to say, the other team members can construct an actual award to present, give it a clever name, and so forth.

STEP I

Before doing anything else, hand each group member an egg. Instruct everyone to hold onto the egg throughout the session. (Just to be safe, you might want to use hard-boiled eggs.) Kids who might be becoming jaded toward Christian truth are the ones who most need to become more sensitive to the leading of the Holy Spirit in their lives. At the end of the session, you can explain that the egg-holding exercise should serve as a reminder of the sensitive nature of the Holy Spirit. We can easily prevent a good relationship with God's Spirit by maintaining improper attitudes: apathy, boredom, self-centeredness, and so forth. If any of the kids' eggs are damaged during the session, your point can be made even stronger.

STEP 3

Before you get into a serious discussion about the various roles of the Holy Spirit, let your kids do a roleplay. One person should act as the President of the United States. The others should be his or her staff of advisors (economic, military, foreign affairs, spiritual, and so forth). Have them suppose that the leader of Aruba called the President a "doofus." The President should be offended and desire to declare war on Aruba and attack. His or her staff should offer advice. (Even though the situation is ludicrous, the advisors should act as if the future of the country actually did depend on their decisions.) While you cannot dictate what decision group members reach, it is hoped that they will realize that the offense certainly doesn't warrant the reaction proposed by the President. Then, as you continue the session and talk about the roles of the Holy Spirit, point out that as we learn to respond to the Spirit in our daily lives, He acts as our own inner staff of advisors to help us make the best decisions possible, rather than acting impulsively and getting into unnecessary trouble.

STEP I

If your group members don't have much knowledge of biblical things, the Holy Spirit can be a very difficult concept to deal with. You can't assume that they know about the Trinity, about how God lives in us, or many other basic concepts that most Christians take for granted. Be very conscious of the words you use and the statements you make. In addition, you may want to make a clear distinction between the "fun" parts of this session and the Bible study portion. If you start out by doing tricks and then shift into a discussion of the Holy Spirit, group members might get confused. Also deal with the meaning and implications of the word *spirit* as soon as possible. When they hear the word used, many of these kids may think in terms of Casper the Friendly Ghost or the characters in Dickens' *A Christmas Carol*—neither of which will be helpful as they approach this important biblical truth.

STEP 3

When you get ready to read John 14:15-27, take your time in describing the context in which these words were spoken. Explain that Jesus had spent about three years teaching His disciples, healing sick people, performing other miracles, and showing us how we should live. However, He knew He would soon be killed. Ask: **If you had left behind your home, business, and family, and had devoted three whole years of your life to following Jesus around, how do you think you would feel at this point?** Only after group members realize, to some extent, the fears and feelings of the disciples will they be able to understand the importance of Jesus' sending the Holy Spirit to help us out in His absence.

STEP I

If you usually sing as part of your meeting time, focus on songs that deal with the Holy Spirit. Some well-known songs include "We Are One in the Spirit," "Father, I Adore You," "Sweet, Sweet Spirit," "Holy Holy," and so forth. Even if you don't usually sing, it would be appropriate to do so as part of this session. If your group members are up to more of a challenge, have them create a song of their own after the session. Many choruses are only three or four lines with a simple tune. Many musically inclined students should be able to come up with something creative. Or, if you wish, have them write new words to an existing tune.

STEP 5

Rather than hoping group members will think of the Holy Spirit by associating His presence with the opening of something in their daily routines, allow time at the end of the session for them to create a more tangible reminder. Provide a variety of craft items (paints, modeling clay, paper, markers, etc.). Ask each person to create something that would symbolize the presence of the Holy Spirit. This may be a bit of a challenge, since the Holy Spirit cannot be seen. Yet most kids should be able to think of something. Try to make yourself available to help anyone who just can't seem to formulate a symbolic concept. When everyone finishes, have each person show what he or she has drawn, sculpted, carved, or built, and explain the symbolism used. Encourage group members to keep their creations in plain sight as reminders during the weeks to come of the Holy Spirit's presence in their lives.

MOSTLY GIRLS

STEP 3

Instead of having your group members write down the qualifications for #3 on "The Spirit of the Spirit" (Repro Resource 6), ask them to prepare a team speech. Assign each of four teams one of the awards listed. Instruct each team to discuss the qualifications needed for someone to win that award. Have each team give a name to its winning person. Each team member should then come up with a statement about that person. Explain that each team is to present its "award winner," with each team member playing a part in the process. The teams may choose to present their information as a "cheer," as a choral reading with a leader and response, or as a speech with each person saying a part.

STEP 4

Before the session, write the six situations on a separate index cards. Instead of saying the situations, distribute the six cards to six volunteers. Have each volunteer present her situation, adding a few additional comments to further explain the dilemma. Then ask the rest of the group members to come up with some ways the Holy Spirit can help, and some things the Holy Spirit will *not* do, in those situations.

MOSTLY GUYS

STEP 3

When dealing with a subject as complex as the Holy Spirit, try to use a lot of analogies that would help explain His nature and function. A group of mostly guys will probably relate to baseball. So you might say: **When a player is taken out of a game for some reason, or is unable to continue, another person is sent in to play in his place. What are the requirements of who can go in as a substitute?** (He must be on the same team, have the same goals, be willing to work hard to win, and so forth.) **How does this compare to Jesus sending the Holy Spirit?** (When Jesus had completed the job He came to do and could no longer assist His team [all believers] in person, He "sent in" the Holy Spirit who could indwell all believers at once. Jesus and the Holy Spirit had the same nature and purpose, yet different forms and styles of ministry.)

STEP 5

With a group of guys, you might want to emphasize that in addition to the wisdom skills provided by the Holy Spirit (counseling, guiding, teaching, and leading into truth), He also provides power. Ask: **What are some of the things guys do to try to show how manly or macho they are?** (Take foolish dares; refuse to cry, no matter how much they are hurt; put down other people—especially women; etc.) These are all nonproductive wastes of energy. In reality, such behaviors reveal weaknesses rather than prove strengths. Explain that since we possess the Spirit of God, we don't need to act tough. To become truly strong, we must learn to tap into the power we have at our disposal. Then we will truly be (or at least become) strong. Only by the leading of God's Spirit will we ever be able to become tough enough to withstand intense pressure while remaining sensitive to the needs and feelings of others. That's a winning combination for success in life that too few guys will ever discover.

EXTRA FUN

STEP 2

Bring in several balloons and two sets of long underwear. Divide into two teams. Each team should choose one person to wear the long johns over his or her clothes. At your signal, everyone else should blow up balloons, tie the ends, and stuff the balloons into the long underwear. After four or five minutes, you should signal again for everyone to stop. Count the balloons accumulated by each team (perhaps by popping one at a time with a straight pin, through the long underwear) and declare a winner. Refer to the unusual appearance of the volunteers as they were stuffed with balloons as you explain that this may be the image some people have when they hear references to "God living in their hearts" or "being temples of the Holy Spirit." It seems unnatural, and indeed, it is. It's supernatural. But allowing the Holy Spirit to be part of one's life is a simple matter of willing obedience—and the results are better than we might expect.

STEP 5

Divide into teams for a relay race. You'll need a two-liter bottle of cola for each team. The bottles should be set at the opposite end of the room from where the teams are lined up. The first person on the team should run to the bottle and remove the cap. The next several team members should drink the cola, with each person chugging as much as possible in one trip. (If group members don't want to drink after each other, provide cups for them.) When all the cola is gone, the next person in line is responsible for filling up the bottle with water. (Have some on hand, or let the players run to a nearby sink or fountain.) When the bottle has been filled with water, the next person in line should put the cap back on. Afterward, explain how this activity symbolizes God's Spirit coming into a person's life. The old ways, sinful and dirty, can be replaced with new, godly ways. The transition is not instantaneous in experience—it's something we should work on throughout our lives.

STEP 2

Preview and show a video clip of a film in which the plot revolves around a main character having something inside of him or her. Then have group members brainstorm other examples they can think of. A few to get them started are *Rosemary's Baby* (the child of the devil), the *Alien* series (evil space aliens), *The Hidden* (another evil space alien), *Sybil* (multiple personalities), *Star Wars* (the "force"), *The Terminator* (a cyborg underneath human-looking skin) and, of course, *Peter Pan* (if you count the crocodile that swallowed the ticking clock as a main character). It seems that Hollywood is somewhat fascinated with this theme. But movie makers have yet to come up with anything as powerful or exciting as the Holy Spirit, who resides within each person who puts his or her faith in Jesus.

STEP 3

To follow up your discussion of the Holy Spirit, have your group members create an episode of "In Search Of" or some related sensationalistic investigative-reporting TV show. Many kids have probably seen reports on topics such as the Loch Ness monster, Bigfoot, UFOs, or other strange phenomena. But their topic now should be: "In search of . . . the Holy Spirit. No one has ever seen Him, yet thousands of people insist He exists." Let group members determine how they might go about proving the existence of the Holy Spirit (through interviews, observations of changed lives, etc.). Videotape their efforts so that later they can take a look at how well they did.

STEP 1

Performing a series of tricks is an effective opener, yet can be time consuming. As an alternative, you might want to consider having a number of packages sitting on the table as students arrive. When the meeting begins, let a few volunteers each choose one. Explain that some of the packages might have good stuff inside, some might have bad stuff, and some might be empty. (A few of your packages should appear very fancy—shiny paper, ribbons, bows, the works. A few should be wrapped in old newspapers or simply placed in brown paper bags. Others should be in between. Take great care in seeing that the good prizes, bogus prizes, and empty packages are divided among all of the kinds of wrapping so that no patterns can be detected.) Let all of the volunteers open their packages at once and show what they got, if anything. Ask a few of them why they chose the package they did. Explain that this session will deal with the Holy Spirit. Point out that people are like these packages—if you judge only from outward appearances, you aren't usually able to tell who does or doesn't have God's Spirit dwelling within him or her.

STEP 3

You can save additional time by simply reading and discussing John 14:15-27 as a group, rather than using Repro Resource 6. If it looks as if you still won't have time to finish, you can select just one of the six examples from Step 4. (The key is to keep up the pace as you go through the steps on the handout. The rest of the session isn't very time consuming.)

STEP 2

If your teens are unfamiliar with the term "Holy Spirit," consider comparing Him to the following:

• a tutor

• a tour guide at a museum

• a stagehand who throws the spotlight on the star (Jesus)

• a paramedic who comes to help or rescue someone

• a psychologist

• a bodyguard

STEP 5

If you cannot easily obtain shelled peanuts for this activity, a couple of bags of peanut M & Ms will serve equally well.

STEP 3

Perhaps no wish is as strong or as common among junior highers as the desire to have a driver's license. Ask: **What things will you be able to do when you get a driver's license that you can't do now? Which of the things that you've mentioned do you plan to do?** Encourage group members to be as specific as possible in their responses. Don't let them get by with "I'll get out of the house!" Press them to find out exactly where they'd like to go and what they'd like to do. Then, as you introduce the topic of the Holy Spirit, try to explain that there are things we want to be able to do as human beings that we can never accomplish without the help of God's Spirit (such as become good, forgive parents, like ourselves for who we are, overcome strong temptations, reach our maximum potential, etc.). Receiving God's Holy Spirit in our lives provides us with the freedom to get beyond where we have become "stuck"—much like a driver's license provides the freedom to get out of our parents' house.

STEP 5

In addition to sending your junior highers home to find their own reminders of the Holy Spirit, give them a head start as well. Hand out boxes of Cracker Jack to everyone. Perhaps your group members are a little too old to look forward to the prize in the box, but they will probably remember the excitement they felt as younger kids. Point out that the Holy Spirit in the life of a Christian is a truly valuable prize—not like a plastic figure or washable tattoo. But the concept is the same. We have something inside us that we (and others) can get excited about if we know enough to look for it.

STEP 2

Students willing to dig a little deeper than most might enjoy seeing exactly how important the tabernacle (and later the temple) was to God's people. This was no pup tent pitched in haste as the people moved through the wilderness. If you have good reference books with pictures and easy-to-understand articles, try to have them on hand for one group to examine. Let another group skim through Exodus 25–31; 35–40. The members of this group will see the incredible detail and some of the symbolism that went into planning the tabernacle and its furnishings. A third group can skim through I Kings 5–8 and see the similar attention given to Solomon's temple. After this kind of examination, it should mean a bit more when group members hear that *they* are temples of the Holy Spirit.

STEP 3

We may tend to use the term "Holy Spirit" without too much thought. But it can be helpful for willing students to do a word study to find out more about what "holy" and "spirit" mean, as well as to discover more about the Holy Spirit Himself. You might also want to deal with the theological concept of the Trinity, since the session doesn't do so. Provide Bible dictionaries and concordances. First, come to some agreement on good working definitions for the terms, and then go to the concordances for other biblical examples and information. (You may wish to single out a few key verses ahead of time for students to explore, or you might want to devote an entire additional meeting to this option.)

DATE USED:

APPROX. TIME

STEP 1: *Tricked!* _____
- ❏ Small Group
- ❏ Heard It All Before
- ❏ Little Bible Background
- ❏ Fellowship & Worship
- ❏ Short Meeting Time
Things needed:

STEP 2: *An Awesome Fact* _____
- ❏ Extra Action
- ❏ Large Group
- ❏ Extra Fun
- ❏ Media
- ❏ Urban
- ❏ Extra Challenge
Things needed:

STEP 3: *Meet the Holy Spirit* _____
- ❏ Small Group
- ❏ Large Group
- ❏ Heard It All Before
- ❏ Little Bible Background
- ❏ Mostly Girls
- ❏ Mostly Guys
- ❏ Media
- ❏ Short Meeting Time
- ❏ Combined Junior High/High School
- ❏ Extra Challenge
Things needed:

STEP 4: *Expectations* _____
- ❏ Mostly Girls
Things needed:

STEP 5: *A Look Inside* _____
- ❏ Extra Action
- ❏ Fellowship & Worship
- ❏ Mostly Guys
- ❏ Extra Fun
- ❏ Urban
- ❏ Combined Junior High/High School
Things needed:

How Do I "Walk" with God?

YOUR GOALS FOR THIS SESSION:
Choose one or more

☐ To help kids recognize the importance of having someone to help them through life's everyday problems.

☐ To help kids understand how the Holy Spirit can help us with our everyday problems.

☐ To help kids commit to "walking in the Spirit."

☐ Other:_____
_____

Your Bible Base:

2 Corinthians 1:19-22
Galatians 5:16-26

Making It Through

(Needed: Large boxes, newspapers, chairs, rolls of tape, large bandannas or scarves, prizes [optional])

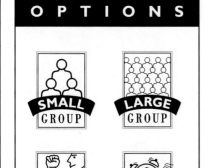

O P T I O N S

SMALL GROUP

LARGE GROUP

MOSTLY GUYS

SHORT MEETING TIME

Have group members form two teams. Assign each team one half of the room. Instruct each team to use whatever objects are available in the room—including shoes, jackets, and the supplies you've provided—to make an obstacle course. [NOTE: Make sure you identify the things in the room you do *not* want used.]

After the teams have completed their courses, the members of Team A (one at a time) will run through Team B's course as quickly as they can without moving or knocking over any of the obstacles. However, the members of Team B may handicap members of Team A by blindfolding them, putting their arms in slings, or anything else (within the realm of safety) that will make it more difficult to get through the course.

After all the members of Team A have run Team B's course, the members of Team B will run Team A's course. Team A will then get to "handicap" the members of Team B.

After both teams have finished running the courses, you may want to award prizes for the most creative or difficult obstacle course.

Then ask: **Have you had a day recently that seemed like an obstacle course? If so, what were some of the obstacles you faced?** (Group members might mention things like a pop quiz, disagreement with parents, needing money for something but not having it, etc.)

How did you feel at the end of your "obstacle course" day? (Depressed, disgusted, angry, tired, etc.)

Say: **When we face this kind of day, we have two choices. We can try to make it through alone, or we can get some help. Let's talk about the kinds of help that are available to us.**

Very good

STEP 2

When You Need a Friend

(Needed: Cut-apart copies of Repro Resource 7)

Before the session, you'll need to cut apart the cards on "Walk with Me" (Repro Resource 7). Distribute the cards to eight volunteers. (If your group is small, you can give more than one card to each volunteer.) One at a time, have the volunteers read aloud their cards (in numerical order 1-8).

After each card has been read, have your group members explain how they might react to that situation. Then have group members suggest how their responses might be different if someone else were facing the situation with them.

For instance, for #4, a group member's reaction might be to say a few choice words to the cafeteria workers and then complain bitterly about the food at the lunch table. However, if another person were facing the situation too, the two of them might joke about it and vent their frustrations through laughter. *Good*

Afterward, ask: **Have you ever gone through a tough experience alone that would have been easier to deal with if you'd some help? Explain.**

Has someone ever helped you get through a tough time? Explain. Encourage responses from several group members.

Summarize: **Having someone around who is truly helpful can save us energy, time, stress, and can sometimes even spare us from deep sorrow or distress.**

OPTIONS

SMALL GROUP

LARGE GROUP

HEARD IT ALL BEFORE

FELLOWSHIP & WORSHIP

MOSTLY GIRLS

EXTRA FUN

SHORT MEETING TIME

JR. HIGH HIGH SCHOOL COMBINED

STEP 3

The One Who Walks with Us

(Needed: Bibles, dictionary)

Say: **It's great to have good friends or loving family members to help us along the way. But sometimes, we need more help than they can give. We need the help of Almighty God. And His help can come through the Holy Spirit, who, as we've discussed, lives in each Christian. The Holy Spirit is here to walk through each day with us. Let's find out what that means.** *read A*

Have volunteers take turns reading aloud Galatians 5:16-26. Then ask: **What instructions are we given in verses 16 and 25?** (To live by the Spirit.)

What do you think it means to "live by the Spirit?" If group members don't mention it, point out that the passage defines it further as not gratifying "the desires of the sinful nature" (vs. 16) and keeping "in step with the Spirit" (vs. 25). Some might also say that it means to obey what the Holy Spirit says to do, follow His guidance, and do what is right.

According to this passage in Galatians, what can happen if we don't live by the Spirit? Some acts of the sinful nature are listed in verses 19-21. Have each group member read and then define in their own words one of the acts of the sinful nature. Allow group members to use a dictionary if they need help.

After each word is defined, have group members give a "thumbs-up" sign if the act is something that kids today might be tempted to participate in.

You may want to summarize the passage by reading the following definitions from the Living Bible: "impure thoughts, eagerness for lustful pleasure, idolatry, spiritism (that is, encouraging the activity of demons), hatred and fighting, jealousy and anger, constant effort to get the best for yourself, complaints and criticisms, the feeling that everyone else is wrong except those in your own little group—and there will be wrong doctrine, envy, murder, drunkenness, wild parties, and all that sort of thing."

Say: **This list of sin seems to go on and on. It's amazing that so much evil can result from disobeying God.** Point out that since most of these activities are still tempting for us today, we *need* to walk in the Holy Spirit.

O P T I O N S

EXTRA ACTION

HEARD IT ALL BEFORE

LITTLE BIBLE BACKGROUND

MOSTLY GUYS

EXTRA FUN

MEDIA

URBAN

JR. HIGH / HIGH SCHOOL COMBINED

What are the benefits of living by the Spirit? (Love, joy, peace, patience, kindness, goodness, faithfulness, gentleness, and self-control [vss. 22-23].)

Encourage group members to give specific examples of each of the fruit of the Spirit. After each example is given, have group members give a "thumbs-up" sign if they would like to experience that fruit in their own lives or if they're already experiencing it.

STEP 4

Giant Steps

(Needed: Copies of Repro Resource 8, pennies or paper clips, prizes [optional])

Distribute a copy of "Backward or Forward" (Repro Resource 8) and a paper clip or penny to each group member.

Explain: **On your sheet, you have two lists—a list of the acts of the sinful nature and a list of the fruit of the Spirit. You also have a game board. Put your penny/paper clip on the "Start" square.**

I'm going to read several situations. After I read each one, you'll decide whether it's an act of the sinful nature or a fruit of the Spirit. Then you'll look at the appropriate list on your sheet and decide which act of the sinful nature or fruit of the Spirit is being described. The first person to stand and give the correct answer gets to move his or her playing piece to the next square. If you identify an act of the sinful nature, you'll move backward. If you identify a fruit of the Spirit, you'll move forward. The first person to reach either end square is the winner.

You may want to award a prize to the winner. If no one reaches one of the end squares before you run out of situations, award the prize to the person who is closest to one of the end squares. Point out that there may be more than one correct answer for each situation.

The situations are as follows:

(1) You watch an X-rated video at a friend's house. (Act of the sinful nature—sexual immorality, impurity, or debauchery.)

(2) You are so anxious to get a car that you agree to sell marijuana to make some money. (Act of the sinful nature—idolatry or selfish ambition.)

O P T I O N S

EXTRA ACTION

MEDIA

URBAN

EXTRA CHALLENGE

(3) You invite a kid of another race who's new at school to eat lunch with you. (Fruit of the Spirit—love, kindness, or goodness.)

(4) You start going to meetings where kids say they can help you gain magic powers. (Act of the sinful nature—witchcraft.)

(5) When one of your friends tells someone else a secret you told him or her in confidence, you plan ways to get even with him or her. (Act of the sinful nature—hatred, discord, or fits of rage.)

(6) Instead of blowing up at your kid brother when he comes into your room for the fifth time and asks you to play with him, you keep your cool and promise to do so after dinner. (Fruit of the Spirit—patience, love, kindness, goodness.)

(7) Because you're angry with your parents for grounding you, you keep complaining about little things your family members do. (Act of the sinful nature—hatred, discord, or fits of rage.)

(8) You have to give a speech in assembly and you're scared, but you pray and sense a calmness growing inside. (Fruit of the Spirit—peace.)

(9) You blew up and cussed out your sister because she took the car after your dad said you could have it this evening. (Act of the sinful nature—hatred, discord, or fits of rage.)

(10) You were very angry because your sister took the car after your dad said you could have it, but you prayed to keep control and took a long walk to calm down. (Fruit of the Spirit—patience or self-control.)

(11) You wish you were dating your best friend's boyfriend or girlfriend. (Act of the sinful nature—envy or jealousy.)

(12) You and another kid at school are competing for the same job. You lie to your potential employer by making up a terrible lie about your competitor. (Act of the sinful nature—selfish ambition.)

(13) You obey God even though you are cruelly made fun of for it by kids at school. (Fruit of the Spirit—love or faithfulness.)

After you've declared a winner, go through the "acts of the sinful nature" situations again. Have your group members suggest ways they could "walk in the Spirit" in each situation, rather than giving in to the sinful nature.

Use the following ideas to supplement group members' responses.

(1) Pray for courage to say no to the X-rated video and for creativity in coming up with a better idea.

(2) Pray about your desire for the car and for the patience to wait for what God wants you to do.

(4) Heed God's Word and run fast in the other direction when black magic or witchcraft is mentioned.

(5) Let the person know how angry you are, but that you're also asking God to help you forgive him or her.

(7) Obey your parents; pray for self-control in handling your anger.

(9) Apologize to your sister; ask God's forgiveness.

(11) Ask God to forgive you for envying your friend and to give you the patience to wait for the person He may have for you.

(12) Tell your potential employer you lied. Apologize to your competitor, if wise Christians counsel you to do so. Ask God to forgive you for lying and for your selfish ambition.

Ask: **Are you taking steps backward or forward in your walk with God? If you're having sex with someone, losing your temper, causing problems at home, you know the answer.**

If you aren't a Christian, you need to turn to God. If you are a Christian, you need to let the Holy Spirit change you by obeying Him.

Spend time with God regularly—in the Bible and in prayer. Try listening to Christian music. As a result of being with God, you'll begin to love God. Then you'll want to walk with Him. You might ask group members to name other suggestions for ways to "walk with God."

STEP 5

Count on It

Good

O P T I O N S

LITTLE BIBLE BACKGROUND

FELLOWSHIP & WORSHIP

MOSTLY GIRLS

EXTRA CHALLENGE

(Needed: Bibles, chalkboard and chalk or newsprint and markers)

Have your group members quickly name five things they can count on about school. (For example: I can count on having homework; getting in trouble if I disobey the rules; having tests; getting a report card; being bored; etc.)

Then have someone read aloud 2 Corinthians 1:19-22. As a group, list five things from the passage God says we can count on. Summarize the answers on the board as follows:

1. God means what He says.
2. God does what He promises.
3. God is faithful.
4. God helps us become strong.
5. God has given us His Spirit.

Point out that there are five points, one for each finger. As time permits, have group members memorize the five points and recite them to the person sitting next to them.

Summarize: **If we choose to walk in the Spirit, we can count on the fact that He will always be our "inside Friend." He'll keep His promises to help with our decisions and to provide courage when we need it. All we have to do is ask.**

Close the session in prayer, thanking God for giving us His Holy Spirit and asking for His help in "walking in the Spirit.

You Teens are not the Church
of tomorrow - You are the Church
of today! God gives you gifts
you need to find out what they
are & use them.
What are the gifts
how can you use them?

Walk with Me

1. At breakfast you spill grape juice on the jacket you have to wear for a school choir concert today.

2. Even though you're running late for school, your dad won't let you take the car.

3. Because you're late for school, you miss a quiz and have to make it up after school. That means you can't go horseback riding with your friend.

4. For lunch in the cafeteria, all they have are wiener roll-ups. You hate wiener roll-ups. You have a few choice words you'd like to say to the cook.

5. When you get home from school, your mom reminds you that you have to rake leaves. You moan and groan. She doesn't seem to care about the bad day you had.

6. While you're raking leaves, the pesky kid next door comes over to watch—and ask a hundred questions. You want to tell him to get lost.

7. Your mom serves liver for dinner. You hate liver and she knows it.

8. After dinner you go to your room to sulk. Just to annoy everyone, you blast your stereo. Life is one big pain.

BACKWARD OR FORWARD

SINFUL NATURE

SEXUAL IMMORALITY
Impurity
Debauchery
IDOLATRY
Witchcraft
Hatred
Discord
Jealousy
Fits of rage
Selfish ambition
Dissensions
Factions
Envy
Drunkenness
Orgies

FRUIT OF THE SPIRIT

Love
Joy
PEACE
Patience
Kindness
Goodness
FAITHFULNESS
Gentleness
Self-control

START
Backward   Forward

STEP 3

A good way to demonstrate the challenge to "keep in step with the Spirit" is to have a three-legged race. Have group members pair up, stand side-by-side, and tie their inside legs together. If you still have your obstacle course set up, perhaps you can adapt it for this relay. Otherwise, just set up a start and finish line in a large open area. When the race is over, have the winners share the secret of their success; then let the others discuss some of the difficulties they faced in trying to keep in step with their partners. Move from this into some of the obvious spiritual applications for keeping in step with the Holy Spirit.

STEP 4

The "Backward or Forward" game in Repro Resource 8 can easily be adapted into a more active exercise. Let kids serve as their own game pieces, standing shoulder-to-shoulder in the center of the room. You can play the game the same way, or you might choose to provide people with pens and paper to write down their answers to each question. Allow all those who answer correctly to move, rather than limiting the opportunity to the first person to raise his or her hand.

STEP 1

A small group split in half may not provide enough people to construct two challenging obstacle courses; so you might want to set one up yourself, before the meeting. Or perhaps you know of a good obstacle course in a park or playground in your area. If so, it may take less time to pile your group members into a car and go to where the obstacles are than to try to construct a course of your own.

STEP 2

If performed as directed, Repro Resource 7 requires 10 people. It can be adapted to your group, of course, but here's another alternative. After you deal with the topic of physical, tangible obstacles (in Step 1), ask kids to brainstorm the other kinds of obstacles they face. They should consider all areas of their lives—home and family, school, work, church, and so forth. List all of the obstacles on the board as they are named, without making comments or observations on them. Then, after you have a good list, go through it one obstacle at a time and let each person express how much of a problem it is in his or her life. (An easy way to do this is to have group members rate each item on a 1 to 10 priority scale [with 10 being highest], holding up the appropriate number of fingers to indicate their answers.) Not only will group members be able to quickly see how many others share their personal concerns, but you will be able to determine which are the major problem areas. You can then plan future sessions to deal with the specific needs of your group.

STEP 1

Divide into teams of four or five. Except for the members of one team, have everyone stand in the center of the room. Members of the designated team must wear some kind of hat. Set a time limit. The object of the game is to see how many times team members can run from one end of the room to the other without having their hats pulled off. The runners may not hold onto their hats; the people in the center may not hold or impede the runners. A point is scored for each time someone makes it all the way across. (A runner may score as many points as possible within the time period.) When time is up, the team's points are totaled. The team then switches places with a team in the center. Continue until all the teams have served as runners; then declare the winners.

STEP 2

A large group may need more involvement than is provided by Repro Resource 7. If that's the case with your group, try the following activity. Have everyone stand in the center of the room. You will name a category. Group members should then divide into the groups you specify for that category. For example, you might say: **The category is age. Find everyone else in the room who is your age.** You might want to make a contest of this by awarding points to the people in the first group to form, and taking away points from the people in the last group to form. Here are some other categories to use:
• Month of birth
• Day of birth
• School attended
• Street address (even numbers vs. odd)
• Hair color
• Amount of money in pockets, wallet, or purse (over $5 vs. under $5)

Afterward, point out that other people probably share a lot of our problems, anxieties, and fears. Perhaps we just need to look a bit harder when we think we're alone in our sufferings.

STEP 2

Instead of using Repro Resource 7, focus more on the follow-up to the obstacle course activity. Distribute paper and pencils. Instruct group members to write "Obstacles, Obstacles, Obstacles" down the left side of their papers. Then have them think of as many obstacles in their lives as possible that begin with those letters. (Allow them to use adjectives if they wish. For instance, if they would like to write "parents" but don't have a "P," they can write "ornery parents.") When group members finish, try to get them talking about the most common and most annoying obstacles they've listed. Then discuss how things might be different if they had a constant companion who could help them through difficult situations.

STEP 3

Before looking at Galatians 5:16-26, have group members do a roleplay. Before the session, write out the sins of the sinful nature listed in verses 19-21 on separate slips of paper (with definitions, if needed). Give one to each group member and ask him or her to assume that characteristic. Have one other volunteer roleplay an average high school student going to a party. The people assuming the sinful characteristics should greet him or her, one or two at a time, and be as creative as possible in demonstrating their "nature." The "innocent" volunteer should wander from person to person, listening to their comments and deciding whether or not to do the things they suggest. Afterward, ask: **Did any of these people remind you of real people you know? How would you like to be in a situation like this one? How can we keep from finding ourselves in such circumstances?** In discussing the Galatians passage, help group members see that this was the kind of thing Paul was trying to warn us about. If we don't allow God's Spirit to provide us with positive "fruit," we won't just be *exposed* to sins like those in the skit—we will be the ones *doing* them.

STEP 3

Long-time Christians may be familiar with terms like "walking in the Spirit" and "keeping in step with the Spirit," but other people might not be. These aren't exactly the easiest things to understand for someone who is trying to absorb these truths for the first time. One thing that might be helpful would be to first speak in terms of Jesus and His disciples. Say: **When Jesus was on earth, He walked along the shores of Galilee and taught His followers important things. They learned from Him, laughed with Him, prayed with Him, and did everything together. When Jesus left, they pretty much fell apart for a while. But Jesus had promised to send them the Holy Spirit. After the Spirit came to live inside the followers of Jesus, all of those people became dynamic individuals even though the earthly Jesus was no longer there. The same is true today. The Spirit of God lives inside all Christians. We are able to talk to Him, walk with Him, and communicate with a real, live person. Sure, it's a little more difficult to learn to interact with an invisible, intangible Spirit, but it becomes easier with practice.**

STEP 5

Second Corinthians 1:19-22 is not an easy passage to understand at first reading—or second, or third. If your kids aren't used to biblical language or concepts, you might want to explain just the five things to remember and where they came from. Also, don't expect your group members to make their own applications as more experienced churchgoers might. Even though they can memorize the five things as instructed, it would probably be very helpful for you to talk them through some specific examples of each one. As good as these promises are, they won't mean much if kids aren't able to relate them to real life.

STEP 2

Rather than moving through Repro Resource 7 as just another step in the session, take a few minutes to build fellowship. One at a time, ask group members to express the current obstacles in their lives. Be patient during this time. If kids aren't used to opening up about the things that bother them, they may be reluctant at first. Perhaps you could list several things from your own life to get everyone started. As other individuals begin to share, make a master list of the obstacles of your group. During the next week, make copies to hand out to everyone the next time you meet. Ask group members to commit to pray for each other during the next few weeks (beginning today). Their obstacles will be more easily overcome when they are aware that several other people are relating to the things they are experiencing.

STEP 5

After you read 2 Corinthians 1:19-22 and have group members memorize the five things they can count on God doing for them, let them go one step further. Provide paper and pens and ask them to complete sentences based on each of the things they've memorized. For example:

• **Because God means what He says, I will . . .**

• **Because God does what He promises, I . . .**

• **Because God is faithful, I can count on Him to . . .**

• **Because God helps me become strong, I am able to . . .**

• **Because God has given me His Spirit, I . . .**

This exercise helps group members create some personal applications for the things they've learned. If some kids are willing, let them share some of the things they've written; but don't put pressure on anyone. It's enough for them to make personal commitments based on what they've learned.

STEP 2

You'll need lunch bags and markers for this activity. Have your group members make very simple paper-bag puppets. The puppets are made by turning the flat bag upside down and drawing a mouth at the fold created by the bottom. Operate the puppet by inserting one hand into the bag and grasping the fold, pressing the fingers toward the palm and/or opening them to make the mouth move. After the puppets are made, have group members form teams of two to four. Distribute a copy of "Walk with Me" (Repro Resource 7) to each team. Instruct the teams to use their puppets to respond to the obstacles in that day. Give the teams a few minutes to work; then have them present their puppet shows. Afterward, discuss the questions at the end of the step.

STEP 5

As you discuss the five things group members can count on about God, ask: **How does knowing these things affect how you feel about God? Which of these things best helps you understand that God is a part of your life and not just a powerful Spirit removed from everyday situations?**

STEP 1

With a mostly masculine group, you might want to be a lot more aggressive with the obstacle course activity. It may even be difficult to construct something within the room that would be sufficiently challenging for them. If so, consider adding the element of physical exercise along the way. ("Crawl through the empty box and then do 25 sit-ups. Go through the door backward and then do a dozen pull-ups on the overhead beam. Limbo under the table and then do 10 push-ups.") As each person runs the obstacle course, you might let the others attempt to impede his progress by throwing balls at him, placing new obstacles in his path, or whatever. Better yet, let your guys come up with their own challenges and see what happens.

STEP 3

When you get to Galatians 5:19-21, take your time discussing the significance of the sins listed there. Most of the things in the list are "guy sins"—things that are especially indicative of or tempting to teenage guys. Don't generalize these things too quickly and move on to the fruit of the Spirit. In fact, you might want to go through the list one at a time and let group members come up with all of the specific instances of that problem that they've encountered during the previous week. Before doing so, however, make sure that they know you will not be overly shocked by anything they say, and that whatever they mention will be held in confidence. Only when they are allowed to deal more deeply with the specifics of their own sinful natures will the fruit of the Spirit seem more like a valid answer for them.

STEP 2

Before you begin this step, arrange chairs in a circle. Have everyone sit in the chairs except for one person, who will stand in the center. There should be an empty chair in the circle. The goal of the person in the center is to sit down. However, the rest of the seated people will try to make sure that he doesn't have that opportunity. As the center person moves toward the open seat, the others should shift seats and fill in the space. Of course, one seat is always open. When the center person is finally able to sit in the open chair, he designates someone else to go to the center. After you play for a while, point out how frustrating it is when some of our closest friends become obstacles for us. Then move into Repro Resource 7 and see how people can help us overcome our obstacles, rather than making them worse.

STEP 3

Have group members arrange their chairs in a circle. As you go through the list of the acts of the sinful nature in Galatians 5:19-21, read one sin at a time. Ask group members to move one chair to either the right or left (your discretion) for every time today (or this week) they've either committed that sin or come into contact with it. (They need not say which.) Of course, soon people will begin to pile up in certain chairs while other chairs remain empty, but that's OK. Just go to the next one on the list and do the same thing. For several of the sins listed, you might want to include examples as well as definitions of the terms used. After you go through the list of sins, have group members return to their original chairs. Then do the same thing for the list of characteristics of the fruit of the Spirit (vss. 22, 23).

STEP 3

Most video stores contain "blooper" videos of various sports. These make very entertaining (and enlightening) examples of what happens when people get "out of step" in some kind of sport. The application then becomes apparent as to what happens to us on a spiritual level when we get out of step with the Holy Spirit in our lives. Sometimes it's not a pretty sight. [NOTE: If the video you choose is labeled "For private use only," it is not intended to be shown in a group setting. Many publishers don't mind as long as you aren't charging admission to see it, but it is still appropriate for you to write them for permission to use specified portions in your group.]

STEP 4

Instead of doing Repro Resource 8, provide several magazines for your group members to go through. After you've discussed the acts of the sinful nature in Galatians 5:19-21, ask group members to examine the ads for suggestions of any of these characteristics. It shouldn't be too hard to find examples of lust, selfish ambition, or envy. And with a little effort, you should be able to find several others on the list as well. In several secular magazines aimed at teens, some of the ads can be quite graphic. And be forewarned—some of these ads occasionally include partial nudity (bare breasts or buttocks), so you might want to look through the magazines first to avoid any surprises.

STEP 1

After your group members run the obstacle course, skip to Step 3 and discuss the Galatians 5 list of sins. Explain that these things are obstacles in our lives. Ask: **Which of the things on this list are the hardest things for you to deal with? Do you think some are worse than others?** (Perhaps, but sin is sin as far as God is concerned.) **How do you think you can get over or around these obstacles?** Let the discussion lead to the rest of the passage, in which the fruit of the Spirit is introduced. Then spend the rest of the time discussing these questions: **What has God done to help us get around all of these obstacles? Based on what He has done, what can we do to keep from being tripped up by any of these things?**

STEP 2

Another option is to eliminate the opening obstacle course, since it can be time consuming. Also skip Repro Resource 7, since it is a follow-up exercise. Begin with the questions at the end of Step 2 and move right into Step 3. Depending on the time you have remaining, Step 4 can be optional. (Rather than playing the game on Repro Resource 8, you may want to simply select a couple of examples to show kids specifically what kinds of things they might expect and how they can choose to respond.) Then conclude with Step 5 as written.

STEP 3

After you've discussed the fruit of the Spirit, ask your group members to consider (a) how they can be applied to the city in general, and (b) what type of urban people need the fruit being applied most. For example, love may be needed by runaways and prostitutes, while kindness may be needed by those who use their riches to oppress, rather than to bless.

STEP 4

Here are some urban-centered scenarios you might use for the activity:

(1) You take a gun or knife to school for protection. (Act of the sinful nature—hatred, fits of rage, factions.)

(2) You volunteer for a soup kitchen after school. (Fruit of the Spirit—kindness.)

(3) You decide to get out of an abusive relationship before things get further out of hand. (Fruit of the Spirit—peace, self-control.)

(4) You are sixteen and involved in a sexual relationship with a person who is thirty-four years old. (Act of the sinful nature—sexual immorality, impurity, discord, selfish ambition.)

STEP 2

If you have a group of mostly junior highers, you might want to replace Repro Resource 7 with a discussion of the following questions: **What are some obstacles that junior highers face that no one else does? What things do you go through that other people just don't seem to understand?** Your group members may not have thought much about this, but have them spend some time coming up with the things that are particularly challenging for them: going through puberty; having a desire to get out and get around, but not being able to drive; being treated like kids half of the time and adults the other half; too much parental control; etc. After you help group members zero in on some specific things, the rest of the session may seem more applicable to them.

STEP 3

When you get to the Galatians 5 list of acts of the sinful nature, junior highers may need considerable more explanation of the definitions of some of the terms. But they might also need a little incentive to differentiate one from the rest. One way to hold their attention is to give them a list of the words (as on Repro Resource 8). Then read one definition at a time from a dictionary. Let kids try to match each definition you read with the appropriate term on their lists. This is a relatively quick way to cover all of the definitions you need to review with your junior highers.

STEP 4

At the end of this step are a number of ideas to supplement group members' previous responses. For an extra challenge, have your students think of an appropriate Bible verse or passage that will support each of the ideas. In cases where they cannot think of one, have them use a concordance to find one. It's one thing to "Pray for courage and say no to the X-rated video"; but it can be even more assuring to reaffirm the truth of Philippians 4:13: "I can do everything through him who gives me strength." And when the kids generate their own biblical support, they are likely to remember the passages longer than they would if you supply them.

STEP 5

When you read 2 Corinthians 1:19-22, explain that this was a message Paul was trying to communicate to the Corinthian church in the first century. However, it may be a bit hard to understand for teenagers in the twentieth century. Challenge group members to paraphrase Paul's message as they might explain it to their friends. This can be done either individually or in small groups.

DATE USED:

Approx. Time

STEP 1: *Making It Through* _____
- ❑ Small Group
- ❑ Large Group
- ❑ Mostly Guys
- ❑ Short Meeting Time
Things needed:

STEP 2: *When You Need a Friend* _____
- ❑ Small Group
- ❑ Large Group
- ❑ Heard It All Before
- ❑ Fellowship & Worship
- ❑ Mostly Girls
- ❑ Extra Fun
- ❑ Short Meeting Time
- ❑ Combined Junior High/High School
Things needed:

STEP 3: *The One Who Walks with Us* _____
- ❑ Extra Action
- ❑ Heard It All Before
- ❑ Little Bible Background
- ❑ Mostly Guys
- ❑ Extra Fun
- ❑ Media
- ❑ Urban
- ❑ Combined Junior High/High School
Things needed:

STEP 4: *Giant Steps* _____
- ❑ Extra Action
- ❑ Media
- ❑ Urban
- ❑ Extra Challenge
Things needed:

STEP 5: *Count on It* _____
- ❑ Little Bible Background
- ❑ Fellowship & Worship
- ❑ Mostly Girls
- ❑ Extra Challenge
Things needed:

NOTES

Unit Two: Free Gifts for Everybody!

Discovering Your Spiritual Gifts

by Ray Johnston

"Millions of Christians live in a sentimental haze of vague piety, with soft organ music trembling in the lovely light from stained glass windows. Their religion is a pleasant thing of emotional quivers, divorced from the will, divorced from the intellect and demanding little except lip service to a few harmless platitudes. I suspect that Satan has called off attempts to convert people to agnosticism. After all, if a person travels far enough away from Christianity, they are liable to see it in perspective and decide that it is true. It is much safer from Satan's point of view to vaccinate a person with a mild case of Christianity so as to protect them from the real disease."

—Chad Walsh, *Early Christians of the Twenty-first Century*

During the first few years of my youth ministry, I produced apathetic kids. I didn't have a plan for developing apathy; it just happened naturally. During this time, one of my seminary professors changed my ministry for life when he said, "Ladies and gentlemen, if you want to have an effective ministry, find out what your spiritual gifts are and build your whole life around them."

That one sentence was a turning point in my ministry. I returned to my youth ministry convinced that for shaking up apathetic kids, maximizing impact, preventing youth worker burnout, and assuring effectiveness in youth ministry, there was nothing better than helping people discover and develop their gifts.

For years, teenagers have been robbed of the chance to discover and use their gifts by living off the antiquated (and unbiblical) philosophy that "teenagers are the church of *tomorrow*." The results have been devastating. For many churches, teenage discipleship is a distant dream. Gifted teenagers with contributions to make are locked out of discovering the joy of being used by God, and adolescent spirituality is an oxymoron, on par with jumbo shrimp, cafeteria food, or Plymouth Reliant.

The goal of these sessions is to help turn that trend around. *Free Gifts for Everybody!* should come with a warning label: "Caution! Putting these sessions into practice could change the lives of your group members!"

I think the apostle Paul would agree. Writing to the Corinthians (a group of people who were acting very much like contemporary high school students), he declared, "Now about spiritual gifts . . . I do not want you to be ignorant" (1 Corinthians 12:1). Youth workers who give high priority to helping teenagers discover and develop their spiritual gifts often experience four major benefits:

• *Discovering spiritual gifts can help your kids develop confidence.* Confidence and self-esteem are critical components for healthy adolescent development. As kids begin to use their gifts, self-esteem often flourishes as they gain a new sense of significance and competence.

• *Discovering spiritual gifts can shake up apathetic teenagers.* When asked which adjective best describes "church," the average young person replies with the word "booooring." A recent study of churched kids in Canada found that 97% felt *under challenged* by the church!

• *Discovering kids' spiritual gifts helps prevent youth worker burnout.* Most of us are too busy. Like Martha in the Gospels (a great youth worker in her day), we get overwhelmed by responsibilities, distracted by all of our preparations, and stressed out by all we have to do.

Sound familiar? Gifted young people can help lighten the load. I've had group members making flyers, planning meetings, leading games, giving talks, teaching Sunday school, handling setup and cleanup, arranging transportation—often better than I would have done the job. When kids discover and use their gifts, this often gives you, the exhausted youth worker, the one thing we all need more of—time.

- *Discovering spiritual gifts develops servanthood.* American teenagers have been described as the "Kodak Generation," overexposed and underdeveloped. As kids discover, develop, and deploy their gifts, they begin to acquire the kind of spiritual vitality that only comes by moving from being spectators to being servants.

Unwrapping Gifts

Here are some tips to lessen the risk of failure and help your teenagers have a reasonable chance of success as they explore their gifts:

- *Let kids grow at their own pace.* A quick glance at any youth group gives you an idea of the tremendous spectrum of maturity, both physical and spiritual, among high school students. Perhaps your group members fit somewhere in these three categories:

Level 1—Ready to discover their gifts. For younger group members or new Christians, it may be a while before they are ready to use their newfound gifts. These kids need information, motivation, encouragement, and a lot of patience.

Level 2—Ready to develop their gifts. Now it gets exciting! Ready for on-the-job training, these young people will benefit from a youth leader who helps them get involved in specific ministries that correspond to their newly discovered gifts.

Level 3—Ready to deploy their gifts. Ready for involvement and wanting to make an impact, these group members will grow to the extent that we are willing to delegate personal and program responsibilities that match their gifts.

- *Start small.* Don't turn over your entire ministry and then expect things to tick along like the gear wheels in your Rolex. Start by letting kids be responsible for pieces of the puzzle—setting up chairs, making one announcement, leading one game, planning part of a meeting, leading a couple of songs, passing out song sheets, setting up a skit, reading Scripture verses, etc. Slowly increase their opportunities to use their gifts as their confidence level rises.
- *Saturate your kids with affirmation.* American teenagers are bombarded with negative information. Most are ridiculed at school and intimidated by the media. Many teenagers may be willing to believe in their gifts only after someone else believes in them.

I recently sat with a group of teenagers at my dining table. They had just finished taking their first spiritual gifts test. I then had each teenager sit at the head of the table and take notes while the whole group shared with him or her what they thought his or her gifts were. The atmosphere was electric! For some of these kids, it was the first time in years they had heard positive information about themselves. Some of the group members still haven't recovered from that night. Their interest in their gifts was heightened. Their confidence level rose. Their willingness to support each other was cemented. A little encouragement (even if you have to arrange it) will go a long way.

- *Allow your group members to assist you.* Kids will learn how to use their gifts more effectively if they are able to help you use yours! Kids with teaching gifts can help you prepare your talks. Kids with encouragement gifts can help you make phone calls. Kids with administrative gifts can help you plan meetings. Kids with the gift of faith can go to the church board and negotiate your 50 per cent raise. It's been years since I planned, programmed, or pulled off any youth ministry event by myself. Letting a few kids help improves the quality of the event while developing their gifts. It's also more fun!

- *Stay in touch.* The roles here are reversed. Now group members are using their gifts and you are in the role of helping them. As your kids begin to use their gifts, you may want to meet with them during the week to help them prepare.
- *Build a climate of grace—allow kids to fail.* During my first year in youth ministry, I took up the guitar. (I thought song leading was a youth ministry requirement.) After six months of practice, the faith-filled leaders in our church asked me to lead music in our small Sunday evening service. That night is still a legend in the church. Tape sales skyrocketed because the music was so bad it was funny. The atmosphere of grace, acceptance, and encouragement in our small church relieved me of any feeling of failure and freed me to try other gifts.

Babe Ruth struck out seven times for every home run he hit. Henry Ford went bankrupt three times. Thomas Edison failed hundreds of times before the light bulb worked. Failure is not fatal, but the fear of failure can be. The only way to discover and develop gifts is trial and error. For your teenagers, gift discovery will mean experimentation, risk, and occasional failure. Creating a relaxed climate of grace will allow your group members to risk trying their gifts. Let them try, fail, and try again. Who knows? The next great song leader just may be in your group. It surely isn't me!

Pitfalls to Avoid

As you get started, let me warn you of a couple of pitfalls to avoid:

- *Don't expect problem-free success.* In a perfect world, chocolate would be calorie-free, troublemaking kids would sit in the front row, church vans would never break down, taxes would never rise ... and your teenagers would never drop the ball. When failure comes (and it will), stay loose and keep your eyes on what the kids can become, not on what they're like right now!
- *Encourage, but don't rescue.* We learn a lot from failing if we are given time to process the lesson. Allow kids to fail, then meet with them and pick up the pieces.
- *Don't focus all of your attention on superstar kids.* Many of your kids are diamonds in the rough. Guard against the temptation to focus only on the kids whose gifts are obvious.
- *Don't underestimate your kids.* Kids can and do serve Christ in remarkable ways. Ben and Stacey, two high school students in El Dorado Hills, California, have started a lunchtime Bible study that is drawing up to 34 students—the gift of teaching in operation.

Jim, 13, in Denver, Colorado, has developed a great relationship with an elderly grandfather in a convalescent home near his house. Visiting twice a week, this eighth grader is the gift of mercy in action.

Suzanne and Stacey, two sophomores in Jackson, Mississippi, lead a lunchtime Bible study for seventh and eighth grade girls that has grown from 2 to over 50 in a year. One of the fastest-growing junior high ministries in the South is being lead by two high schoolers putting their gifts of evangelism into action.

I recently had a conversation with a high school principal in Denver, in charge of a student body of 2,000, who told me that he was led to Christ by a sophomore girl at his school.

These young people all have one thing in common—a youth worker who believed that their gifts were worth discovering and developing! Teenagers are capable of having an incredible impact for Christ, and that capability is often unlocked when an adult finds an area of strength and calls attention to it. May God bless you as you begin this task!

A graduate of Azusa Pacific University and Fuller Theological Seminary, Ray Johnston is currently president of Developing Effective Leaders, an organization that sponsors leadership training seminars for student and adult leaders. He is also on the staff of Lake Hills Community Church in Folsom, California.

The images on these two pages are designed to help you promote this course within your church and community. Feel free to photocopy anything here and adapt it to fit your publicity needs. The stuff on this page could be used as a flier that you send or hand out to kids— or as a bulletin insert. The stuff on the next page could be used to add visual interest to newsletters, calendars, bulletin boards, or other promotions. Be creative and have fun!

Do You Feel Gifted?

If you're a Christian, God has given you some important, unique gifts to use to benefit His church. So how do you find out what your gifts are?

How do you put them to work?

What happens if you don't use your gifts?

You'll find the answers to these and other questions when you join us for a new series called *Free Gifts for Everybody!*

Who:

When:

Where:

Questions? Call:

Unit Two: Free Gifts for Everybody

Don't be a Lone Ranger with your spiritual gifts.

Tell your friends.

Do you have a grasp of your spiritual gifts?

What Are They For?
(The Purpose of Spiritual Gifts)

YOUR GOALS FOR THIS SESSION:
Choose one or more

☐ To help kids discover the meaning and purposes of spiritual gifts.

☐ To help kids recognize the differences between gifts, natural talents, and fruit of the Spirit.

☐ To help kids choose a personal prayer request related to the function of spiritual gifts in their group.

☐ Other:_____
_____

Your Bible Base:

Exodus 35:30-35
Romans 12:3-8, 13
1 Corinthians 12:4-11, 27-31
Ephesians 4:7-16
Colossians 1:9-12
1 Peter 4:9-11

STEP 1

The Silly Skills Show

(Needed: Various props for talent show performers to use—balloons, clay, paper and crayons, juggling balls, rubber chicken, kitchen utensils, toys, etc.)

Start with an impromptu crazy-talent-show icebreaker that relates (at least indirectly) to your theme for the course. You'll be making the distinction between talents and spiritual gifts later in the session. But for now, raise the theme of talents, and give your group members a chance to display some of theirs. Explain to your group members that they may display any talent—telling a joke, drawing a picture, curling their tongue, etc. Then invite the whole group to vote on various awards, such as "craziest body talent" (for example, the ability to cross eyes, touch tongue to nose, touch thumb to forearm), "scariest face-maker," "most creative use of a prop," or "most likely to become a circus performer." You may also wish to offer an award for the most "serious" talent demonstrated (for example, for those who play musical instruments or who show genuine artistic ability).

The point is to make sure that everyone has a chance to demonstrate—or at least talk about—some skill or talent, whether silly or serious, great or small. If any kids can't think of anything to do, make it clear that they can just talk about an ability they have. Offer suggestions by asking questions like the following: **Do you have the ability to watch TV and do homework at same time? The ability to fall asleep within 10 minutes?** Be ready to affirm any talent you see, including the ability to dress colorfully, the ability to be a good conversationalist, the ability to drive safely to youth meetings, etc.

Then ask: **How many of you were surprised by how much talent we have in this group?** Ask volunteers to talk about their reactions to others' talents. Find out who had talents that no one knew about before.

How do talents and abilities help us in life? (We might use them to make friends, get jobs, and enjoy ourselves.)

How can our abilities help others? (We could use our abilities to encourage a friend, to make things for people to use, to entertain people, to produce art or literature, etc.)

In your opinion, what percentage of these talents could be used in a church, to help people grow in Christ? This question may bring some laughter. The percentage will no doubt be low; but some talents could probably be used.

STEP 2

Not Seeing . . . Isn't Knowing

(Needed: Paper, pencil)

Let kids watch you from a distance as you pencil in a small black dot in the center of a sheet of paper. Then gather group members in a circle and hold up the sheet of paper, bringing it close to people's faces.

Ask: **What do you see?** (A dot, a black mark.)

Then say: **Actually, what I'm holding up is a sheet of white paper! How come nobody** (or **so few of you**) **saw that?** Get a few responses.

Explain that the point of this little object lesson is that sometimes when we look at ourselves, we don't see all that is there. For example, we're often blind to our abilities.

Say: **Suppose you had a hidden talent. Wouldn't you want to know what it was—so you could use it? The point is that God has given all Christians special abilities or "spiritual gifts" for Christian service. But many Christians don't know what those gifts are. In our next session, we'll work on discovering what gifts God has given to each of us personally, but today we first need to know what gifts are actually available. In other words, we need to become familiar with the "pool of possibilities" when it comes to spiritual gifts.**

OPTIONS

SMALL GROUP

MOSTLY GIRLS

MEDIA

STEP 3

Developing a Gift List

(Needed: Bibles, copies of Repro Resource 1, pencils, chalkboard and chalk or newsprint and marker)

Say: **Suppose you had to make up a gift list for a friend or relative—one that included all of the things you'd like him or her to have, if money were no object. What things might be**

OPTIONS

on your list? Get several responses. Then suggest that the list is a "pool" of possible gifts.

Then ask: **What is the "pool of the possible" when it comes to "gifts" for us Christians to have—abilities that God gives us to use in His service?** Get a few responses.

Distribute copies of "Pool the Possibilities" (Repro Resource 1) and pencils. Ask group members to choose two of the columns to work on, or assign columns so they are distributed equally. Go over the instructions on the sheet to be sure everyone is clear about the task.

Circulate among group members as they work, offering guidance as needed. When everyone has finished, work together as a group to develop a "master gift list" on the board. Do this by asking kids to call out one gift at a time, having the rest of the group members cross off that gift on their lists, until all possibilities have been listed.

Possible responses for Repro Resource 1 might include the following:

Romans 12:3-8—Prophesying, serving, teaching, encouraging, giving, leading, showing mercy

I Corinthians 12:4-11—Wisdom, knowledge, faith, healing, doing miracles, prophesying, distinguishing spirits, speaking in tongues, interpreting tongues

I Corinthians 12:27-31—Being an apostle, being a prophet, being a teacher, doing miracles, healing, helping, administrating, speaking in tongues

Ephesians 4:7-16—Being an apostle, being a prophet, being an evangelist, being a pastor, being a teacher

The following is a suggested "master list" of gifts that you may want to use for the rest of this course:

1. Proclaiming the Truth—includes prophesying, preaching, and persuading (I Cor. 12:10, 28)
2. Serving (Rom. 12:7)
3. Teaching—includes wisdom and knowledge (Eph. 4:11; I Cor. 12:8)
4. Encouraging (Rom. 12:8)
5. Giving (Rom. 12:8)
6. Leading—includes shepherding or pastoring (Eph. 4:11)
7. Having faith (I Cor. 12:9)
8. Working miracles/healing (I Cor. 12:28)
9. Discerning—includes "distinguishing between spirits" (I Cor. 12:10)
10. Speaking languages/interpreting (I Cor. 12:10, 28)
11. Administrating—includes organizing and managing people (I Cor. 12:28)
12. Evangelizing (Eph. 4:11)
13. Showing mercy (Rom. 12:8)
14. Offering hospitality (Rom. 12:13; I Peter 4:9-10)
15. Praying for people (Col. 1:9-12)
16. Using craftsmanship (Exod. 35:30-35)

As your group members consider the master gift list, ask: **Can you recall another Christian helping you in one of these ways? If so, what happened? Were you aware at the time that this person was using a God-given ability to help you grow as a Christian?** Get a couple of responses, if possible.

Follow up your discussion by making the point that there are still tough questions about spiritual gifts to which Christians will give different answers. Supplement your discussion time by raising any or all of these tough questions for consideration, as time permits.

Tough Question #1—**How many spiritual gifts are there?** Point out that lists of gifts can never be exact. Mainly because we don't know if the Bible intends to name them all. For example, hospitality is not named specifically as a gift, but it seems to function as a gift in many believers' lives. And what about "modern" abilities, such as computer programming skills, with which a person could organize a church office?

Tough Question #2—**Should we look to the Old Testament to discover spiritual gifts?** Point out that some have suggested that craftsmanship ought to be considered a spiritual gift (see Exod. 35:31).

Tough Question #3—**Are any gifts no longer valid for this age?** Some Christians say yes. They point to the gift of apostling as an example. Others would say that being an apostle today simply means being a missionary. Many churches deny the modern validity of the so-called miraculous gifts. They would say that God only ushers in new eras with the miraculous—such as the beginning of the church age; therefore, gifts such as apostleship, tongues, healing, and miracles have now ceased. Others disagree. What position does your church take?

Tough Question #4—**Should we distinguish between spiritual gifts and positions in the church?** This is unclear. Some groupings of the gifts do distinguish among the "motivations," "ministries," and "manifestations," based on the statements in 1 Corinthians 12:4-6. This might limit the actual gifts to seven—proclaiming truth, serving, teaching, exhorting, giving, ruling, and showing mercy. At least 10 ministries would draw upon those 7 gifts—apostle, prophet, evangelist, pastor, teacher, worker of power, healer, helper, administrator, and linguist.

The important point to keep in mind when exploring such questions is that we need to be open to how the Holy Spirit wishes to work among us, as long as everything that is done is for the building up of the church and the maturing of believers. Also, any gift should be exercised with loving motives and in an orderly way.

STEP
4

Getting Gifts in Gear

(Needed: Copies of Repro Resource 2, pencils)

Emphasize that Christians differ in their views about how many spiritual gifts there are and to what extent some of them are valid today. But the key point to remember is that we need to be aware of the gifts God has given us and be ready to use them. We are all a part of Christ's body, and though Jesus is not still here with us physically, He has filled us with His Spirit and equipped us to keep doing His work on earth with our spiritual gifts.

Ask: **How does it look when we actually use our gifts? Let's consider the case of Jason.**

Hand out copies of "Avoiding Concept Confusion" (Repro Resource 2). If necessary, go over the distinctions between gifts, talents, and fruit of the Spirit. Then ask group members to mark their sheets with "G," "T," or "F," as instructed toward the bottom of the sheet.

After a couple of minutes, go over group members' responses, suggesting the following answers:

- Jason's natural talent is described in the first statement.
- In the second statement, Jason is using his spiritual gift of service— or perhaps encouragement or craftsmanship (or a combination of these)—in conjunction with his talent.
- In the third statement, Jason displays the fruit of patience, faithfulness, self-control, and probably love.

Don't Forget Your Purpose!

(Needed: Copies of Repro Resource 3, previously composed prayers)

Distribute copies of "Gift Goals" (Repro Resource 3). Emphasize the three primary purposes for spiritual gifts: to minister to one another, to bring the church to spiritual maturity, and to glorify God.

Explain: **In the next session, we'll look at the purpose for each specific gift and begin to think about which gift(s) we may have. But for now, let's consider which of the three overall purposes of the gifts you most want to experience in the future. In other words, according to the handout, are you a #1, a #2, or a #3?**

Give kids a chance to choose one category on the sheet that best represents their desire before God. Designate a place in the room for each of the three groups to stand, with heads bowed, for a closing prayer. In advance, prepare a specific prayer for each group. Read your prayers now, beginning as follows: **Lord, for those in Group #1, I pray for . . .** Ask kids in each group to raise their hands as you mention their specific group number.

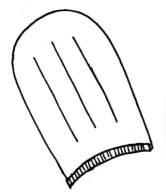

POOL THE POSSIBILITIES

• First, for two of the columns below, read the Bible passage and list the spiritual gifts you find.

Romans 12:3-8	I Corinthians 12:4-11	I Corinthians 12:27-31	Ephesians 4:7-16
_____	_____	_____	_____
_____	_____	_____	_____
_____	_____	_____	_____
_____	_____	_____	_____
_____	_____	_____	_____
_____	_____	_____	_____
_____	_____	_____	_____
_____	_____	_____	_____
_____	_____	_____	_____
_____	_____	_____	_____
_____	_____	_____	_____
_____	_____	_____	_____

Second, seek out others in the group who chose the other two columns. Add their gift lists to your blank columns.

Third, compare the lists and cross out any gift descriptions that seem to duplicate others.

FINALLY, WORK WITH THE REST OF THE GROUP TO CREATE A "MASTER GIFT LIST."

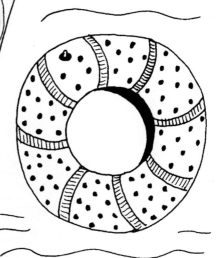

Avoiding Concept
Confusion

Gifts of the Spirit
A spiritual gift is a God-given ability for Christian service. It includes *natural talent* from birth and *supernatural ability* given at the time of salvation. Gifts are given to believers so that the believers may specialize in ministries that meet specific needs in the church. Through using their gifts, believers carry out the kingdom work of the church.

Talents of Individuals
A talent is similar to a spiritual gift, but not the same. Talents are also given by God and can be used to bring glory to God—or they can be used for purely selfish goals. For example, a natural talent for teaching becomes a spiritual gift when it is dedicated for a specific purpose in the church, to help other believers grow in Christ.

Fruit of the Spirit
The fruit of the Spirit are character qualities that every Christian should display. The fruit are listed in Galatians 5:22, 23—"love, joy, peace, patience, kindness, goodness, faithfulness, gentleness and self-control." According to I Corinthians 13, love is the most important quality for a Christian. The gifts are temporary, but the fruit of love is eternal.

Put a G, T, or F next to each of the situations below to indicate whether Jason is demonstrating a spiritual gift, a talent, or fruit of the Spirit.

___ Jason plays awesome piano. Most kids at school think he should major in music when he goes to college next year. Not only does he play keyboard for a rock band, but he also won first place in a state classical music competition.

___ Jason once prayed, "Lord, I know that playing the piano can help other Christians experience your love and joy. Help me to do it for that purpose, as Your servant." People often tell Jason after church, "Your playing really blessed me today."

___ Whenever Jason plays the piano for a church service, he usually seems happy to do it. Even when a soloist is not as talented a musician as he is, Jason patiently helps the singer find the right notes by providing the perfect tempo and chords.

Gift Goals

What are spiritual gifts for? Check out these three big purposes or goals.

To serve one another . . .
(I Peter 4:10)

so the church will be built up . . .
(Ephesians 4:12, 13)

which brings praise to God.
(I Peter 4:11)

My Prayer Request

1. I'd like to experience more of what it means to "serve one another" in practical ways in this group. I want to give and receive more encouragement, help, and friendship with others.

2. I want to become a better Christian and learn how to help others grow in their faith too.

3. I hope to see what a group of teens is like when it is bringing praise to God. I want more than just "fun" out of this group.

STEP 1

Begin the session with a slightly modified version of "Simon Says." Start out with some simple instructions like **Simon says touch your nose.** Then throw in a few twists. First, introduce the topic of spiritual gifts by saying, **Simon says that today we're going to talk about spiritual gifts.** Then start giving some commands that deal with spiritual gifts like **Simon says if you think leading, encouraging, and praying for others are spiritual gifts, then sit down** and **If you think playing the organ in church is not considered a spiritual gift, then sit down.** (Oops! Simon didn't say.) If you're creative with your commands, you can get across some important information while still making the game fun for your kids.

STEP 3

Have kids form two teams for a "spiritual gifts relay race." Instruct the teams to line up at one end of the room. Set up two easels, each with a large piece of newsprint on it, at the other end of the room. Give each team one marker. Explain that the object of the game is to see which team can write down all 16 of the spiritual gifts listed in the session. At your signal, the first person on each team will run to his or her team's easel, write down one of the spiritual gifts, run back to his or her team, and hand off the marker to the next person in line. That person must then run to the easel, write down another gift, and return to the line to hand off the marker to the next person, and so on. The first team to write down all 16 spiritual gifts is the winner. To help teams out, you might want to give them copies of the list of spiritual gifts from Step 3 in the session.

STEP 1

Sometimes members of a small group feel "on the spot" if too much attention is placed on them. In the opening exercise, adapt the talent show. Hand out paper and pencils. Have group members write "THINGS I DO WELL" down the left side of the sheet. Then instruct each person to think of an activity that he or she does well that begins with each of the letters in the phrase. (For example, one of your group members might write down talents like typing, hosting parties, icing cakes, and so forth.) After a few minutes, have each person read his or her list. In most cases, kids will somehow work in their primary talents. But also provide them the opportunity to discuss any talents they have that they didn't get to write down.

STEP 2

Before the meeting, hide a small gift for each person somewhere near where the person will be sitting. (The easiest thing to do would be to tape a dollar bill in an envelope underneath each person's chair.) At the point in this step when you begin to discuss hidden talents, point out that the kids have had "hidden gifts" all along. Explain that when it comes to *spiritual* gifts, sometimes we're unaware that we have them at first. More often, however, we know what our gifts and talents are, but choose to keep them hidden from others.

STEP 1

Write on individual index cards some of the spiritual gifts listed in Step 3 of the session. Make sure that each gift is written on two different cards. Also make sure that you have one card for each group member. So if you have 16 kids, prepare 16 cards (using 8 of the spiritual gifts, each written on 2 cards). Put the cards in a container. To begin the session, have kids draw a card. Explain to each of your kids that one other person in the group has a card with the same spiritual gift on it. The object of the game is to find the person with the matching card. However, the lights will be off as kids search. And to make things a little more difficult, kids may not say what their gift is. When the lights go off, kids must walk around the room, saying things that identify what their gift is. For example, if someone's gift is encouragement, that person might say things like "You're doing great!" and "I'm rooting for you!" After a few minutes, turn on the lights to see f everyone is matched up. Then ask volunteers to share some of the things they said to indicate their spiritual gift.

STEP 3

Have kids form teams. Write the spiritual gifts listed in Step 3 on individual slips of paper. Have each team draw a slip of paper. Then instruct each team to make up a "school cheer" about the spiritual gift it chose. For example, if a team drew the gift of leading, it might come up with a cheer like this: "Leading, leading, that's the plan; lead us to the promised land. Lead us as no other can, with your gift from God's own hand!" Give teams a few minutes to make up their cheers; then have each team perform its cheer in front of the rest of the group. After all of the teams have performed, vote as a group on the best cheer.

STEP 3

Using the "master list" of spiritual gifts in Step 3, create a word search puzzle that contains all 16 of the spiritual gifts. Make the words as hard to find as possible by listing them diagonally, vertically, or backward. Or you might add some other words to the puzzle to try to trip up your church "veterans." If you want to make the activity a little easier for your kids, give them a list of the words they'll be looking for. Award a prize to the first person to find all 16 words.

STEP 4

Hand out paper and pencils. Rather than having your kids simply talk about the various spiritual gifts (which they've surely done before), try a different approach. Explain that you're going to read the names of some Christians. As you read each name, group members should write down the spiritual gift(s) that they associate with that person. For this activity, you might name some characters from the Bible, some Christians in today's society who are nationally known, or some Christians from your own church or community. Give each group member a copy of the list of spiritual gifts from Step 3 so that he or she can see his or her choices. When you're finished, let group members share which gifts they wrote down for each person and why.

STEP 1

If your opening activities usually include singing, try to do everything possible to show what music would be like without variety and diversity. For example, if your kids have a favorite round, sing it—but don't let them break into the different parts. If someone starts singing harmony, stop and make everyone sing the same part. Include a song in a high register, and make everyone try to hit the high notes together. In other words, do everything you can to try to frustrate your group members. Afterward, explain that when it comes to music, we see the value of diversifying and combining talents. (Your kids' favorite groups would be kind of dull if everyone in the band played the same instrument.) Yet sometimes we miss out on the fact that when it comes to spiritual matters, the same principle applies.

STEP 3

You can probably expect a number of questions after your kids finish Repro Resource 1. One obvious concern should be that they begin to realize the potential spiritual importance of the things they do well and see that it is the work of the Holy Spirit to help Christians identify and use their specific gifts. But on an even more basic level, kids who are new to Scripture may find it particularly unusual to think of "gifts" in terms of encouraging other people, having faith, giving, praying for people, and so forth. Commands? Yes. Disciplines? Sure. Obligations? OK. They understand such things. But they may need help understanding that some people are specifically gifted in these areas. If your kids don't ask a lot of questions during this part of the session, you need to do so to make sure that they understand what they're learning.

STEP 1

You may want to kick off this course by reading a story about discovering—and using—one's special talent. Pick up a copy of *Tales of the Kingdom* (available from Chariot Books at your local Christian bookstore). Read "The Apprentice Juggler." After you've read the story to your group, ask: **Do any of you ever feel that you have a different rhythm from the rest of the world, even from other Christians?** Get several responses. Then explain that God created each of us to be unique and gave us special gifts and abilities—gifts that you're going to be looking at in this series.

STEP 5

Many of your kids may already be aware of and are developing their talents. Put together a short worship service, drawing on any talents available in your group (playing the piano, reading aloud well, writing, etc.). Be sure to emphasize that this is an impromptu event, and though we always want to offer our best effort to God, we don't have to fear failing. He still loves us even when we aren't perfect.

STEP 2

After discussing the black dot object lesson, ask: **What are some of the things we focus on that don't allow us to see our whole selves or the whole selves of others?** (Physical appearance, intelligence, and wealth.) **Why do you think this happens? What can we do about it?** Allow time for discussion. Your girls will certainly know what things people tend to focus on, but they may never have thought about what's behind it or what they can do about it. Challenge your girls to take some of the steps they discussed.

STEP 3

Just as churches hold varying opinions on whether or not some spiritual gifts are still valid, there are also varying opinions on how women may receive or use some of the gifts. While respecting the views of your church, have your girls go through the "master list" of spiritual gifts and discuss practical, realistic ways they or other women may use each gift in service to God.

STEP 3

Don't let your guys assume that gifts are gender-specific. Some people believe that God intends guys to be responsible for some gifts (teaching, leading, etc.) and girls to take care of others (offering hospitality, serving, and so forth). To avoid the many traps involved with this way of thinking, go through the list of spiritual gifts that your guys compile. For each gift listed, ask: **What are some ways that we as men can apply this gift?** Encourage your group members to be specific about possibilities in each area. It may be that some of your guys have gifts such as showing hospitality, encouraging, and showing mercy; if they do, they should not be made to feel less-than-masculine.

STEP 4

After your guys complete Repro Resource 2, have them do some roleplays. One person should play the role of Jason, the guy described on the sheet. Others should play the roles of people who, in some way, try to get Jason to question the use of his spiritual gifts. For instance, a football coach who knows that Jason is also a good receiver might subtly try to convince him to spend more time on the football field and less in the practice room. A jealous friend might suggest that piano playing is not for *real* men. A manager might try to enlist him as a keyboard player for a high-paying band that plays a lot of dates when Jason would normally be in church or youth group. These roleplays should help kids see that spiritual gifts can be rendered ineffective if we allow them to be. Whenever we identify something we believe to be a spiritual gift, we need to give it a high priority rather than listen to influences that might prevent us from developing it and using it for the glory of God and for the good of others.

STEP 1

Begin the session by having kids play a murder mystery game. Most such games require eight people and about 45-60 minutes to play, so you may need to make special arrangements to do this. In these games, each player is given unique information that must be shared with the other players before the guilty person among them can be brought to justice. Afterward, draw a comparison to spiritual gifts—when you discover something significant that God has given you, it should be shared with the rest of His body.

STEP 5

Before the session, wrap several items that would make good gifts for young people—toys, games, books, knickknacks, dollar bills, and so forth. In addition to the "fun" items, wrap a few plaques that say things like "A large dose of patience," "Complete peace of mind for a month," and "Increased knowledge at school." Let each person select one wrapped gift. After the gifts are opened, have each person show what he or she received. Ask for a show of hands to see who would like to exchange gifts with someone else in the room. Check to see if anyone who received character qualities wants to trade for a "real" prize. If so, point out that the same thing happens in real life. Some people are given spiritual gifts that they sacrifice for money, fame, possessions, or any number of things. Also try to show kids that characteristics like patience, peace, and knowledge *can* (but don't necessarily) lead to material benefits. Patience might help someone wait for just the right job, college, or marriage partner. Peace cuts down on medical bills in the long run as people avoid stress and ulcers. And knowledge can pay off in many ways. The point is not to learn to capitalize on one's spiritual gifts, but to trust that God knows what is best as He assigns them.

STEP 2

Bring in a copy of the video "The Grinch Who Stole Christmas." Play the scene in which the Grinch ends up giving back the gifts to the people of Whoville. Afterward, ask: **When you think of God giving people spiritual gifts, what kinds of images come to mind? Do you think it's at all similar to the Christmas scene that we just watched?** Encourage several group members to offer their opinions. Then move on to Step 3.

STEP 5

Have kids form pairs. Give each pair a stack of old newspapers and news-magazines. Assign each pair one or more (depending on the number of pairs) of the spiritual gifts listed in Step 3. Instruct the members of each pair to find pictures and articles that relate to their assigned gift(s). For example, an article about someone claiming to know when the end of the world will take place could relate to the gift of prophesying (although it's a false prophecy). An article in which someone bad-mouths someone else could be used to show a *lack* of encouragement. After a few minutes, have each pair share its findings. Spend some time talking about how Christians using their spiritual gifts might affect our society.

STEP 1

Replace Steps 1 and 2 with a shorter opener. Hand out paper and pencils. Ask: **What's the best gift you've ever received?** Instruct each group member to write down his or her response, sign his or her name on the sheet, and turn it in to you. After shuffling the papers, read the gifts aloud one at a time. Let group members guess who received each gift. Continue until all of the gifts have been guessed. Then introduce the topic of spiritual gifts. Point out that *everyone* gets a spiritual gift when he or she becomes a Christian.

STEP 4

Rather than using Repro Resource 2, simply point out that spiritual gifts shouldn't be confused with individual talents and the fruit of the Spirit (Gal. 5:22-23). In Step 5, after kids choose a category on Repro Resource 3, encourage them to pray silently, asking God to help them identify their spiritual gifts.

STEP 3

Write each of the spiritual gifts listed in Step 3 on a separate index card. Make copies of the cards so that you have several for each gift. Randomly assign each spiritual gift a dollar value. A few of the gifts should cost $3; the rest should cost $2 or $1. Make sure that the "price" of each spiritual gift is on the card. Give each group member $5 in play money—preferably in five $1 bills. Instruct group members to "buy" the spiritual gifts of their choice. Because group members have only $5, they will be forced to think about their purchases. (NOTE: Emphasize that the dollar values for the spiritual gifts were assigned randomly. You are *not* suggesting that some gifts are more valuable than others!) After a few minutes, ask volunteers to explain why they purchased the spiritual gifts that they did. Perhaps some of your kids chose the ones that interest them most and that coincide with their own natural talents and abilities. Perhaps other kids went "bargain shopping," trying to get the most for their money.

STEP 4

Rather than using Repro Resource 2, try another option. Explain that you will call out the names of celebrities or other people with whom your kids are familiar. Group members should then call out the talent or ability that they most associate with each person. For instance, if you were to name Michael Jordan, group members might call out "Playing basketball (or baseball)." Other names you might use are Janet Jackson (singing/acting), Ice Cube (rapping), Carl Lewis (running/long jump-ing), and Denzel Washington (acting). You might even want to throw in the names of some of your group members who have special talents or abilities. Afterward, emphasize that there's a difference between talents and abilities and spiritual gifts—although spiritual gifts can be utilized by God through one's talents and abilities.

STEP 3

Have kids form teams to work on Repro Resource 1, making sure that you have both junior highers and high schoolers on each team. Encourage team members to work together in completing their two columns on the sheet. When they're finished, have the junior highers and high schoolers on each team split up to circulate among the members of other teams to get the necessary information to fill in the other two columns on their sheet. The junior highers should be responsible for filling in one column; the high schoolers should be responsible for filling in the other. After a few minutes, have team members reassemble to share their information. When everyone is finished, work together as a group to create the "master list."

STEP 4

Distinguishing between natural talents, spiritual gifts, and the fruit of the spirit may be difficult for some of your junior highers. When you hand out Repro Resource 2, pair up each junior higher with a high schooler, and have them work through the sheet together. After everyone has completed the sheet, be sure to discuss the information on it thoroughly. Open the discussion for questions; then challenge kids to come up with other scenarios in which spiritual gifts, talents, and the fruit of the spirit are used.

STEP 3

You'll need to have a variety of creative supplies—construction paper, pencils, colored markers, modeling clay, tape, glue, etc.—available. Instruct each group member to choose one spiritual gift from the master list in Step 3. Group members should not tell anyone else which gift they chose. Instruct group members to draw, sculpt, or create something that represents the gift they selected. After a few minutes, have each person stand and display his or her work. The rest of the group must then try to guess which gift the person is depicting. The artists should be prepared to explain their work and how it relates to their chosen gift.

STEP 4

Come up with a list of situations similar to the ones on Repro Resource 2. For each situation, have your group members tell you whether a spiritual gift, a talent, or a fruit of the Spirit is being demonstrated. If possible, try to come up with some "borderline" situations that could fit any of the three categories. (For example, you might use the following situation: "After a family in her church lost all of their possessions in a house fire, Shawna organized a clothing drive for them.") Encourage debate among your group members as to which category each situation fits in. Ideally, this activity might spur some interesting and informative discussion.

DATE USED:

Approx. Time

STEP 1: *The Silly Skills Show* _____
- ❏ Extra Action
- ❏ Small Group
- ❏ Large Group
- ❏ Little Bible Background
- ❏ Fellowship & Worship
- ❏ Extra Fun
- ❏ Short Meeting Time
Things needed:

STEP 2: *Not Seeing . . .*
Isn't Knowing _____
- ❏ Small Group
- ❏ Mostly Girls
- ❏ Media
Things needed:

STEP 3: *Developing a Gift List* _____
- ❏ Extra Action
- ❏ Large Group
- ❏ Heard It All Before
- ❏ Little Bible Background
- ❏ Mostly Girls
- ❏ Mostly Guys
- ❏ Urban
- ❏ Combined Junior High/High School
- ❏ Extra Challenge
Things needed:

STEP 4: *Getting Gifts in Gear* _____
- ❏ Heard It All Before
- ❏ Mostly Guys
- ❏ Short Meeting Time
- ❏ Urban
- ❏ Combined Junior High/High School
- ❏ Extra Challenge
Things needed:

STEP 5: *Don't Forget Your Purpose!* _____
- ❏ Fellowship & Worship
- ❏ Extra Fun
- ❏ Media
Things needed:

What's My Gift?
(Recognizing Your Spiritual Gifts)

YOUR GOALS FOR THIS SESSION:
Choose one or more

☐ To help kids learn the gift-discovery process.

☐ To help kids understand why it's important to discover their spiritual gifts.

☐ To help kids choose gift possibilities to explore further.

☐ Other:_____
_____

Your Bible Base:

Exodus 35:30-35
Romans 12:7-8, 13
I Corinthians 12:8-10,
   13, 28
Ephesians 4:11
Colossians 1:9-12
I Peter 4:9-10

How Are You Wired?

OPTIONS

(Needed: Paper, pencils, copies of a wiring diagram for an appliance or machine, prizes)

Have kids form pairs for a quick activity. Hand each pair a sheet of paper, a pencil, and a folded photocopy of a wiring diagram for an appliance or machine (perhaps a furnace or a washing machine), which group members must not look at until you say so. Explain that on your signal, they will have 30 seconds to write down a guess as to what kind of appliance or machine the wiring chart diagrams. Display the prizes that the winners will receive for a correct guess. Emphasize that the guesses must be exact. After each pair has written a guess, collect the sheets, check for correct responses, and award the prizes.

Then ask: **How does a wiring diagram help us understand an appliance?** (The diagram shows the basic way it works; it shows the purpose and function.)

When you think about your place in the church and in the world, how would it help you to know how you are "wired"? (To know what special abilities God has built into us would help us know what we're supposed to do with our life; we'd be aware of our function and purpose in the church—how God could use us.)

Summarize: **God has "wired" us from birth—with our natural talents and abilities from our physical birth and our spiritual gifts from our second birth. As we discover these talents and gifts and use them for God's glory, we find the greatest fulfillment in life. Our "spiritual-gift wiring" points to who we are and what we are called to do. In other words, knowing how a thing is wired or put together helps us better understand its purpose and function. This is true of us, too, as we seek to know our place in the body of Christ. So it's very important for us to recognize our individual spiritual gifts.**

If you have time, supplement your discussion with any of the following information that you deem appropriate or that will help your group members better understand why they need to discover their spiritual gifts.

Why Do You Need to Discover Your Spiritual Gift(s)?

1. To find God's will for your life. God will call you into areas of service that make the most of your spiritual gifts. What He calls us to do, He equips us to do.

2. To feel confident about saying yes and no. With a clear understanding of our gift-wiring, we'll be able to say yes to and volunteer for ministry work that fits us. And we won't have to feel guilty about saying no to things that don't fit our particular gift-mix.

3. To build your self-esteem. As we've seen, God has given every Christian at least one spiritual gift and at least one place of ministry among the body of believers in the church. No one is inferior and no one is left out. All of the gifts are equally important and crucial to the functioning and growth of the church.

Gift Charades

(Needed: Cut-apart copies of Repro Resource 4, pencils, paper clips or rubber bands)

Before the session, you'll need to cut apart several copies of "Wired for Service" (Repro Resources 4a and 4b)—one copy for each group member. Bind each 16-card set with a paper clip or rubber band. Distribute the card sets at this point in the session.

Have group members gather in a circle for a game of Gift Charades. Explain that one person will choose one of his or her cards, go to the center of the circle, and act out (without speaking) a situation in which a person is exercising that particular spiritual gift. Emphasize that the actors may use you as a prop. For example, for "Showing Mercy," an actor might ask you to lay on the floor as an accident victim who needs medical attention. Allow fifteen seconds for the person to perform. The rest of the group members will then hold up the card of the spiritual gift they think the actor is portraying. Declare winners after the actor announces the correct answer.

Then read the spiritual-gift card aloud, supplementing your discussion with any additional information you may have about that gift. Continue this activity, using different actors, until all 16 cards have been acted out. The point of this activity is not so much competition as it is to help group members become familiar with the various gifts.

Afterward, ask: **Which of these spiritual gifts were easiest to act out? Which were hardest? Why?**

Which gifts seem easiest for you to understand? Which seem hardest? Why?

Which spiritual gifts seem the most interesting to you personally? Which seem least interesting? Explain.

STEP
3

Making the Connections

(Needed: Copies of Repro Resource 5, pencils)

Distribute copies of "Start Your Gift-Discovery Project" (Repro Resource 5). As a group, go through the seven basic steps listed Part I of the sheet. As needed, offer brief explanations about the overall process of gift discovery. Use the following information to supplement your discussion.

The Basic Steps of Gift Discovery

1. Become familiar with the biblical gifts and their ministry uses. Every Christian should have a basic definition in mind of each of the various gifts and should be familiar with key New Testament passages that deal with spiritual gifts (Rom. 12; I Cor. 12; Eph. 4; I Peter 4).

2. Pray for God's guidance as you begin your discovery process. God is the one who gives the gifts through the Holy Spirit. And it is God who will enlighten us about the gifts we have. Yet we are called to seek insight. Read James 1:5.

3. Think about who you are. Usually God gives gifts that are in line with our natural abilities and talents. It would be hard to imagine, for instance, a person having the spiritual gift of teaching without enjoying research and study. So encourage group members to think about their interests and inclinations, past and present.

4. Ask other Christians what they see in you. This is a key point. No one is to be a loner Christian, deciding in isolation which gifts he or she has. Giftedness can only be confirmed when other believers say, "What you are doing is a blessing to me, helping me grow, encouraging me." With gifts that extend the kingdom of God into the world, such as evangelism, other Christians should be able to see the results of the evangelism—that is, new converts to Christ.

5. Experiment by trying various kinds of ministries. This is the practical side of gift discovery. No one should be ashamed to attempt something that he or she thinks God wants him or her to do. That person will

learn whether he or she has a particular ability and should be ready to develop the gift or give up the ministry. Of course, first attempts may give us the indication that we need more training to enhance our natural skills and our spiritual effectiveness.

6. *Evaluate your effectiveness.* The Holy Spirit is the power behind the working of the gifts, and His working will be successful. Therefore, it is proper to focus on spiritual results. Yet we must realize that sometimes we make progress in spiritual growth at levels that do not appear on the surface to be successful. For example, what might be labeled as failure in a person's life may actually be building patience and perseverance in that person. An encourager would come alongside that person in his or her apparent failure to help the faith-building process along.

7. *Dedicate your gifts to service in God's Kingdom as you seek places of ministry.* The gifts do not have a power of their own. They are abilities that we offer to God for His use. To use gifts effectively, we must be motivated by His power, dedicated to Him.

As you move on to Part II of the sheet, invite your group members to make some personal connections. Have them spend a few minutes in silence, jotting responses under each of the four headings on the sheet. Emphasize that this is very preliminary thinking and that no one is expected to be able to immediately identify his or her spiritual gifts. In some ways, discovering spiritual gifts is a lifelong search. However, encourage group members to come up with at least one gift that they feel may deserve further exploration in the future. After a few minutes, ask a couple of volunteers to share what they came up with.

Then ask: **At this point, how willing would you say you are to explore your gift possibilities further? What do you think might be a next step?** Get several responses.

Friendly Feedback

(Needed: Cut-apart copies of Repro Resource 4, copies of Repro Resource 5)

OPTIONS

SMALL GROUP

LARGE GROUP

HEARD IT ALL BEFORE

FELLOWSHIP & WORSHIP

MOSTLY GIRLS

MOSTLY GUYS

MEDIA

SHORT MEETING TIME

Direct group members' attention back to the "Others' Feedback" column on Repro Resource 5. Emphasize the importance of this step. Then say: **Let's spend a few minutes giving and receiving some feedback with others in our group right now.**

Have group members pair up again with their partners from Step 1. Ask kids to take a minute to review the spiritual-gift cards from Repro Resource 4. Instruct them to choose two cards to give to their partner, as if to say, "Here are a couple of spiritual gifts that I think I see hints of in you. Why not explore these gift possibilities further?"

After everyone has exchanged gift cards, ask: **How many of you are surprised by your partner's choices? Why?**

How many of you feel your partner has affirmed a gift that you have suspected you might have? Explain.

How many of you had a partner affirm one of the gift possibilities you wrote down on Repro Resource 5?

When you are ready to explore your possible gifts further, what ministries do you think you might consider trying in the future?

What areas of ministry seem to be needed right now in our church or in our youth group?

Explain to your group members that the next step for them is to pray about these things during the coming weeks of the course. They should not attempt to "pigeonhole" themselves into any one or two gifts, but to use the information from this session as "prayer fodder" for seeking guidance from God.

Wired for Service

Prophesying *(I Cor. 12:10, 28)*
Definition: The ability to speak God's truth directly and persuasively
Desire: To convince others of biblical truths
Ministry examples: Preaching, public speaking, witnessing projects, outreach work

Serving *(Rom. 12:7)*
Definition: The ability to joyfully help others in practical ways, often behind the scenes
Desire: To meet needs and be involved, usually involving a hands-on approach
Ministry examples: Lending a hand with fix-up projects, sending thank-you cards, setting up a stage for a play

Teaching *(Eph. 4:11; I Cor. 12:8)*
Definition: The ability to help others learn, making complicated things interesting and easy to grasp
Desire: To study, analyze, and present truth in a systematic way
Ministry examples: Teaching a class, helping a friend learn to tune up his car, coaching a team

Encouraging *(Rom. 12:8)*
Definition: The ability to motivate people for service through encouraging words
Desire: To work with people one-on-one to inspire and build their confidence
Ministry examples: Being a friend, counseling, coaching a team

Giving *(Rom. 12:8)*
Definition: The ability to give generously, with a joyful heart
Desire: To use money and talents wisely to accomplish God's work
Ministry examples: Helping to fund youth group projects with monetary gifts, directing a fund-raising project

Leading *(Eph. 4:11)*
Definition: The ability to envision goals and inspire people to reach them
Desire: To help a group accomplish its goals
Ministry examples: Serving as a committee chairperson, organizing a project that involves other people

Having faith *(I Cor. 12:9)*
Definition: The ability to trust in God's power and working, even in the face of opposition
Desire: To recognize the working of God in situations that seem impossible
Ministry examples: Starting new ministries, leading a prayer group, encouraging a discouraged friend

Working miracles/healing *(I Cor. 12:28)*
Definition: The ability to be used by God for his miraculous workings
Desire: To see God do the miraculous
Ministry examples: (if valid for today): Leading in healing ministries, inspiring others to have greater faith

Wired for Service

Discerning (1 Cor. 12:10)
Definition: The ability to know the difference between true and false teachings; insight into others' personalities and spiritual condition
Desire: To keep a group of Christians doctrinally pure
Ministry examples: Calling insincere of phony Christians to account, being a counselor, teaching, giving advice

Languages (1 Cor. 12:10, 28)
Definition: The ability to learn languages quickly or to speak a "prayer language"
Desire: To translate the Word of God for people to understand it; to glorify God with unlearned utterances
Ministry examples: Being a Bible translator, working with Christian literature, leading a prayer service that involves speaking in tongues and interpreting

Administrating (1 Cor. 12:28)
Definition: The ability to organize people and systems to accomplish God's work
Desire: To avoid wasteful effort in accomplishing God's will
Ministry examples: Being a director, organizing a project, keeping track of paper work

Evangelizing (Eph. 4:11)
Definition: The ability to present the Gospel in ways that produce new converts
Desire: To see people accept Christ as Savior
Ministry examples: Public speaking, counseling, being a friend, winning people one-on-one

Showing mercy (Rom. 12:8)
Definition: The ability to offer care and comfort to the suffering
Desire: To help the hurting
Ministry examples: Working in a hospital, visiting the sick or elderly, working in a food pantry

Offering hospitality (Rom. 12:13; 1 Peter 4:9-10)
Definition: The ability to help people feel welcomed and comfortable when they are guests
Desire: To include people, making them feel at ease
Ministry examples: Being a friend, inviting people into your home, serving refreshments

Praying (Col. 1:9-12)
Definition: The ability to persevere in intercession
Desire: To see answers to prayer on behalf of others' needs
Ministry examples: Being in a prayer group, spending time in prayer, learning new ways to pray, teaching others how to pray

Using craftsmanship (Exod. 35:30-35)
Definition: The ability to make things with skill and beauty
Desire: To create and build things for ministry use
Ministry examples: Being an artist, writer, carpenter, actor, painter, etc.

START YOUR GIFT-DISCOVERY PROJECT

Part I: The Basic Steps of Gift Discovery

1. Become familiar with the biblical gifts and their ministry uses.
2. Pray for God's guidance as you begin your discovery process.
3. Think about who you are. What have you enjoyed doing within the body of Christ? What were you good at? What things have seemed to "bless" other believers?
4. Ask other Christians what they see in you. What do they say are your special abilities?
5. Experiment by trying various kinds of ministries.
6. Evaluate your effectiveness. Has the Holy Spirit given you some level of success in your efforts?
7. Dedicate your gifts to service in God's Kingdom as you seek places of ministry.

Part II: What Connections Can You Make?

My Insights	*Ministry Attempts*	*Others' Feedback*	*Needs in the Church*
When I consider my inner desires, my apparent abilities, and my present ministries, what "clues" do I have concerning possible spiritual gifts?	Which of the things I've done in the past have "felt right"? Which things seemed to help or encourage others? Which things didn't seem to "fit" me?	What have others said about my ministry attempts? Jot down any specific phrases or comments that come to mind.	What are some of the needs in my youth group? What are some of the needs in my local church? What are some of the needs in my community?

Gifts involved: Gifts involved: Gifts involved: Gifts involved:

_____ _____ _____ _____
_____ _____ _____ _____
_____ _____ _____ _____

Based on my own insights, my attempts at ministry, feedback I've received from others, and my recognition of the needs in my church, I make this connection:

The following are some gifts that deserve further exploration:

STEP 1

Bring in a small gift-wrapped package. Tape a note to the package that says, "God's will." Ask a volunteer to leave the room. While he or she is gone, hide the package. Then bring the person back in to try to find the hidden package. Time him or her to see how long it takes. Continue the activity with three or four other volunteers, each time hiding the package in a different place. See who can find it in the least amount of time. Use this activity to introduce the idea of finding God's will for our lives. Point out that what God calls us to do, He equips us to do. So using our spiritual gifts (or striving to discover our spiritual gifts) can lead to finding God's will.

STEP 3

Have kids form pairs to play "The Spiritual Gift Game" (a variation of the TV game show "The Newlywed Game"). Have one person from each pair leave the room. Hand out four sheets of poster board and markers to each of the remaining players. Ask each to answer four questions according to how he or she think his or her partner would respond; have them write each answer on a sheet of poster board. For each question, name four of the spiritual gifts from the "master list" (in Step 3 of Session 1); ask each person to choose which of the four his or her partner will say that he or she (the partner) most likely possesses. With four questions, you'll be able to cover all 16 gifts on the master list. After players have written their responses, bring in their partners. Ask the partners the same four questions; see how their responses compare to their partners' guesses. The pair with the most matching responses is the winner. Afterward, point out that one of the ways to find out your spiritual gift(s) is to see what attributes and gifts other people notice in you.

STEP 3

The fifth step of gift discovery may be difficult for kids in a small group that offers little opportunity to try various ministries in a structured way. Many times small groups have a fairly rigid structure. They find something that works and stick with it. And while there's nothing wrong with that approach, perhaps it is more effective for kids with certain spiritual gifts than for those with others. You might want to organize group meetings that will help kids experiment with various spiritual gifts. One meeting might focus exclusively on prayer. Another might offer an opportunity to participate in a service project. Another might concentrate on hospitality—perhaps hosting another youth group. If you let kids come up with ideas for future meetings, you're more likely to have their full support and cooperation.

STEP 4

A small group will probably have time to do feedback on everyone in the group. Rather than using the spiritual gift cards, have kids write the 16 spiritual gifts down the left side of a sheet of paper. Across the top, kids should list the names of all group members, including themselves. Instruct kids to use a scale of 1 to 10 for rating signs of each spiritual gift in the life of each person. A "1" indicates little observable sign of the gift. A "10" signifies a strong presence of the gift. Say: **These scores do not indicate "good" or "bad." They are designed to acknowledge whether or not you've seen signs of these gifts in others—and in yourself.** When kids finish, determine each person's average score for each gift. Let kids see their own average scores, but not each other's. Emphasize that the perceptions of fellow group members may or may not be accurate; they are only a starting point for kids who are trying to determine how God has gifted them.

STEP 1

Have kids form two teams. Give each team a large box (if possible, a refrigerator box), a couple of rolls of wrapping paper, scissors, and tape. Explain that the teams will have 90 seconds to wrap their boxes. The team that does the best wrapping job in 90 seconds is the winner. When time is up, judge the packages based on the neatness of their appearance. Award prizes to the winning team. Use this activity to introduce the concept of spiritual "gifts."

STEP 4

With a large group, you have the opportunity to bring together kids who've identified (or had others identify) the same spiritual gifts in themselves. Have group members choose one (rather than two) spiritual-gift card from Repro Resource 4 to give to their partners. After group members receive feedback from their partners, have them form small groups based on the gifts that were identified in them. So everyone whose partner identified the spiritual gift of "encouraging" in him or her should form one group; everyone whose partner identified the gift of "giving" should form another group; and so on. Instruct the members of each group to share with each other their responses to the questions at the end of Step 4.

HEARD IT ALL BEFORE

LITTLE BIBLE BACKGROUND

FELLOWSHIP & WORSHIP

STEP 3

If your group members have grown up in the church, they're probably somewhat aware of at least some of their spiritual gifts. Hand out paper and pencils. Instruct group members to write down one spiritual gift that they are fairly sure that they possess; then have them write down three reasons why they believe they possess that spiritual gift. But don't let anyone share what he or she wrote yet. Wait until after the partners have offered their opinions in Step 4; then have group members compare their partner's opinion with what they wrote earlier.

STEP 4

Bring in a hacksaw and a hollow metal bar. Have group members take turns trying to saw the bar in half. It's likely that they'll struggle with the task. Afterward, discuss why the job was so difficult. Then have someone read aloud Proverbs 27:17 ("As iron sharpens iron, so one man sharpens another"). Ask: **Do you think the process of sharpening iron is any easier than what we just tried to do?** (Sharpening iron may be a little easier than cutting a metal bar in half, but it's still a difficult process.) Discuss as a group how being accountable to other Christians and getting their feedback in areas of your life is like "iron sharpening iron." It's not always easy and smooth, but it can do some great sharpening. Similarly, getting other people's feedback on what they see as your spiritual gift(s) may not always be smooth or pleasant, but it has the potential to do some great sharpening of one's Christian walk.

STEP 1

Begin the session by having group members make a poster that illustrates the theme "This Is Why I'm a Special Person." The poster may include physical attributes, personal interests, and so forth. But explain that everyone must incorporate his or her fingerprints into the poster in some way. It usually goes without saying that our *fingerprints* demonstrate our one-of-a-kind uniqueness. So by starting with something your group members already understand, the following discussion of unique combinations of talents and spiritual gifts may seem a bit less confusing.

STEP 2

After the "Gift Charades" activity, collect a set of 16 cards. Say: **Now that you've seen the various spiritual gifts acted out, let's try to rank them in order of importance.** Have group members offer suggestions for their #1 choices by going through their own sets of cards. Perhaps a few ideas will be offered for things to go at the top or the bottom of the list, but soon your group members are likely to find it difficult to prioritize the cards as individuals—much less come to any kind of mutual agreement. Let kids struggle for a while; then explain that they've proven a point about spiritual gifts. There can be no order of importance because *all* spiritual gifts are important. We need a variety of gifts at work in the church. If we could list them #1, #2, #3, and so forth, no one would be happy if he or she didn't have the #1 gift. Therefore, we should be content to discover and use *whatever* gift(s) we have received.

STEP 1

Have kids form teams. Give each team a length of wire. Instruct each team to create something recognizable or something useful from the wire. After a few minutes, have each group display and explain what it came up with. Then say: **We're going to start investigating our spiritual gifts. In order to do that, we first need to know how God has "wired" us. We'll also discover that He's given us some instructions on our wiring, so we're not totally clueless about how this wiring works.** Read I Corinthians 12:1. Supplement your discussion with the "Why Do You Need to Discover Your Spiritual Gift(s)?" information in Step 1.

STEP 4

Read I Corinthians 12:4-6. Spend some time thanking and praising God for the variety He's created in us and for the fact that He designed it to all work together. Encourage group members to identify specifically at least one gift that they are thankful for—either one that they have themselves or one that someone else has by which they've been blessed.

STEP 1

Have group members form pairs. Give each pair a recipe card that lists the ingredients and preparation instructions for a dish, but doesn't give the name of the dish. Be sure to give each pair a different recipe. Allow 30 seconds for the members of each pair to guess what their dish is. Award prizes for correct answers. Then take a few minutes to talk about the fact that God has given each of us different ingredients along with instructions for how to put the ingredients together. We each have our own unique blend of gifts and talents, and in order to discover and effectively use our spiritual gifts, we need to know what ingredients we're working with.

STEP 4

After your girls have tentatively identified their spiritual gifts, have them get together to brainstorm an activity to which they could each contribute their gift. Discuss and review the definitions, desires, and ministry examples of the gifts as necessary. Encourage your girls to come up with a realistic plan that they can put into action using their gifts.

STEP 1

Ask your guys to talk about males that they admire—not in a physical sense (big muscles, athletic ability, etc.), but rather people who seem to have their lives in order. List the name of each person, along with the characteristics of the person that are admired. Leave the list posted during the session. Later, after you discuss spiritual gifts, come back to your list. See if any of the characteristics that were admired might be the result of a spiritual gift. (In many cases, this will be pure speculation. In other instances, however, the possibility may be more apparent.) Challenge your guys to see beyond things such as fame, power, and physical strength. Most guys crave such things without realizing that they are shallow possessions unless there is a spiritual foundation as well. Encourage group members to *begin* by seeking out their spiritual gifts and then go from there.

STEP 4

If possible, line up a panel of Christian men from your church or community to attend the session. At the end, have your panel members discuss spiritual gifts and address some of the things covered in the meeting. Ask them: **What do you think are your spiritual gifts? How did you find out what your spiritual gifts were? How does a guy go about developing a spiritual gift once he determines what it is? What advice would you give a group of young men for avoiding some of the same mistakes you've made along the way in your search for spiritual maturity?** Group members may be used to hearing *you*. But if you bring in a number of church staff, businessmen, and other males who can discuss this matter openly, your guys may be more willing to open up about themselves.

STEP 1

Instead of using the wiring diagram quiz, have your kids imagine that *they* are appliances. As such, ask them to create an "operation manual" for themselves. This manual should include things such as a schematic diagram of all important parts (an outline of the person's body), instructions on how the appliance operates, warning signs that indicate it isn't working as it should, information on how this particular model stands apart from all others, and a listing of specific benefits provided by this model. Kids should have fun analyzing themselves as if they were machines. But in doing so, they should deal with some of their underlying gifts, talents, and abilities.

STEP 2

While it is clearly the work of the Holy Spirit to assign spiritual gifts, you might want to see how your kids would do it if given the opportunity. Tape the names of your group members in a row across one wall. Instruct kids to assign (using the cards on Repro Resource 4) one spiritual gift to each person. (If your group has fewer than 16 people, some of the cards won't be used; if you have more than 16, not everyone can receive a "gift" from everyone else.) Make it clear that you don't want kids to match a person with gifts they think he or she already has. (This will be done in Step 4.) Rather, kids are to show which people they would choose to be responsible for certain spiritual gifts if they could do so. Afterward, reveal who was selected for which gifts. Discuss the criteria kids used in making their decisions. Then explain that this exercise doesn't really mean a thing. Many times God bestows gifts on people because He knows what is best, and for no other apparent reason. Challenge your kids to be open to considering that God may choose them to receive any of the gifts that are listed.

STEP 2

While you're talking about which spiritual gifts are easiest to understand and which are most difficult to understand, play some songs by Christian artists that refer (either overtly or subtly) to various spiritual gifts. Among the songs you might use are "I'll Be a Friend to You" by Kenny Marks (encouragement) and "Who Will Save the Children" by Randy Stonehill (serving). See if your group members can tell which gift is being referred to in each song.

STEP 4

Rather than having kids give feedback face-to-face concerning possible spiritual gifts they see in each other, allow them to do it privately on videotape. Set up a video camera in another room of your building. Assign each person the name of someone else in the group. One at a time, have group members go to the video room, push the "Record" button on the camera, sit down in a designated spot, say the name of his or her assigned person, and then share which potential spiritual gift(s) he or she sees in that person. Encourage kids to approach this activity seriously. After everyone has recorded his or her message, play all of the messages back for your group.

STEP 1

Rather than using Steps 1 and 2, try a shorter opener. Have kids pair up, preferably with someone they don't know very well. Give the members of each pair three minutes to find out as much about each other as possible. Give kids a minute or two to think of some questions to ask their partners; then begin the activity. When time is up, have each person share what he or she learned about his or her partner. Note the various differences between partners as they share their descriptions. Afterward, point out that God has "wired" each of us differently and has given us unique gifts and talents. Lead in to a discussion of how to discover your gifts (see Step 3).

STEP 4

Rather than going through Repro Resource 5 in Step 3, assign the sheet as a take-home paper. Skip Step 4. While you're explaining the instructions for filling out Repro Resource 5, pass around index cards, each of which has the name of one of your group members on it. Ask group members to write on each person's card one potential spiritual gift that they see in that person. When everyone is finished, give the cards to the appropriate people. Encourage kids to refer to the cards (others' feedback) as they fill out Repro Resource 5. Close the session in prayer, asking God to guide your group members as they seek to discover their spiritual gifts.

STEP 1

Bring in a plastic bowling ball and 16 plastic bowling pins. Write each of the 16 spiritual gifts listed in Step 3 of Session 1 on the bowling pins, one gift per pin. Set up the pins in rows of 1, 2, 3, 4, 3, 2, and 1 (from front to back). Explain that your group members will be participating in a bowling contest. However, the object of the game is not to knock over all of the pins; instead, the object is to knock over all but one pin. Contestants may roll as many times as necessary to knock down all but one pin. Explain that the spiritual gift written on the pin that a person leaves standing becomes that person's designated spiritual gift. After everyone has had a turn, discuss as a group how kids feel about their designated spiritual gifts. Then point out that there's a much better (and more biblical) way to discover one's spiritual gift(s).

STEP 3

Before the session, prepare several sets of lists. Each list should include five items. Four of the items should be related somehow; the fifth should be unrelated. For instance, one of your lists might include the following movies: *Ricochet*, *Malcolm X*, *The Pelican Brief*, *Demolition Man*, and *Philadelphia*. (*Demolition Man* is the movie that doesn't belong here because it stars Wesley Snipes. The rest of the movies star Denzel Washington.) As you read each list to your group members, have them compete to see who can be the first to call out the item that doesn't belong. Afterward, point out that a big part of recognizing your spiritual gifts is recognizing what your spiritual gifts *aren't*.

STEP 1

Have kids form teams of two or three, making sure that each team has at least one junior higher and one high schooler on it. Give each team a wiring diagram for an appliance or machine. If possible, try to have enough different diagrams so that no two teams have the same one. Give teams a few minutes to figure out what their diagrams are for. However, rather than simply announcing what its appliance or machine is, each team must act it out. Working together, the members of team must simulate the appliance or machine in action. The rest of the group must then try to guess what appliance or machine the team is acting out.

STEP 3

Before you look at Repro Resource 5, which may be difficult for your junior highers who are still trying to figure out who they are and what they're good at, spread out a large sheet of paper on which you've drawn the outline of a life-sized body. Read I Corinthians 12:14-26, emphasizing that we all have a place in the body of Christ. As a group, identify gift(s) that each person seems to possess. As you identify a gift for each person, write that person's name in a representative part of the body. (For example, kids with the gift of mercy might have their names placed near the heart.) When you're finished, take a look at the distribution of gifts throughout the body to see what kind of balance God has given your group.

STEP 1

In keeping with the wiring-diagram theme, instruct your group members to create a wiring diagram for a person that indicates his or her spiritual gift(s). For instance, a diagram of a person with the gift of serving might have a label by the eyes that reads "Sees the needs of hurting and needy people"; a label by the hands that reads "Calloused hands from doing physical labor for elderly people in his or her neighborhood"; and so on. Let kids work in pairs or small groups to complete their diagrams. After a few minutes, have each pair or small group display and explain its diagram. Then lead in to a discussion on how we can discover our spiritual gifts.

STEP 3

Hand out paper and pencils. Instruct each group member to write down 5-10 things that he or she enjoys doing. These interests might be serious pursuits or recreational hobbies. They might include things like reading, playing sports, singing, math, English, debate, science, styling hair, playing around on a computer, playing guitar, talking on the phone, or anything else. After a few minutes, collect the sheets. Make a master list on the board of all of your group members' interests. Then, as a group, go quickly through the list one item at a time. Encourage your group members to call out spiritual gifts that might apply to each interest. Afterward, spend some time talking about ways that we can incorporate spiritual gifts into our talents and abilities.

DATE USED:

Approx. Time

STEP 1: *How Are You Wired?* _____
- ❏ Extra Action
- ❏ Large Group
- ❏ Little Bible Background
- ❏ Fellowship & Worship
- ❏ Mostly Girls
- ❏ Mostly Guys
- ❏ Extra Fun
- ❏ Short Meeting Time
- ❏ Urban
- ❏ Combined Junior High/High School
- ❏ Extra Challenge

Things needed:

STEP 2: *Gift Charades* _____
- ❏ Little Bible Background
- ❏ Extra Fun
- ❏ Media

Things needed:

STEP 3: *Making the Connections* _____
- ❏ Extra Action
- ❏ Small Group
- ❏ Heard It All Before
- ❏ Urban
- ❏ Combined Junior High/High School
- ❏ Extra Challenge

Things needed:

STEP 4: *Friendly Feedback* _____
- ❏ Small Group
- ❏ Large Group
- ❏ Heard It All Before
- ❏ Fellowship & Worship
- ❏ Mostly Girls
- ❏ Mostly Guys
- ❏ Media
- ❏ Short Meeting Time

Things needed:

What Do I Do with Them?

(Putting Your Gifts to Work)

YOUR GOALS FOR THIS SESSION:

Choose one or more

- [ ] To help kids identify various forms of ministry that make use of spiritual gifts.

- [ ] To help kids understand why spiritual gifts must be developed and put to use.

- [ ] To help kids respond to unmet needs they see around them, using their spiritual gifts.

- [ ] Other: _____
  _____

Your Bible Base:

Judges 4:4-16
Acts 2:14-41; 6:1—7:15;
  8:26-40; 9:36-39;
  11:21-30; 27:21-26
3 John 1-8

STEP 1

How Far Have We Come?

O P T I O N S

(Needed: Copies of Repro Resource 6, pencils, prizes [optional])

Begin this session with a mini-review exercise. If you've completed the first two sessions of this book, you've covered a lot of information on a tough subject. Check to see what your group members have grasped so far by having them take a short quiz. Distribute copies of "Checking Your Gifts Grasp" (Repro Resource 6) and pencils. To add some excitement to the proceedings, you might announce that the first three people to complete the sheet correctly will receive a prize.

After a few minutes, go through the sheet, asking group members to call out their responses. The correct answers are: (1) false; (2) b; (3) true; (4) a; (5) false; (6) b; (7) true; (8) b; (9) false; (10) true.

After you've reviewed the answers, ask volunteers to share some of their questions regarding spiritual gifts. While you may not be able to anticipate all such questions, we've included some information to help you address three commonly asked questions regarding spiritual gifts. Use the following information as necessary to address kids' queries.

• *Are women given the same gifts as men?* Yes. It's likely that there are many women involved in the ministry of your church. And though the New Testament focuses more on the ministry of men (perhaps for cultural reasons), it also includes stories of Tabitha, who displayed the gift of showing mercy (Acts 9:36); the four daughters of Philip, who displayed the gift of prophecy (Acts 21:8-9); and Phoebe, who used her gift of serving in the office of deacon (Rom. 16:1). Some churches question whether women are to serve as pastors, since the Bible does not use the words "shepherd" (pastor) "overseer" (bishop) or "elder" (presbyter) in conjunction with a woman in the New Testament. However, in the Old Testament, Deborah the judge led the entire nation of Israel (Judges 4:4-16)!

• *Is it possible for people to use their gifts in the wrong ways?* It is possible to abuse spiritual gifts. For instance, one may (1) consider the gifts private, and fail to launch into a ministry on behalf of others; (2) believe that everyone should be able to do what he or she is specially gifted to do, causing others to feel inferior; or (3) emphasize so-called "public" gifts—including preaching, teaching, evangelizing, and leading—as though they are more important than gifts that are used behind the scenes— such as giving, showing mercy, helping, and praying. *All* gifts are important to a maturing church body; *all* must be used for mutual edification.

• *Why do we have ordination, if everyone is gifted with equally important gifts?* Emphasizing the importance of professional, ordained clergy may cause "ordinary" Christians to think that they are to sit back and let the professionals do the work of the church. The key biblical passage related to this question is Ephesians 4:11-12, which indicates that pastors are to act as coaches, preparing the church members to do the work of ministry. Yet this does not rule out the legitimate place of recognized leadership and authority in the church body. This is where ordination comes into play: the body recognizing and submitting itself to the authority of God's chosen leaders.

STEP 2

Muscle Mush

Have group members sit in a circle. Say: **For the next few minutes, let's suppose that you've never learned to use certain muscles in your body. Would it make much difference in how your body worked? Let's see.**

Explain that you will name an action and then point to a person in the circle. That person must perform the action as though he or she has never exercised or developed the muscles involved and doesn't know how to use them.

Here are some actions you might use (feel free to add any others you come up with):
- **Comb your hair.**
- **Hug the person on your right.**
- **Stand up straight.**
- **Pick your nose.**
- **Throw a paper wad.**
- **Do a push-up.**
- **Whistle.**
- **Skip across the room.**
- **Suck your thumb.**
- **Blink.**
- **Clap your hands.**
- **Lick your lips.**

Afterward, ask: **How is exercising and developing our physical muscles similar to and different from developing our spiritual gifts?** (Like underdeveloped physical muscles, underdeveloped spiritual gifts cannot be used to their greatest potential. The difference

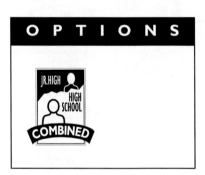

OPTIONS

JR.HIGH
HIGH SCHOOL
COMBINED

between physical muscles and spiritual gifts is that with spiritual gifts, the Holy Spirit is empowering us. Our willingness to be used by Him is what makes us effective in ministry.)

What's the toughest thing about putting our gifts to work—once we know what they are? (We may have a hard time thinking of practical things to do. We may think that the "little" things we can do aren't as important as the "big" ministries that everyone can see.)

Summarize: **Spiritual gifts must be developed and exercised in order to be put to use effectively. To see how this is done, let's take a look at how gifts were used in Bible times.**

STEP 3

Ancient Observations

(Needed: Bibles, copies of Repro Resource 7, pencils)

Have kids form pairs. Distribute copies of "Bible-Time Gift Users" (Repro Resource 7) and pencils. Assign one or more (depending on the size of your group) of the Bible characters on Repro Resource 7 to each pair. Instruct each pair to look up its assigned Scripture passage(s) and write down what gifts each Bible character may have been using and how those gifts helped others and/or glorified God.

After a few minutes, have each pair share what it came up with. Use the following information to supplement group members' responses.

- *Deborah*—Used the gift of leading to help Barak make military decisions to win a major battle.
- *Philip*—Used the gift of evangelism to help the Ethiopian come to Christ.
- *Peter*—Used the gift of preaching to help the church grow by persuading people to believe in Christ.
- *Tabitha*—Used the gift of craftsmanship to help people with the things she made.
- *Paul*—Used the gift of faith to help crew members believe in God's will for them.
- *Stephen*—Used the gift of working miracles to demonstrate God's power to the people.
- *Barnabas*—Used the gift of encouraging to lift the spirits of other church members.
- *Gaius*—Used the gift of hospitality to treat strangers kindly.

Afterward, ask: **In light of these passages, what general impression do you have about how spiritual gifts worked in**

OPTIONS

SMALL GROUP

LARGE GROUP

HEARD IT ALL BEFORE

LITTLE BIBLE BACKGROUND

MOSTLY GIRLS

EXTRA FUN

URBAN

EXTRA CHALLENGE

the early church? If no one mentions it, suggest that the early Christians probably viewed the use of spiritual gifts as being practical and necessary. They found practical ways to serve.

How motivated would you say these people were? How would you summarize their apparent sense of mission? (They appear to have been completely dedicated to the work of God's Kingdom. When they used their gifts, it was for the purpose of church growth.)

How would you judge the effectiveness of these people's use of their gifts? For example, was Stephen a "success," even though he was killed? (When we use our gifts, motivated by the Spirit, we are always successful. Success mustn't be judged only by outward appearances.)

Super Transformations

Say: **How might a young person today actually put his or her spiritual gifts to work? Let's approach that question through a flight of imagination. Enter the Mighty Giftor. Giftor is a spiritual superhero who has the power to transform himself into a teenager with any "gift mix," depending on the needs he encounters. For example, if he sees someone who is seeking God, Giftor can transform himself into a teen with the gifts of evangelism and encouragement.**

Explain to your group members that you're going to read some situations aloud. After you read each one, ask group members to call out what "gift mix" Giftor might use for that situation.

The situations are as follows:

- **Bill and Mike want to go on a mission trip to Guatemala, but they have to each raise $1,000 for their airfare.**
- **After a nasty fight with her parents, Kim Sung stormed out of the house, fell down the stairs, and broke her leg.**
- **Heather sees a lot of drug and alcohol abuse at her school. She wants people to know that they are messing up their lives, but she doesn't know how to make a difference.**
- **The youth group planning council meets every month, but nothing ever seems to get done. Everybody just keeps making the same old suggestions at each meeting.**

O P T I O N S

EXTRA ACTION

LITTLE BIBLE BACKGROUND

MOSTLY GUYS

MEDIA

SHORT MEETING TIME

URBAN

- **Once again, the children's church is going to stage a Christmas play. For what seems like the seventy-fifth consecutive year, the kids are going to dress in the same old costumes, stand in front of the audience, and read Bible verses about Mary, Joseph, and the Baby Jesus.**
- **Sue told Renaldo that she was breaking up with him. Now Renaldo feels depressed and is thinking about getting smashed tonight.**
- **Every time Phil enters church, all he can think about is the dust on the floor, the peeling paint, and the cracked windows. He wonders whether anyone really cares about making this a place of worship.**

Once kids have identified the gifts that Giftor might use in each situation, ask for more detailed explanations about how he would go about using those gifts in the most practical way. The key is to help kids be very practical in describing how the gifts could be put to use in real-life situations. If you have time, ask group members to suggest other possible situations, then do the Giftor exercise with those situations.

As you wrap up this section, emphasize the following strategies for putting spiritual gifts to work:

1. Be open to seeing the needs around you. We must develop sensitivity to see how people are hurting or what needs are not being met in the community of believers.

2. Develop your gifts by seeking training experiences. No one knows how to apply his or her gifts wisely and effectively without some training. Ask people you admire to show you how to do better at teaching, or encouraging, or praying, or strengthening your faith. If you believe you have the gift of evangelism, try leading someone to Christ. Then ask yourself, "What did I learn from this experience that can help me improve next time?"

3. Be yourself. Your unique personality and combination of gifts makes your ministry unique. God will use your personality, just as it is, if you dedicate yourself to Him and seek to please Him in all you do.

STEP
5

Chart the Church

(Needed: A chart of your church's organizational structure)

Say: **We've learned a lot about spiritual gifts so far, but we still need to get more specific about putting our gifts to work. One way to begin would be to ask ourselves, "What kinds of gifts are already being used in our church each week to keep it running and doing ministry?"**

Work with your group members to construct a rough organizational chart of your church's structure. List as many offices and ministries as you are aware of. (It might be helpful for you to do some research on this in advance.) Also see how many names you can put next to offices and ministries.

Ask kids to suggest which gifts are being used by people in the positions you've listed—whether you have specific names of individuals or not. Then discuss any needs that seem to be unmet in your church or youth group—or in your desire to reach out to other people in the community. Think not only of "formal" programs, but of individuals' needs.

Close the session with a period of silent prayer, asking kids to pray about these questions: "Which of these needs seems to speak most directly to me because of what I have to offer?" and "What next step might I take?"

CHECKING YOUR GIFTS GRASP

How much have you grasped about the topic of spiritual gifts? The following quiz is designed to help you get a grip on what you've learned so far.

1. Some Christians don't have a spiritual gift. True or false?

2. Christians can discover their spiritual gifts through . . .
   a. a process of deciding which gifts they like and then declaring their choices.
   b. a process of getting involved in ministry and asking for feedback.
   c. a process of praying for all of the gifts and then using them in private.
   d. a process cheese spread.

3. Some spiritual gifts may not be listed in the Bible. True or false?

4. The main purposes for spiritual gifts are . . .
   a. to serve one another, build the church, and glorify God.
   b. to fund the church, evangelize the world, and prevail against temptation.
   c. to give Christians a chance to show off, feel superior, and control others.

5. Christians earn their spiritual gifts by living a Christ-like lifestyle. True or false?

6. My spiritual gifts are for . . .
   a. my own benefit.
   b. the benefit of others.
   c. a benefit banquet.

7. All spiritual gifts are of significant value. True or false?

8. When using my gift(s), my attitude . . .
   a. doesn't matter, because God is motivating me.
   b. matters, because a ministry must be done in love.
   c. matures, because it grows wiser every day.
   d. mattresses, because a nap can give me renewed strength.

9. Natural talents have no connection to spiritual gifts. True or false?

10. All spiritual gifts are undeserved and given by grace. True or false?

So far, my biggest question about spiritual gifts is . . .

Bible-Time GIFT USERS

Name	Possible Gift(s) in Use	How the Gift(s) Helped Others and/or Glorified God
Deborah (*Judges 4:4-16*)		
Philip (*Acts 8:26-40*)		
Peter (*Acts 2:14-41*)		
Tabitha (*Acts 9:36-39*)		
Paul (*Acts 27:21-26*)		
Stephen (*Acts 6:1-15*)		
Barnabas (*Acts 11:21-30*)		
Gaius (*III John 1-8*)		

STEP 1

The mini-review exercise isn't very active, so you may want to begin the session in a different way. Have kids form two teams. Give each team a gift-wrapped present to hide somewhere in the church (or somewhere around your meeting area). After each team has hidden its present, it should create a list of clues to give to the other team to indicate where the present is hidden. The clues should be hard enough to make the other team do some serious thinking, but should not be impossible to figure out. You should probably check each team's clues to make sure that they're OK. After the teams trade clue lists, see which team can find its opponent's present first. Use the idea of searching for gifts to introduce the spiritual-gift quiz.

STEP 4

Rather than using the "gift mix" situations in Step 4, give your group members an opportunity to determine what needs exist in various areas of your church. First, you might take kids on a tour of the church building—both inside and outside—to look for areas that need work done on them. Perhaps the paint on a hallway ceiling is peeling. Perhaps the carpets need to be cleaned. Perhaps boxes in the church basement need to be put into storage. Next, you might take kids to a missions display in your church to see what kinds of needs your church's missionaries have. Finally, you might take the group to your pastor's office (making sure to arrange the visit in advance, of course) and ask him to share some of the other needs in your church. Afterward, discuss as a group what "gift mix" is required for each need that you identified.

STEP 3

With a small group, the Bible study on Repro Resource 7 will probably be more effective if done together instead of in pairs. The time can be spent interacting with each other as you go along rather than giving reports and asking questions afterward. After you discuss the people listed on the sheet, ask group members to try to think of other biblical characters who used specific spiritual gifts. Challenge kids to think of lesser-known individuals as well as the more common names you would expect to be mentioned.

STEP 5

If you have a small group because you have a small church, the "charting the church" activity may not be much of a challenge. If this is the case, try another option. As you wrap up the session, ask: **In a small church where we don't have all of the programs and opportunities to serve that larger churches have, how do we use and develop the spiritual gifts we've been given?** There may be no easy answers to this question. Perhaps the solution is to use spiritual gifts at other places wherever we can—school, work, with friends, and so forth. Ideally, spiritual gifts should be nurtured and allowed to grow in the church. But when that is not possible, it is still important to do whatever we can, *wherever* we can, to use our gifts for God.

STEP 1

Before you begin the mini-review exercise on Repro Resource 6, give your group members an opportunity to get their "memory juices" flowing a little bit. Have kids sit in a circle. Explain that you will start the activity by saying your name and your favorite flavor of ice cream. Once you've done that, the person to your left must say your name and your favorite ice cream flavor, followed by his or her name and favorite ice cream flavor. Continue the process around the circle, seeing how well your group members handle loads of information. Finally, the last person in the circle must recall everybody's name and favorite ice cream flavor. Proceed from this activity into your review of spiritual gifts.

STEP 3

Have kids form teams. Assign each team one of the characters on Repro Resource 7. Rather than simply having the members of each team fill in the information on the sheet, instruct them to create a brief scenario that illustrates the actions of their character in their assigned passage. However, teams should not mention the name of their character in their scenarios. After each team has performed its scenario, the rest of the group will try to guess which character the team was assigned. Afterward, discuss as a group what possible gift(s) each character might have been using and how that gift helped others or glorified God.

STEP 1

Bring in various tools, utensils, and equipment. You might include things like a hammer, a plunger, a tennis racket, a fork, and a toothbrush. Ask for volunteers to come to the front of the room one at a time, choose an item, and explain to the group what the item is used for. However, rather than explaining the *actual* use for the item, the volunteer should make up something as off-the-wall and as humorous (but not offensive) as possible. For instance, someone might explain that the tennis racket is used by spelunkers (cave explorers) to swat bats. After several volunteers have made their presentations, vote as a group on which explanation was most creative and which was most convincing. Afterward, point out that, like the equipment on display, spiritual gifts have many different uses.

STEP 3

It probably won't mean much to your group members that people like Philip and Stephen used their spiritual gifts effectively *almost two thousand years ago.* So give your kids a chance to update the Bible stories. Have group members form teams. Assign each team one of the characters on Repro Resource 7. Instruct each team to come up with a scenario in which its assigned character uses his or her spiritual gift in a modern setting. Teams may use humor in their scenarios, but the situations should be as realistic as possible. After a few minutes, have each team share what it came up with.

STEP 3

As your kids work through Repro Resource 7, they may feel a bit awkward if they haven't heard of several of the characters. Other than Peter and Paul, the Bible characters on the sheet may be new to kids with little Bible background. Be sensitive to this possibility. One way to help your kids avoid feeling "stupid" is to point out that the Bible is filled with people like these who were mentioned only briefly and cited for their faith. If we feel badly that we don't know them all, we miss the point. It's as if these people were included in God's inspired Word to let us know that He notices when people are faithful to Him and use the spiritual gifts that He has provided. Perhaps if the Bible were being written today, your group members might be named in the place of people like Tabitha, Barnabas, or Gaius.

STEP 4

To help make the Giftor exercise a bit more personal for your group members, and to make sure that they're thinking about what their own spiritual gifts might be, say: **Suppose we were commissioned to build Giftor. We have a mechanical superhero body to use, but his circuits have been erased. He has no "personality" at all—none, that is, except what we as a group can donate to him. So how would you suggest that we try to equip him, using what we can "transfer" to him from members of this group?** For example, perhaps the group would want Giftor to have Sue's sense of humor, Tony's patience, Jane's comfortable way of dealing with people, and so forth. Keep looking for ways to make Giftor stronger as you also draw out the potential spiritual gifts of your own group members.

STEP 1

When kids arrive, have all of the ingredients for pizza sitting out, but not put together. Explain that you were going to have pizza for the meeting this week, but didn't have time to prepare it. Then step back and get involved in preparing something else for the meeting (or leave the room); see what happens. Afterward, discuss what took place. If some kids kicked in and started to put the pizzas together, discuss the process that they went through. If no one did anything, ask why. Explain that life is a lot like the unmade pizzas in that there are always things that can be done—ways we can put our gifts to use—if we're open to and looking for them. But unless we put our gifts to use, they do no one any good. Read Romans 12:3-8. Review briefly how God distributes gifts in a balanced way; then thank Him for the gifts He's given your group. Then get the pizzas in the oven for a hot snack at the end of your meeting!

STEP 5

After group members have thought a bit about the gift(s) they may have, set out paper, pencils, small empty boxes, various types of wrapping paper, scissors, and tape. Say: **God has given us our spiritual gifts as just that—gifts. We can offer those gifts back to Him for His service.** Instruct kids to write what they think may be their spiritual gift(s) on a slip of paper. Then give them the option of wrapping the piece of paper and offering it back to God as a gift for His service. When kids are finished wrapping, close the session in prayer, thanking God for the many gifts He gives us.

MOSTLY GIRLS

MOSTLY GUYS

EXTRA FUN

STEP 1

When you're talking about whether or not women are given the same gifts as men, you may wish to introduce to your girls some women who have the gifts of preaching, serving, teaching, etc., and are using them in service in various ways. (Of course, you'll need to line up these volunteers in advance.) Encourage your group members to ask questions about the use of these gifts after your volunteers have shared.

STEP 3

You may wish to add some more women to the list of "Bible Time Gift Users" on Repro Resource 7. Possibilities might include the following people:

• Mary, the mother of Jesus (Luke 1:26-56)—Using the gift of faith, she believed the angel's message that she was expecting, even though she had no husband.

• Elizabeth (Luke 2:39-45)—Using the gift of prophecy, she knew that Mary's baby was the Son of God before Mary even said anything to her.

• Ruth (Ruth 2:1-8)—Using the gift of serving, she gathered food for herself and her mother-in-law.

• Martha (Luke 10:38-42)—Using the gift of serving, she made preparations for her visitors. [NOTE: This is also an example of a gift being misused. This passage could lead to a good discussion on the need for wisdom in using our gifts.]

STEP 1

If your guys are a competitive bunch, let them create their own review of previous material to begin the session. Have kids form two teams. Let each team write questions to ask the other team. However, players must be able to answer every question they ask. Give your guys a few minutes to brainstorm questions; then let them take turns quizzing the other team members. Any question that can't be answered by the other team and *can* be answered by the asking team should score a point. You should act as judge to make sure that everything asked has actually been covered in the course of previous sessions. After opposing teams run out of questions, see if they've missed anything that's listed on Repro Resource 6; then move on from there.

STEP 4

The situations used in the Giftor section of this step should be rewritten to appeal more to an all-guy crowd. Girls' names can be changed to guys' names in some cases. In addition, you can probably think of several situations that you know your guys are facing. While you don't want to get so specific that you make anyone embarrassed or uncomfortable, you can take this opportunity to help your guys deal with very real problems. No one knows your group better than you do, so put some time into creating some situations that you know will be real and relevant for your guys.

STEP 1

Rather than using Repro Resource 6 for the opening review, you might want to adapt a popular game that will accomplish the same thing. For instance, you might play a Pictionary-type game in which you show key words to one person on a team and have him or her try to draw the word or concept for the other team members. You can adapt Outburst by having teams guess "Ten spiritual gifts," "Ten questions people ask about spiritual gifts," and so forth. You can adapt Wheel of Fortune by having kids guess letters to words or phrases they need to remember. It may be a little more work to put together a fun and creative review, but it's not usually as difficult as you might think. Give it a try and see what happens.

STEP 3

Make a contest out of the activity on Repro Resource 7. Rather than using the sheet as is, take advantage of the unusual names on it. Scramble the letters in the names and make a different handout with the scrambled names and Bible references. You'll probably want to add a few names and references of your own—the more obscure, the better. The first person to correctly unscramble the names and determine what spiritual gift was used by each person is the winner. While Peter and Paul aren't likely to stump many people, names like Gaius are likely to send your group members searching for Scripture references.

STEP 1

Before the session, prepare a video exercise designed to get your group members' "memory juices" flowing before the review quiz. Record brief excerpts from several different TV shows. Make sure that each excerpt includes a familiar character from the show so that the show is recognizable. To begin the session, hand out paper and pencils. While you show the compilation tape, group members should write down the name of the show that each excerpt comes from. If group members don't know the name of a show, they should draw a question mark and wait for the next clip. When everyone is finished, reveal the correct answers. Award prizes to the group members with the most correct answers. Then move on to the mini-review exercise.

STEP 4

Supplement the "gift mix" situations listed in Step 4 with some real-life situations. Before the session, record a TV newscast. As you play back the tape for your group members, ask them to call out spiritual gifts that might be put to use in some of the news stories that are covered. Then ask volunteers to explain what results might occur if spiritual gifts were put to use in those situations.

STEP 4

Rather than reading through the "Mighty Giftor" situations listed in Step 4, ask group members to brainstorm a couple of their own situations, identifying which spiritual gifts could possibly be used in each situation. Encourage group members to explain exactly how a particular spiritual gift might be used. Then very briefly go through the three strategies for putting spiritual gifts to use.

STEP 5

Rather than constructing an organizational chart of your church's structure, try a shorter option. Ask your group members to brainstorm some reasons why people don't attend church or why people dislike coming to church. These reasons might include the following: the people in the church aren't friendly; there's no Sunday school class geared toward me; there's no evangelism program; the songs we sing are too old-fashioned; the sermons are too boring; and so on. After you've come up with a list, ask your group members to consider what spiritual gifts could be applied to some of the various "complaints." Also ask them to consider *how* spiritual gifts might be applied and what some of the possible results might be. Close the session in prayer, asking God to make your group members aware of spiritual gift-application opportunities in your church.

STEP 3

Before the session, write each of the 16 spiritual gifts listed in Step 3 of Session 1 on a separate slip of paper; put the slips into a hat. Bring in a radio or a tape player. Have kids sit in a circle and give one person a tennis ball. Explain that when you start the music, kids should begin passing the tennis ball around the circle. When you stop the music, the person with the tennis ball must draw a slip of paper from the hat and read aloud the spiritual gift that's written on it. The person must then answer this question: **What are some ways that this spiritual gift could be used to minister to people in the inner city?** Encourage the person to be creative and thoughtful in his or her response. Ask the rest of the group to offer their insights and suggestions.

STEP 4

Add the following "Mighty Giftor" situations to Step 4:

• Jermaine knows that several of his buddies have recently joined a gang and are selling drugs to kids after school. He knows that they're heading for serious trouble. He also knows that he wants to make a difference, but he doesn't know where to begin or even whether his efforts would have a lasting effect.

• Shawndra lives with her single mother. One night, her mom came home drunk and started hitting Shawndra, causing Shawndra to suffer some internal injuries. Shawndra is now in the hospital.

• Ronnie and Tommy Lee live in the projects with their families. The living conditions are terrible, with trash, rats, and broken windows everywhere. The two are tired of their living conditions and dream of making the projects a decent place to live.

STEP 2

After your kids have gotten the hang of "muscle mush," set them up in pairs, preferably pairing a junior higher with a high schooler. Have the members of each pair act out for each other what an entire day without muscles would look like. As each person is acting out the events of his or her day, his or her partner should try to guess what each activity is. Afterward, ask: **How difficult would it be to live without using your muscles? Why do you think God created our bodies in such a way that if we don't use our muscles they get weak? Why do you think He created our spiritual gifts to be the same way?**

STEP 5

Rather than setting up an organizational chart, with which your junior highers may not be familiar, have kids form small groups. Instruct each group to draw a rough map of the church. In each room or area of the church, group members should write which spiritual gifts would most likely be put to use there. After a few minutes, have each group share and explain its map.

STEP 1

Begin the session by having your group members play the board game "Scrabble"—with a spiritual gifts twist. Have kids form teams. Give each team a large supply of letter tiles. Explain that before each round, you will announce a spiritual gift. All words formed in that round must somehow relate to that spiritual gift. For instance, if you choose the gift of "encouragement," teams might use words like "smile," cheer," "go," "yes," and "great." Emphasize that teams must be able to defend their words, if challenged. Choose a different spiritual gift for each round. Play as many rounds as you have time for. Award prizes to the team with the most points at the end of the game. Use this activity to introduce the mini-review exercise at the beginning of Step 1.

STEP 3

Expand your discussion of the strategies for putting spiritual gifts to work, giving kids an opportunity to "personalize" the information. Hand out paper and pencils. After you read the first strategy, instruct kids to write down some of the specific needs they've noticed around them. After you read the second strategy, instruct kids to write down some opportunities for spiritual-gifts training—both formal and informal—that they're aware of. After you read the third strategy, instruct kids to write down some personality traits, talents, and abilities that make them unique. Encourage kids to keep their sheets handy for the next couple of weeks to help them discover their spiritual gifts.

DATE USED:

APPROX. TIME

STEP 1: *How Far Have We Come?* _____
❏ Extra Action
❏ Large Group
❏ Heard It All Before
❏ Fellowship & Worship
❏ Mostly Girls
❏ Mostly Guys
❏ Extra Fun
❏ Media
❏ Extra Challenge
Things needed:

STEP 2: *Muscle Mush* _____
❏ Combined Junior High/High School
Things needed:

STEP 3: *Ancient Observations* _____
❏ Small Group
❏ Large Group
❏ Heard It All Before
❏ Little Bible Background
❏ Mostly Girls
❏ Extra Fun
❏ Urban
❏ Extra Challenge
Things needed:

STEP 4: *Super Transformations* _____
❏ Extra Action
❏ Little Bible Background
❏ Mostly Guys
❏ Media
❏ Short Meeting Time
❏ Urban
Things needed:

STEP 5: *Chart the Church* _____
❏ Small Group
❏ Fellowship & Worship
❏ Short Meeting Time
❏ Combined Junior High/High School
Things needed:

Teamwork
(Using Your Gifts in Conjunction with Others)

☐ To help kids explore the relationship between teamwork and effective gift use.

☐ To help kids understand that spiritual gifts cannot be used in isolation.

☐ To help kids set up a telephone chain for increasing their levels of Christian communication.

☐ Other: _____
_____

Your Bible Base:

Romans 12:3-8
1 Corinthians 12:12-26
Ephesians 4:1-6
1 Thessalonians 5:11
Hebrews 3:13

STEP 1

Spoonfuls of Teamwork

(Needed: Fishing pole, plastic spoon, tape, cereal, bowl, prizes)

Begin the session by announcing that you're hungry—and that your group members are going to feed you. Before the session, you'll need to tape a plastic spoon to the end of a long fishing pole. You'll also need a bowl of cereal. Explain that each group member must wrap one finger around the fishing pole. The kids must then work together to feed you at least three bites from the bowl, without dropping any of the cereal.

Announce that all group members will get a prize if they can successfully complete the task. Deduct points for spills or for touching any part of your body other than your mouth with the spoon. The feeders will have to work together, slowly and carefully, to do this right. If they successfully complete the assignment, award prizes.

Afterward, ask: **How did you feel about trying to work together with others on something that you might have been able to do better yourself?**

After you get a few responses, ask group members to name some tasks that they probably wouldn't be able to do very well unless they had the help and support of others.

Then ask: **What group qualities did this exercise require?** (Patience, flexibility, and cooperation.)

What would you say is the common goal of Christians? (To glorify God by living in unity and love, by learning to know Christ and become like Him, and by bringing others to the Lord.)

What kinds of group qualities are required for the body of Christ to accomplish its goals? (Interdependence, humility, patience, the working of spiritual gifts.)

Explain: **Teamwork is important because there are many things that can't get done without it. This is especially true when it comes to being a well-rounded, gift-using Christian.**

STEP
2

Lonesome Translations

(Needed: Copies of Repro Resource 8, pencils)

Distribute copies of "The Lone-Ranger Christian" (Repro Resource 8) and pencils. Give group members a few minutes to work on the sheet. Kids will have to do some creative, abstract thinking in order to translate the cowboy items into the problems of a loner Christian. It may be difficult for some, but let them try.

After a few minutes, go through the sheet, asking volunteers to share what they came up with for each item. Use the following information to supplement group members' responses, adding your own clarifications and explanations to make the point that Christian discipleship—using our gifts for God's glory—requires Christian community.

- *Wears a mask*—Does not open up to others; has no accountability; has no one to share with.
- *Saddled up*—"Saddled" with personal problems, but has no one to pray with.
- *Horsing around*—Vulnerable to temptation and sin because of lack of fellowship, support, encouragement, and accountability.
- *Uses spurs*—Can hurt others with a sharp tongue or with cutting actions.
- *Riding high*—May have an unrealistic view of self and abilities; may believe his or her gifts are more important than the gifts of others; may abuse leadership gifts by not consulting others for their wisdom and guidance.
- *Shoots from the hip*—Has not developed the ability to get along with others; is not developing loving communication through living in Christian community.
- *Silver bullets*—May rely on personal power, rather than the power of teamwork in the body of Christ.
- *Galloping ahead*—Does not stop to consider the advice and guidance of other Christians when attempting to discern God's will; perhaps has no direction in life.

O P T I O N S

SMALL GROUP

HEARD IT ALL BEFORE

LITTLE BIBLE BACKGROUND

MOSTLY GIRLS

MOSTLY GUYS

EXTRA FUN

URBAN

JR.HIGH HIGH SCHOOL COMBINED

STEP 3

The Sitting Challenge

(Needed: Bibles)

Say: **When we Christians act as though we're simply a gathering of individuals, we will find it harder to appreciate spiritual gifts. Gifts are designed to work in conjunction with others in a kind of spiritual teamwork. Not having a close fellowship hinders the effectiveness of spiritual gifts. Let's see how the apostle Paul explains this.**

Ask volunteers to read aloud Romans 12:3-8; I Corinthians 12:12-26; and Ephesians 4:1-6 . Focus group members' attention on I Corinthians 12:18—"God has arranged the parts in the body, every one of them, just as he wanted them to be."

Then say: **Don't move! Notice how everyone is sitting.** Point out that some people are sitting with their legs outstretched or crossed; some are sitting up straight; some are slouching; some have their hands in various positions; etc. Ask: **How many of you think that if we all stood in a circle, facing each other's backs with our hands on the shoulders of the person in front of us, we could all sit on each other's knees if we sat down at the same time?** Take a poll to see how many kids think it could be done; then give it a shot. Keep trying until you're successful—or until you see that the group can't do it.

Afterward, explain: **This is like a mini-picture of the church as the apostle Paul describes it. There are many parts, many individuals, but one circle—one common goal that we all work together to achieve. As Christians, that common goal is God's glory through the growth of the church. Remember that true growth requires both quality—individuals maturing in Christ—and quantity—new people entering because of the love that flows from a community of believers in which spiritual gifts are fully operational.**

STEP 4

Telephone Work

(Needed: Copies of Repro Resource 9, pencils)

Explain: **One way to experience the unity of the body of Christ is to have more contact with each other, interacting more regularly throughout our Christian journeys.**

Hand out copies of "Telephone Teamwork" (Repro Resource 9). Work together as a group to fill in names and phone numbers on the sheet. Talk about whether group members would be willing to commit to using it; then work out the details about how you'll do it. For example, you might commit to sharing joys and concerns with one another for a month. You might share prayer concerns, personal concerns, requests related to individual ministries, or requests that deal with the whole group's outreach efforts.

Be sure to emphasize that the purpose of the telephone chain is not to solve one another's problems. Rather, you are simply putting into practice the biblical principle of "If one part suffers, every part suffers with it; if one part is honored, every part rejoices with it" (1 Cor. 12:26). To apply this, we must actually know what's going on in each other's lives.

As you wrap up this section, emphasize the following points regarding how fellowship or teamwork relates to the effective functioning of spiritual gifts.

1. Teamwork in a church usually requires small groups. Let group members know that the phone chain can eventually lead to deeper face-to-face relationships, perhaps in small groups or other share-and-prayer-based meetings. Only as we get to know each other, beyond the surface levels of small talk and into the areas of one another's needs and struggles, will we begin to depend on one another. That's the key to the use of spiritual gifts—building interdependence, working together to minister to and with one another.

2. Programming goals will flow from our fellowship goals. God wants to build a community of love and mutual support. This is a greater priority than any program the church or youth group may develop. When everyone is in unity, working together, programming naturally follows. And since programming will be directed by the Holy Spirit, it will be creative—and not necessarily conventional. The key is to build a healthy, loving group, and then to be ready to follow God's leading for methods and organization.

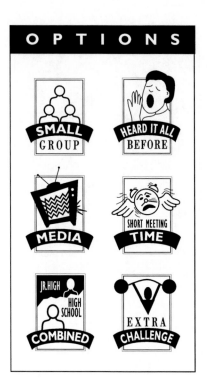

O P T I O N S

SMALL GROUP

HEARD IT ALL BEFORE

MEDIA

SHORT MEETING TIME

JR. HIGH / HIGH SCHOOL COMBINED

EXTRA CHALLENGE

STEP 5

Come Together

Say: **We've seen that teamwork is essential to using our spiritual gifts because the church is one body with many parts. But one point still needs to be clear: Though we have individual gifts, that doesn't mean we can ignore the gifts we don't have. We still have roles to play in the church that may call for us to pray, be encouraging, lead, show mercy, and so on. The gifted person may be better at doing these things and may focus most of his or her energy in these areas, but all Christians need to be ready to respond to God's call to play such roles in certain situations. We'll have a hard time discovering our spiritual gifts unless we are open to serving God in *all* areas of service. Let's apply this specifically to the area of encouraging one another. This is something we're all called to do.**

Have volunteers read aloud I Thessalonians 5:11 and Hebrews 3:13. Then ask group members to find a place in the room in which they are (1) as far from the center of the room as possible and (2) as far away from every other group member as possible. Instruct kids to close their eyes and keep them closed.

Then say: **We're far apart now, just as it would be if we attempted to be "lone-ranger Christians." But the Bible tells us that we belong to one another and that we should live like that is true. So, keeping your eyes closed, find your way to the center of the room and join with your fellow believers for a group hug before we close.**

After all group members have made it to the center of the room with their eyes closed, explain that you all will be standing together for a moment to symbolize the way the body of Christ really is—one faith, one Lord, one baptism, living together in unity and love. Then give kids a few minutes to offer words of encouragement and affirmation to each other. Each person should make a statement that (1) says something good about how the group has ministered to him or her, (2) says something encouraging or affirming about another individual in the group, or (3) says something about his or her hopes for the group or for someone in it. After everyone has had a chance to share his or her statement, close the session in prayer.

THE
LONE-RANGER CHRISTIAN

Imagine trying to live the Christian life all by yourself! Suppose you never met with other Christians, never prayed with a friend, never used your gifts with others to work toward the common goal of God's glory. You'd be a Lone-Ranger Christian—and you'd definitely have some problems. Using some of the items below to spur your thinking, identify some of the problems that a Christian loner might face. (One example has already been done for you.)

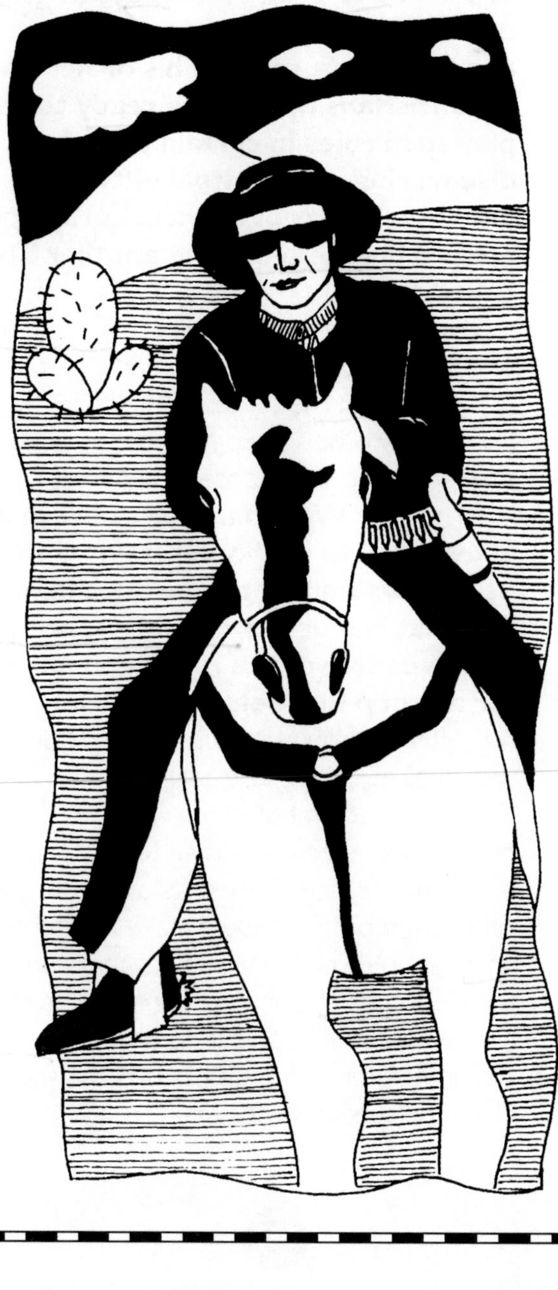

Wears a mask

_____
_____
_____
_____
_____

Saddled up

_____
_____
_____

Horsing around

_____
_____
_____
_____

Uses spurs

_____
_____
_____
_____

Riding high

_____
_____
_____
_____

Shoots from the hip
Hasn't developed the ability to get along with others; hasn't developed loving communication through living in Christian community

_____
_____

Silver bullets

_____
_____
_____

Galloping ahead

_____
_____
_____

Telephone  Teamwork

"There should be no division in the body, but that its parts should have equal concern for each other. If one part suffers, every part suffers with it; if one part is honored, every part rejoices with it."

—I Corinthians 12:25, 26

Name: _____ Name: _____ Name: _____
Phone number: _____ Phone number: _____ Phone number: _____

Name: _____ Name: _____ Name: _____
Phone number: _____ Phone number: _____ Phone number: _____

Name: _____ Name: _____ Name: _____
Phone number: _____ Phone number: _____ Phone number: _____

Name: _____ Name: _____ Name: _____
Phone number: _____ Phone number: _____ Phone number: _____

Name: _____ Name: _____ Name: _____
Phone number: _____ Phone number: _____ Phone number: _____

NOTES

EXTRA **ACTION**

Step I

Set up a volleyball net in your meeting area (or outside, if possible). Have kids form two teams for a friendly game of volleyball. However, rather than using a volleyball for the game, use a large mushball (a ball that's about five feet in diameter). You may need to contact a school or a YMCA to secure the use of a mushball. Explain that both teams will try to push the ball over the net without letting it hit the ground on their side. Once you start playing the game, you'll see how the mushball humbles those who think they can hit it over the net by themselves. In fact, it will take several people to hit the ball over the net. Let kids play for several minutes. Afterward, point out that just as it took teamwork to get the mushball over the net, so also it takes teamwork to make spiritual-gift use most effective.

Step 3

To emphasize the fact that Christians are all working together as parts of one body, have your group members work together to form a "human machine." Ask one person to stand in the middle of the room. Encourage him or her to start doing something—anything—in a repeated rhythm (as if he or she were a windup toy that did the same thing over and over). Emphasize that the person may not stop what he or she is doing until the end of the activity. Once the first person has begun doing something, ask another group member to venture out to the middle of the room and start doing something that complements the first person's actions. Continue adding group members one at a time until everyone is part of the "machine." Afterward, compare working together as a "machine" with working together as part of Christ's body.

SMALL **GROUP**

Step 2

Explain that the concept of a "Lone-Ranger Christian" can also apply to a "Lone-Ranger Christian youth group." Sometimes a small group can isolate itself and miss out on spiritual gifts and opportunities that other people and groups might be able to offer. To make sure that this isn't a problem in your group, use this opportunity to plan an event that will allow your group members to interact with young people from other Christian groups. Perhaps there's a local conference you can plan to attend. If not, you might decide to host a dinner, a film, a volleyball tournament, or any number of things that would attract other Christians in your community. Preferably you can incorporate a number of other small groups who may have the same limitations that your group must cope with. If things go well at the initial get-together, you may want to make it a regular event.

Step 4

In a group with only a few members, a telephone chain may not be such a big deal. Mention it as one option, but see if your group members can come up with a more intimate alternative that would encourage them on a more personal level. A small group should have more flexibility than a larger group. Is there a time during the school day when all of your group members can meet together for three minutes to offer encouragement to one another and see if anyone needs special attention? Can you buy kids breakfast or lunch once or twice a week? Can you pack into a minivan and go somewhere, more for the drive than for the ultimate destination (a park, movie, ice-cream store, etc.)? Challenge your group members to think creatively; see what they can come up with.

LARGE **GROUP**

Step I

Divide kids into two teams. Have the teams form two single-file lines. Give the first person in each line a medium-sized gift-wrapped box. At your signal, the first person in line must pass the box over his or her head to the next person in line. That person will then pass the box between his or her legs to the next person in line. Team members will continue alternating "over" and "under" passing until the box reaches the end of the line. The first team to successfully get its box to the end of the line is the winner. Afterward, discuss how teamwork was needed to be successful in the relay race. Similarly, teamwork is needed to be successful in effectively using our spiritual gifts as Christians.

Step 5

If possible, bring in a parachute. If you can't find a parachute, bring in a few large bedsheets that you've sewn together. Also bring in a volleyball (or a ball of similar size). Have kids form two teams. Letting one team go at a time, have team members stand around the edge of the parachute, holding it taut. Place the ball in the middle of the parachute. Explain that the object of the game is to see which team can "whip" the ball highest simply by waving the parachute in a rippling motion. Ideally, the slack from the waving of the sheet will send the ball high into the air. To do this, kids will have to work together to get the waving process going. Give each team five chances to toss the ball. The ball that goes the highest (according to your keen eye) is the winner. However, the team must catch the ball in the parachute without letting the ball touch the ground in order to make the toss count. Afterward, explain that similarly, Christians need to work together to both strengthen each other and to successfully minister to others with their spiritual gifts.

STEP 2

The fact that Christians are supposed to work together will probably come as no surprise to most of your group members. So rather than using Repro Resource 8, try approaching the topic from the opposite direction. Ask your group members to list the "top 10 reasons why the Christian life should be lived alone." Let group members suggest reasons like "You'd be able to sleep in on Sunday mornings instead of going to church" and "You wouldn't have to eat potluck food at fellowship dinners." Then have group members list the "top 10 benefits of sharing the Christian life with other believers." Afterward, compare the two lists to see which one is preferable.

STEP 4

The telephone chain is simply one way to unite your kids. As a group, brainstorm some other practical suggestions for developing a "team spirit" among your group members. For example, kids might form small-group Bible studies, plan occasional retreat activities, meet at a local restaurant for weekly "resharpening" meetings, and so on. After kids have settled on one particular course of action, encourage them to commit to it for at least a month. When the month is up, plan a time of sharing in which group members can share how their "opening up" with each other about the struggles and joys of their Christian walk has affected their lives.

STEP 2

After kids complete Repro Resource 8, make sure that they understand what you've been discussing by having them create characters who properly exercise their spiritual gifts. Have kids form small groups. Instruct each group to design a previously unheard of hero (or heroine) who properly uses his or her God-given gifts and talents for the good of others. Many of your kids have probably read enough comic books that this won't be much of a problem for them. But if some need help, give them a few ideas.

• Sponge Man, who "wrings himself out" for others in times of need, and then regains strength as others surround him so that he can absorb the benefits of their various gifts.

• The Jigsaw Warriors, a race of mutant characters whose arms and legs interlink with each other like jigsaw puzzle pieces. The bigger the challenge they face, the more of them who join forces to defeat it.

STEP 3

An activity frequently done in youth groups is identifying which "body parts" members might be in the "body of Christ." Though this may be overdone in some groups, it can still be effective in groups that haven't done it before. After you read and discuss I Corinthians 12:12-26, have each person select a body part that he or she thinks is descriptive of himself or herself. After a few minutes, have kids reveal the parts they selected and explain why. Point out that while you certainly have a good start, many parts are still missing. (List several obviously important body parts that weren't mentioned.) For kids with very little Bible background, this simple exercise may be more effective in helping them understand spiritual gifts than anything else.

STEP 1

During the week prior to the meeting, contact your group members and ask each of them to bring some type of potluck dish, explaining that you're going to share a meal together to kick off the session. (If possible, you may wish to have a sign-up sheet ready at the preceding meeting.) When kids arrive, set up a buffet-style spread, lead the group in a prayer of thanks for the food, and dig in. When kids are close to finishing their meal, ask: **What do you think is the significance of sharing a meal together? And in light of what we've been discussing the past few weeks, why is a pot-luck meal significant?** (With everyone working together and contributing various talents, you came up with quite an array of food that made a better meal than just one person could have put together.) Explain that using our spiritual gifts involves a lot of teamwork, which is what you're going to discuss today.

STEP 5

First Corinthians 13:4-13 is probably the most frequently used Scripture passage concerning love, but seldom do we hear it in the context of the passages that surround it. The "Love Chapter" is nestled in with Paul's teaching about spiritual gifts. Point out this fact to your group members; then read aloud some of the surrounding passages. Afterward, ask: **Why do you think Paul started talking about love in the middle of all of this stuff about spiritual gifts?** (Because if our gifts aren't used in love, they're worthless.) **Are you surprised to find out this love is referring to service and the use of our gifts? Why or why not?** Get a few responses. Then challenge kids to examine their attitudes toward serving and working with others. Close in prayer, thanking God for the chance He's given us to work together.

MOSTLY **GIRLS**

MOSTLY **GUYS**

EXTRA FUN

STEP 2

As you work through the parts of your Lone Ranger Christian (Repro Resource 8), ask your girls to think of situations they or their friends have been in that would fit the descriptions given. (For example, perhaps Joy is "wearing a mask" as she tries to pretend that everything is fine even though her parents are getting a divorce.) As your group members bring up examples, talk about which gifts could be put to use to help those people, and how the help could be offered. Be sure to point out how different gifts can work together to solve the same problem.

STEP 3

After reading I Corinthians 12:18, ask: **What do you think would happen if our body parts suddenly decided to rearrange themselves?** Have kids form teams. Give each team a "Mr. Potato Head" figure. Explain that you're going to have a contest to see which team can come up with the strangest configuration for Mr. Potato Head's body parts. After a minute or two, have each team display its work; then declare a winner. After you've had a good laugh, talk about how well a body that is put together incorrectly would function. (Not very well!) Then point out that the body of Christ is the same way. It's designed to fit and work together in a certain way, and if people aren't working together as God intended, the body won't function properly.

STEP 2

The Lone Ranger gets picked on quite a bit in this step, almost to the point of making him a bad guy instead of a good one. So after going through the exercise and discussing traits to watch out for, let your guys discuss the Lone Ranger's positive points. For example, he became the Lone Ranger because all of his colleagues were massacred. His two main options were to give up or to go it alone, and he made the courageous choice. The mask may indeed signify lack of vulnerability, but it is also something that helps him remain anonymous and humble. Have your guys identify the positive aspects of the Lone Ranger and then discuss how it is important to find the right balance between opening yourself up to other people and getting a job done (even if you occasionally need to do it yourself).

STEP 5

You may want to use a more "masculine" closing than the one in the session. It's likely that many of your guys are most "centered" and committed to teamwork when they stand in a huddle. So try to devise a huddle activity. You should act as the motivator, trying to get your guys excited and ready for action. Have guys form a tight circle and join hands. Bark out questions such as **Are we ready to operate as a single body? Are you up to this challenge? Are your eyes on the goal line? Are you willing to sacrifice yourself for the others in this group?** After each question, group members should offer loud and enthusiastic affirmation.

STEP 1

To begin the session, have kids form teams. See which team can create the most inventive "human machine." Explain that the actions of each machine part (each person) should interact with the next part, and so forth. The "machines" need not actually produce anything or serve a purpose. The goal is rather to establish the most intricate interaction group members can design. After teams have formed individual machines, see if you can assemble one large machine using the entire group. This activity will lead naturally into the "one body" concept discussed later in the session.

STEP 2

After group members complete Repro Resource 8, have them conduct an impromptu skit. The story line should be that every group member is the Lone Ranger in his or her own part of the country. But all of the Lone Rangers happen to ride into the same town at the same time. They are all looking for other people to help, but they suddenly find out that there are many of them. Have the characters discuss what to do. (Should they work together as the "Group Rangers"? Should they work in teams of twos or threes? Should they keep working alone, but plan a Lone Ranger Convention once a year?) Have fun as group members give each other new law enforcement techniques, directions to a discount mask store, information on the best ointments to use for saddle sores, and so forth.

STEP 1

Before the session, put together a video compilation of several excerpts from TV shows, movies, and sporting events that show some form of teamwork. In addition to the obvious examples from the world of sports, you might include scenes like the one in the movie *Witness* in which the Amish people work together to build a barn. To begin the session, show the compilation tape to your group members. Ask kids to guess what the various scenes have in common. If no one mentions it, bring up the topic of teamwork. Lead in to a discussion of how teamwork can affect the effectiveness of our spiritual gifts.

STEP 4

As group members work on Repro Resource 9, play a couple of songs by Christian artists that address the topic of teamwork among Christians. You might consider using songs like "Shoulder to Shoulder" (Allies) and "Holy Hand" (Morgan Cryar). Afterward, ask: **What are some of the things that prevent a "team spirit" from developing among Christians? How can we combat these things to allow teamwork to develop?** Get several responses.

STEP 1

Replace Steps 1 and 2 with a shorter opener. Instruct kids to think of something or someone that doesn't seem right all by itself or without another item. For instance, someone may say that bacon doesn't seem right without eggs. Another person may say that Laverne doesn't seem right without Shirley. Someone else may say that a member of a rock group who decides to pursue a solo career doesn't seem right without his or her old band. After a few minutes, ask kids to share what they came up with. After everyone has shared, ask: **What if I said that a Christian doesn't seem right without something else? What would you say is that "something else"?** If no one mentions it, suggest that a Christian doesn't seem right without other Christians. Point out that Christians should provide encouragement, strength, and comfort for each other. Then move on to Step 3.

STEP 4

Rather than having kids take the time to fill out Repro Resource 9, simply ask them to suggest some ideas for building unity and teamwork in the group. After you've got a list of ideas, ask group members to vote on which idea they'd like to put into practice within the next week. Then make the necessary arrangements to follow through on the idea. Skip Step 5.

STEP 1

Use some examples from the world of professional sports to emphasize to your group members the importance of teamwork. Ask your group members to name the champions of the National Basketball Association, National Hockey League, National Football League, and major league baseball. If your kids are really into sports, you might ask them to talk about some of the players on the various championship teams. Point out that these squads had several different people contributing and building each other up with their efforts. Then point out that just as teamwork is important in sports, Christian fellowship (or teamwork) is important in making effective use of our spiritual gifts.

STEP 2

Have your group members consider the following scenario: **Tyrone feels all alone. He recently became a Christian. At first, he felt like he could conquer the world; but lately, the world has been pounding on him. He finally quit the football team after being seriously harassed by his teammates for his faith. Now the gangs in the neighborhood are starting to target him. His mom and dad recently split up. He quit his job, lost his girlfriend, and is starting to feel like "this Christianity stuff just isn't worth it." Why do you think Tyrone feels this way? What are some things that might help him?** Spend some time discussing things that could improve Tyrone's situation. Brainstorm some specific plans of action that might help inner-city Christians effectively use their spiritual gifts in their difficult environment.

STEP 2

Junior highers may find the connections between the Lone Ranger's silver bullets and the Lone Christian's desire for personal power too difficult to make on their own. To help them with this exercise, make an enlargement of the picture of the Lone Ranger and put it up in front of the group where everyone can see it. Then work together as a group, or divide into teams that combine junior highers and high schoolers, to make the connections listed for Repro Resource 8. Be sure to discuss the sheet thoroughly and allow time for questions.

STEP 4

Younger members of your group may not be mature enough to handle sharing concerns in a telephone chain. So instead of using Repro Resource 9, read each of the following scenarios and discuss as a group which spiritual gift(s) could be used to help that person and how.

• Brian was psyched for his senior year of cross-country. During his junior year, he had done very well. The coach was now looking to him to be a state champ this year. However, at the beginning of the season, Brian found out that he has mono and will be out the rest of the season.

• When they started school this fall, Kristi and Cheryl were best friends. Cheryl's now found a new group of friends—one in which Kristi isn't welcome.

• Cathy's mom had been diagnosed with cancer, but she's just had another checkup and things seem to be clearing up. The doctors are ready to give her a clean bill of health.

STEP 3

Rather than simply assuming that kids will agree that teamwork for Christians is natural and easy, spend some time talking about why working as a team is sometimes difficult. Ask: **What are some things that you prefer to do on your own as a Christian? Why? What aspects of being part of the same body as other Christians make you most uncomfortable? What would it take for you to feel completely comfortable about being part of the same team as other Christians?** Encourage your group members to respond openly and honestly to these questions.

STEP 4

Encourage kids to keep a journal of their telephone-chain experiences. How did they feel after hearing the personal concerns and prayer requests of others in the group? Do they feel confident in their ability to offer support, encouragement, and prayer for their fellow group members? Are they unsure about how to respond to a person who's sharing a heavy burden? How did they feel about sharing their own personal concerns and prayer requests with others? Did they feel supported and encouraged by the others? Ask kids to continue tracking their thoughts and feelings as they continue the telephone chain to see if things change over time.

DATE USED:

Approx. Time

STEP 1: *Spoonfuls of Teamwork* _____
❏ Extra Action
❏ Large Group
❏ Fellowship & Worship
❏ Extra Fun
❏ Media
❏ Short Meeting Time
❏ Urban
Things needed:

STEP 2: *Lonesome Translations* _____
❏ Small Group
❏ Heard It All Before
❏ Little Bible Background
❏ Mostly Girls
❏ Mostly Guys
❏ Extra Fun
❏ Urban
❏ Combined Junior High/High School
Things needed:

STEP 3: *The Sitting Challenge* _____
❏ Extra Action
❏ Little Bible Background
❏ Mostly Girls
❏ Extra Challenge
Things needed:

STEP 4: *Telephone Work* _____
❏ Small Group
❏ Heard It All Before
❏ Media
❏ Short Meeting Time
❏ Combined Junior High/High School
❏ Extra Challenge
Things needed:

STEP 5: *Come Together* _____
❏ Large Group
❏ Fellowship & Worship
Things needed:

Use Them or Lose Them?

(What Happens if You Don't Use Your Gifts)

YOUR GOALS FOR THIS SESSION:
Choose one or more

☐ To help kids explore what can happen in the church when spiritual gifts aren't functioning.

☐ To help kids understand that not using their gifts can seriously hinder the church's ministry.

☐ To help kids decide to keep their gifts in active use.

☐ Other:_____
_____

Your Bible Base:

I Timothy 4:12-16
2 Timothy 1:3-14

STEP 1

A Wrench in the Works

(Needed: Table, index cards, pencils, wrench)

Have kids form pairs. If possible, have all of the pairs sit around a large table. Give each pair 10 index cards. Instruct the pairs to write on each card one way in which a spiritual gift might be used in the church to promote growth. After all of the cards have been filled in, have each pair build a house of cards with its ten index cards. Emphasize that the pairs must not disturb each other's building projects.

After all (or most) of the structures have been completed, instruct group members to slowly and carefully sit back in their chairs. Then take a wrench out of your pocket and slide it across the table, trying to knock over as many of the structures as possible.

Afterward, say: **There's a well-known phrase for what I just did. Who knows what it is?** If no one mentions it, point out that you just "threw a wrench into the works."

Let the moans and groans die down before you make your point. Say: **The point of this little demonstration is simple: When a church is built on the workings of spiritual gifts, it has a strong foundation and can remain healthy. But when members refuse to identify, develop, and use their gifts, they throw a wrench into the works. That is, they weaken the fellowship and increase the potential for disastrous consequences. Let's take a look at how this might happen.**

OPTIONS

EXTRA ACTION

SMALL GROUP

LARGE GROUP

FELLOWSHIP & WORSHIP

EXTRA FUN

MEDIA

SHORT MEETING TIME

URBAN

EXTRA CHALLENGE

STEP 2

Message Mess-Up

(Needed: Paper, pencil)

Have group members sit in a circle. Explain that you're going to to test their accuracy in relaying a message by conducting four rounds of the old telephone-message game. You will jot a brief message on a piece of paper (large enough for all to read) and then whisper that message into the ear of the teen sitting on your left. That person will then whisper the message to the person on his or her left, and so on. After the last person in the circle receives the message, he or she will repeat it aloud while you compare it to your original message. Offer a prize to your group members if the final message exactly matches the original one.

What your group members won't know, however, is that you've arranged beforehand to have one person in the group change the message completely when he or she passes it on. For instance, if your original message is "Use your spiritual gifts or lose them," the person might change the message to something like "My dog wears banana-flavored earmuffs."

Continue this activity for four rounds. After each round, playfully scold the players, encouraging them to try their best to get the message right in the next round and reminding them of the prize at stake.

Before the last round, state that you think someone is deliberately trying to mess up the activity for the whole group. Ask for guesses as to who that person might be. Then suggest that players do one round completely out loud to find out for sure which person is not contributing to the team effort.

Afterward, ask: **In what other areas of life have you noticed that it is possible for one person to mess up a whole group's effectiveness?** Ask for numerous examples, perhaps from sports or classroom activities at school.

Then ask: **How is it possible that the entire body of believers suffers if a person doesn't use his or her gifts?**

After you get at least a couple of responses, say: **Let's try to answer this question by looking at the Bible and then relating what we find there to the concept of "choking" in the world of sports.**

STEP 3

Handling the Pressure

(Needed: Bibles, copies of Repro Resource 10, pencils, paper, masking tape, wastebasket, candy bars)

O P T I O N S

EXTRA
ACTION

HEARD IT ALL
BEFORE

LITTLE
BIBLE
BACKGROUND

MOSTLY
GIRLS

MOSTLY
GUYS

SHORT MEETING
TIME

URBAN

Give kids a chance to "choke" by setting up a free-throw situation, using a wastebasket and a large paper wad held together by masking tape. Pick five volunteers to compete. Their ability to stay cool under pressure will determine the fate of the rest of the group.

Give everyone a candy bar. Explain that group members will either be able to keep the candy or will have to turn it back in to you, depending on how well the free throw shooters handle pressure. If they choke, the whole group will lose its candy bars.

Put the pressure on by calling each shooter to the line with a different instruction that involves a consequence or reward for the whole group. Here are five instructions you might use:

- For Shooter #1: **You must make one out of two shots or everyone loses the candy.**
- For Shooter #2: *(If Shooter #1 didn't come through)* **You must make three out of five shots to get the candy back.** *(If Shooter #1 did come through)* **You must make four out of five shots or everyone loses the candy.**
- For Shooter #3: *(If Shooter #2 didn't come through)* **You must make two out of three shots to get the candy back.** *(If Shooter #2 did come through)* **You must make five out of five shots or everyone loses the candy.**
- For Shooter #4: *(If Shooter #3 didn't come through)* **You must make one out of five shots to get the candy back.** *(If Shooter #3 did come through)* **You must make five out of five shots or everyone loses the candy.**
- For Shooter #5: *(If Shooter #4 didn't come through)* **You must make one out of one shot to get the candy back.** *(If Shooter #4 did come through)* **You must make one out of one shot or everyone loses the candy.**

Afterward, ask: **How does it feel to be responsible for everyone's fate? Have you ever been in a position like this before? If so, how did you feel? What happened?** Get a couple of responses.

If the Christian community depends on all of its members' gifts to function, how is not using your gifts like "choking" in

sports? How is it different? (It's similar because in both situations, we are not "coming through" for others. It's different because in using our gifts, we don't depend on our own willpower or self-esteem; we open our lives to God's leading and the Holy Spirit's empowering. The results are ultimately in God's hands.)

In your opinion, how serious is it to fail or refuse to discover, develop, and use your spiritual gifts? Get a couple of responses.

Distribute copies of "The Pressures of Timothy" (Repro Resource 10) and pencils. Have volunteers read aloud I Timothy 4:12-16 and 2 Timothy 1:3-14. Explain that Paul was writing to encourage the young leader to keep teaching and preaching in the face of growing opposition.

Give group members a few minutes to read "The Pressures" section and to fill in "The Commands" section on the sheet. Then briefly discuss the two sections. The answers to "The Commands" section are as follows:

- "Fan into *flame* the *gift* of God" (2 Tim. 1:6).
- "Do not be *ashamed* to *testify* about our Lord" (2 Tim. 1:8).
- "*Join* with me in *suffering* for the gospel" (2 Tim. 1:8).
- "Keep . . . the pattern of sound *teaching*" (2 Tim. 1:13).
- "*Guard* the good *deposit* [of Christian doctrine] that was entrusted to you" (2 Tim. 1:14).

Then focus your discussion on the question at the bottom of the sheet: "What do you think might have happened to the church if Timothy had 'choked'—if he'd neglected his gifts and left the church in the hands of someone else?" Supplement group members' responses with the following information, as necessary:

What Happens When Christians Fail to Use Their Gifts?

1. Slowed growth. It's hard to imagine a growing, vibrant church or youth group in which spiritual gifts are not being used. For example, even one person with the gift of evangelism or teaching who chooses not to get involved hinders the growth of the church. There would be fewer converts who, in turn, could get involved and begin developing and exercising their own gifts.

2. A loss of true fellowship. Churches may begin to base their reason for existing on things other than the unity of the Spirit, as demonstrated by the functioning gifts. Then the church is in danger of becoming a kind of social club in which people may get together to have fun, but never really share their lives with each other. For spiritual life to blossom, we have to use our gifts and recognize that our unity comes from the bond of the Spirit, not the bond of similar likes and dislikes or similar social status.

3. Worker burnout. When Christian young people refuse to involve their spiritual gifts, they place a greater burden on those who must take up the slack. This can lead to tired, discouraged leaders—those who feel they must keep things going for the people who sit back and expect to be served.

4. *The possibility of dormancy.* We can let our gifts "cool off" and become ineffective through lack of use. Timothy was exhorted to "fan into flame" the gifts that God had given him. We must do the same. Use them or lose them!

STEP 4

Fanning the Flame

OPTIONS

Refer again to 2 Timothy 1:6—"I remind you to fan into flame the gift of God." Work together as a group to determine what "fanning the flame" means (in practical terms) for a Christian young person today. Use the following case studies to supplement your discussion.

Case Study #1
Pat knows that she has administrative and leadership gifts, but when she was asked by her youth pastor to head up a big hunger project, all she felt was fear—fear of failure. The youth pastor said, "This project has got to fly or people are going to question why we even have a youth group in our church. So, are you going to take the lead here or not?"

If you were Pat, how would you respond? Why?

What's the best possible response for Pat, assuming that she knows the importance of using her gifts and the importance of "political" success for her youth pastor?

Case Study #2
Kids at school have started to discover that Larnell is active at church. A kid on his soccer team made a wisecrack, saying, "Hey, maybe we should call you Rev. You know, The Holy Reverend. What's with all the church stuff, anyway?"

If you were Larnell, how would you respond? Why?

What's the best possible way for Larnell to handle the conflict between his desire to use his gifts and his desire to stay cool with his buddies at school?

Case Study #3
The youth choir director said to Chris, "You're so musically talented, why aren't you in the choir?" Actually, Chris is aware of five different jobs she could do in the church if she'd just volunteer. But then she thinks, *When would I ever*

study, work, or have any time for myself? **She hesitates for a moment before responding.**

    If you were Chris, how would you respond?

    What's the best possible answer Chris could give, in light of what we've learned about spiritual gifts?

The Potential for Fire

(Needed: Charcoal briquettes)

    Hold up an unused charcoal briquette in one hand and a used one in the other hand. Ask: **How are these two briquettes alike?** (Both are made of the same substance.)

    How are they different? (One has potential; the other doesn't. One can't burn.)

    How are two Christian teens different if one is actively developing and using her spiritual gifts and the other one isn't? (One has the potential for contributing to the church's ministry; the other can't "get on fire" until she opens up to God's leading.)

    What is the next step for the "inactive" young person to take? Ask group members to think about this question for a moment, applying it to their own lives. After a brief discussion, close the session in prayer, asking God to "stir up" the gifts in your group.

The PRESSURES of *Timothy*

Consider Timothy's call to continue using his spiritual gifts in the church. Timothy was under a lot of pressure. It probably would have been easy for him to give in to the pressure, neglect his gifts, and leave the church in the hands of someone else. Let's look at Timothy's situation a little more closely.

The Pressures
Check out a few of the pressure situations that Timothy faced.
• Some people may have thought Timothy was too young for the job (I Timothy 4:12).
• Timothy had to confront false teachers (I Timothy 1:3, 4; II Timothy 2:16-18).
• He had to deal with blasphemers (I Timothy 1:20).
• He had to identify and train leaders in the church (I Timothy 3:1-12).
• He faced liars and legalists (I Timothy 4:1-5).
• He may have had some health problems that caused him to get sick a lot (I Timothy 5:23).
• He had to handle arrogant rich people (I Timothy 6:1, 2).
• He faced the constant threat of persecution (II Timothy 1:8; 2:3).
• He had to resolve conflicts and opposition in the church (II Timothy 2:23-26).
• He was hassled by the godlessness around him (II Timothy 3:1-9).
• He was bothered by Alexander the metalworker (II Timothy 4:14, 15).

The Commands
Fill in the blanks to discover five commands that Paul gave to Timothy.

• "Fan into _____ the _____ of God" (II Timothy 1:6).

• "Do not be _____ to _____ about our Lord" (II Timothy 1:8).

• "_____ with me in _____ for the gospel" (II Timothy 1:8).

• "Keep . . . the pattern of sound _____" (II Timothy 1:13).

• "_____ the good _____ [of Christian doctrine] that was entrusted to you" (II Timothy 1:14).

What do you think might have happened to the church if Timothy had "choked"—if he'd neglected his gifts and left the church in the hands of someone else? Explain.

_____

_____

NOTES

STEP 1

Begin the session with a basketball-like game. You'll need dozens of paper wads and a trash can for this activity. Explain that the object of the game is to shoot as many paper wads as possible into the trash can. Designate different "point areas" in your room. For example, if a person hits a shot from right next to the trash can, it might be worth two points; if a person hits from a little farther out (use objects in your room to designate boundary lines), it might be worth three points; and so on. Assign half of your kids to be "active" players; assign the other half to be "passive" players. Explain that the active players may run anywhere in the room to retrieve or shoot paper wads; the passive players must stand in one spot for the entire game. Passive players may bend over to pick up any paper wads that land in their vicinity, but may not take a step in any direction to retrieve or shoot a paper wad. Allow kids to play for a few minutes. When time is up, compare the scores of the active players with the scores of the passive players. Use this activity to introduce the difference between actively using one's spiritual gift(s) and passively allowing one's spiritual gift(s) to go unused.

STEP 3

To add some action to the free-throw activity, change the consequences for a missed shot. Instead of offering candy bars for made shots, announce that the entire group will have to run 15 wind sprints (or do 50 sit-ups or perform some other difficult physical action) if the necessary shots aren't made. See how the prospect of negative consequences affects your shooters.

STEP 1

In a small group, you might want to let everyone work on the same house of cards. This will accomplish several things. It will make it easier for you to knock the house down with your wrench. If group members succeed, it will show them what they can do by working together. If they have problems working together because of one person's clumsiness or impatience, it will give you a good example for later in the session when you discuss "choking." In a small group, anytime you can get people focused on doing the same thing, it's usually a good growth experience.

STEP 2

The telephone-message game (sometimes known as "Gossip") won't work well with a small group. Instead, put one person at one end of the room, one person in the center, and everyone else at the opposite end. Give the person by himself or herself at the end of the room a message to try to communicate to the people at the other end. It is the job of the person in the center to prevent that message from going through in any way possible (yelling, humming, banging things together, or whatever). When the message is at last successfully transmitted, give other people the opportunity to try to communicate and to interfere.

STEP 1

Bring in as many dominoes as you possibly can. Begin the session by having your group members work together to set up a domino course. They may make the course as elaborate or as simple as they wish. When all of the dominoes are set up, knock the first one over and watch the chain reaction. Point out that this is similar to what happens when Christians use their spiritual gifts together—an interesting chain reaction occurs in which one person's gift(s) directly affect another person. Have your group members set up the domino course again. However, this time remove one domino from a critical place in the course. Knock the first domino over and see what happens. Ideally, the chain reaction should stop at the place where the domino was removed. Point out that this is similar to what happens when a Christian doesn't use his or her spiritual gifts—other people are affected as a result.

STEP 5

Take your kids outside. Have them form three teams. Give each team a small grill, a can of lighter fluid, and enough charcoal briquettes to make a small fire. Have team members douse the charcoal with lighter fluid; then hand out matches. Instruct one person from each team to light just one of the soaked briquettes. As that one briquette catches fire, ask team members to observe what happens next. The fire should begin to spread to the other briquettes, until a blazing fire is created. Point out that, just as the one lit briquette spread its fire to the other briquettes, one very active spiritual gift user can inspire others to use their gifts. Afterward, roast some hot dogs and marshmallows over your fires.

STEP 3

Your group members have probably heard dozens of times about the importance of using one's spiritual gifts. So make the point in a different manner. Ask: **How many people or things do you depend on in your life?** (Among other things, group members probably depend on a parent to supply food and shelter; they probably depend on their teachers at school to give them a quality education; they might depend on their friends to provide acceptance; and so on.) Then ask: **How many people depend on you?** Ask group members to consider whether other Christians depend on them to use their spiritual gifts.

STEP 4

The case studies in Step 4 may seem rather obvious to kids who've heard it all before. So instead of using the case studies in the session, ask your group members to brainstorm the most difficult, complicated case studies that they can think of—situations that reflect the real-life problems and feelings that kids experience when they think about using their spiritual gifts. After group members have come up with a couple of case studies, discuss them as a group.

STEP 3

If your group members are still discovering the elemental truths of Scripture, Paul's letters to Timothy may be of less interest to them than further discussion of many of the things you've already talked about. If you've gone through the entire series and are concluding it with this session, you may prefer to spend this time in review. Before the session, prepare a short review to make sure that your group members are absorbing the things you want them to know. By this point, kids should be better equipped to understand concepts that were new and confusing to them a month or so ago.

STEP 5

This session (and series) was probably not an easy one for kids who have little Bible background. So before you close the session, hand out index cards and pencils. Say: **If you have questions remaining about any of the things we've discussed in regard to spiritual gifts, please write them down. You need not sign your name to them.** Collect the cards. Then say: **Now I'd like you to think of one thing you can do to put into effect something we've discussed during this series** (or **session**). **If you will commit yourself to try it sometime in the future, write it down and hand it in.** After collecting both sets of cards, read the cards aloud so that kids can see what questions and goals everyone has. Spend the remaining time dealing with kids' questions and challenging your group members to follow through on the things they've committed to do.

STEP 1

Before the session, recruit one of your group members to help you with an object lesson. As kids arrive, this person should walk up to various group members and ask, "Are you using your _____?" (it could be any item that the person is carrying or holding—a comb, pen, Bible, etc.). If the person responds no, your recruit should grab it and walk away. After a minute or two (before any fighting breaks out), call the group together, return the "stolen" items, and talk about what happened. Ask: **How did it feel to be "robbed" of something that was yours? Do you think the fact that you weren't using it makes any difference?** Get a couple of responses. Then ask: **Do you think if we're not using our spiritual gifts that God will just take them back? What do you think happens when we don't use our gifts?**

STEP 5

Set out some creative supplies—construction paper, colored markers, tape, glue, magazines, scissors, etc. To wrap up your series on spiritual gifts, have your group members create a large mural that celebrates the various spiritual gifts represented in your group. After group members complete the mural, spend a few minutes praising God for the gifts with which He's blessed your group. Ask Him to keep the gifts in your group active and growing.

STEP 2

After playing the telephone-message game, ask your group members to role-play some real-life situations in which one person ruined something for a whole group. (Do not, however, allow the role-play activity to turn into a "bashing" event. Ask girls to change the names in their roleplays to protect the not-so-innocent.) When each roleplay reaches a critical point, stop the action. As a group, talk about actions that could be taken to achieve a more positive outcome. Then have group members continue the roleplay, putting the advice to work. Afterward, say: **Sometimes just as one person can ruin an event for others, so can one person turn it around into something good.** Challenge your group members to be a positive influence on their friends this week.

STEP 3

After you've discussed ways in which a church or youth group can be negatively affected when spiritual gifts aren't used, talk about the flipside of the equation. As a group, discuss some of the things that might happen in a church or youth group when spiritual gifts are used. Challenge your girls to identify the gifts they possess. Discuss ways in which those gifts could be put to use to make your youth group come alive. Encourage your girls to start making an effort to use their spiritual gifts.

STEP 3

Most guys are likely to prefer a more action-oriented setting if they're going to choke. Try to meet in a gym or outdoors, where your guys can shoot baskets, try to complete football pass patterns, kick field goals, toss Frisbees, or do something unusual and different. In each case, start with simple things that everyone can do; then gradually make the challenge more difficult. In many cases, the guys will begin to choke from nervousness rather than inability. After giving them the opportunity to "sweat it out" (in more ways than one), reassemble inside and continue the session.

STEP 4

If time and space permit, plan a campfire to accompany the session. Try to build it the "Boy Scout" way, in which no more than two matches (and no flammable liquids) are allowed. When the match is lit and applied to the kindling, much care must be taken to ensure that the flame does not go out. Group members should all be expected to contribute wood and kindling to get the fire started and to keep it going. Soon, however, they should be able to feel the heat they have helped generate. Discuss how "fanning into flame" can be applied to spiritual growth as well as to campfires.

STEP 1

Explain that today's topic is the proper use of spiritual gifts. And while nowhere can it be found that "creating fun" is a gift, have your group members suppose that it is. Ask them to spend the next 10 minutes creating all the fun they can, using whatever methods they can think of. Perhaps they will discover that creating fun is harder than it looks, and will develop a greater respect for your well-planned sessions. On the other hand, maybe they will surprise you with what they come up with. Challenge them to do whatever they can to continue to generate fun *wherever* they are—at youth group, school, home, and so forth.

STEP 5

Since you're going to the trouble of bringing charcoal briquettes, why not be prepared to throw them on a grill and close the session with a cookout of some sort? If nothing else, fire up a few coals on which group members can roast some marshmallows. Add some graham crackers and chocolate bars to make s'mores. End your discussion of spiritual gifts by showing how well various elements can blend together for a treat that none of the ingredients could accomplish alone. Also challenge your kids to begin to "blend together" more completely and more regularly than they have in the past.

MEDIA

SHORT MEETING TIME

URBAN

STEP 1

Bring in a video designed to enhance relaxation in the viewer—a video with scenes that show nothing but a mountain stream or some other pastoral setting. Before you play the tape, create some excitement about it. Say: **I'm going to show you one of the coolest outdoor action scenes you've ever seen in your life. You won't believe your eyes.** After getting kids excited about the video, play the tape. When kids express their disappointment or boredom, ask: **What's wrong?** Kids will probably mention that nothing is happening onscreen—there's no action. Use this activity to lead in to a discussion of what happens when there's no action in a Christian's life—at least in the area of putting spiritual gifts to use.

STEP 5

As you wrap up the session, play one or more Christian songs that address the topic of "being on fire for the Lord" or spreading one's "fire" to other believers.

STEP 1

Replace Steps 1 and 2 with a shorter opener. Have kids form two teams to compete in a game of volleyball (or some other two-team competition). Secretly recruit one player from each team to subtly sabotage his or her team's chances of winning. For instance, in a volleyball game, the person might miss every ball that's hit to him or her. After the game is over, explain to the group what your recruits were doing. Point out that just as one person negatively affected his or her entire team, so too can one Christian who doesn't use his or her spiritual gifts negatively affect the entire body of believers.

STEP 3

Rather than using five shooters, simply use one. Give him or her a paper wad. Say: **You have one shot at the trash can. If you make it, everyone in the group gets a candy bar; if you don't, no one gets anything.** Afterward, discuss how the shooter felt about having all of that pressure on his or her shoulders. Then compare "choking" in sports with Christians who don't use their spiritual gifts.

STEP 1

Rather than using the index-card activity, begin the session with a "do-nothing" contest. See which of your group members is best at doing nothing for three minutes. Watch each person carefully, looking for blinks, facial twitches, muscle movements, eye movements, etc. After three minutes, award a prize to the person you judge to be best at doing nothing. Use this activity to lead in to a discussion of the problems of doing nothing with one's spiritual gifts.

STEP 3

Rather than having group members shoot paper wads into a wastebasket, take the activity outside to a basketball court near your meeting area. Have your volunteers shoot a real basketball into a regulation-size hoop to determine whether group members get candy bars or not. If you think you can keep your group members' attention, finish the session on the basketball court. Then take on all challengers in a game of "Horse."

COMBINED

STEP 4

Divide your group into two teams—a junior high team and a high school team. Instruct the members of each team to make a list of what they see as their biggest obstacles or stumbling blocks to using their spiritual gifts. Kids may refer to Repro Resource 10 for some examples of obstacles that Timothy faced. After a few minutes, have each team share its list. Then, as a group, talk about ways that kids can overcome those obstacles. Allow some time for your junior highers to pray for the things on the high schoolers' list and vice versa.

STEP 5

Ask your group members to think back over the past few weeks and identify one spiritual gift that they feel they may have. Hand out paper and pencils. Challenge group members to write a prayer to God, offering their gift for His use. Encourage them to be specific and honest in their offering to God, reminding them that if we make an offer or promise to Him, He expects us to keep it. If you think your kids would be comfortable with it, have each junior higher pair up with a high schooler; instruct the members of each pair to share their spiritual gifts with each other and pray for each other.

EXTRA CHALLENGE

STEP 1

Challenge your group members to consider what might happen if some of the people in your church suddenly stopped using their spiritual gifts. For instance, what if your pastor suddenly stopped using his or her spiritual gifts? What if your song leader suddenly stopped using his or her gifts? What if you (the youth leader) stopped using your gifts? Finally, ask your group members what might happen if they didn't use their spiritual gifts. Encourage several kids to offer their opinions.

STEP 5

As you wrap up the session, have kids form teams. Give each team a piece of poster board and a set of markers. Instruct each team to create a poster that encourages Christians to put their spiritual gifts to use. The posters may be informative (a how-to approach), humorous, creative, or any combination of the three. After a few minutes, have each team display and explain its poster. If possible, hang these posters in different areas of the church, where they'll be seen by most church members. If it's not possible to hang the posters in the church, hang them in your meeting area.

PLANNING CHECKLIST

DATE USED:

Approx. Time

STEP 1: *A Wrench in the Works* _____
- ❏ Extra Action
- ❏ Small Group
- ❏ Large Group
- ❏ Fellowship & Worship
- ❏ Extra Fun
- ❏ Media
- ❏ Short Meeting Time
- ❏ Urban
- ❏ Extra Challenge

Things needed:

STEP 2: *Message Mess-Up* _____
- ❏ Small Group
- ❏ Mostly Girls

Things needed:

STEP 3: *Handling the Pressure* _____
- ❏ Extra Action
- ❏ Heard It All Before
- ❏ Little Bible Background
- ❏ Mostly Girls
- ❏ Mostly Guys
- ❏ Short Meeting Time
- ❏ Urban

Things needed:

STEP 4: *Fanning the Flame* _____
- ❏ Heard It All Before
- ❏ Mostly Guys
- ❏ Combined Junior High/High School

Things needed:

STEP 5: *The Potential for Fire* _____
- ❏ Large Group
- ❏ Little Bible Background
- ❏ Fellowship & Worship
- ❏ Extra Fun
- ❏ Media
- ❏ Combined Junior High/High School
- ❏ Extra Challenge

Things needed:

NOTES

Unit Three: Going Against the Flow

To Go Against the Flow

by Mike Yaconelli

There are two kinds of people who are difficult to find in this day and age—people who love high school students and people who love God. I feel like I am standing on holy ground to be writing to people who have both of these characteristics (actually, I am sitting on a holy computer seat). It is an honor for me to introduce the book *Going against the Flow* to people like you. I have been ministering with high school students for 34 years now, and I know what it costs in time and effort to teach *and* how important it is to teach what matters. This topic matters—how to *live* the Christian life in the *real* world. This topic matters because of the two words in italics—live and real.

The Christian life is about believing and living. Believing and living are one and the same thing (you live what you believe and you believe what you live)—but it is very difficult for adolescents to understand what believing looks like when it's lived. A large amount of curriculum deals with what young people *ought* to believe and what faith *ought* to look like, *but there is very little material out there on what real belief looks like in the real world!*

The real world of today's adolescent is very different than it was just a few years ago. The issues are no longer whether or not to go to the prom or kissing on the first date. This is a world of gangs, guns, violence, AIDS, divorce, abortion, abuse—coupled with intense pressure to compete in every area of life. If Christianity is true, then it is not just true on the pages of the Bible, but is also true when it comes to parents, friends, and sex. What is the shape of faith? What form does it take? What acts are defined by our faith?

The subtitle of this book is "When Being a Christian Feels Weird." Weird is a weird word. It sounds like what it means—strange, unusual, different, odd. The Christian faith feels weird because it is weird. Someone has said, "You shall know the Truth and the Truth shall make you odd." There is a built-in oddness to faith.

So what does this oddness mean? How is this oddness lived? *Going Against the Flow* addresses these questions head-on. Session 3 helps high school students explore the difference Christ makes in our everyday behavior, and Session 1 helps kids figure out what to do when people notice the difference. When to talk about your faith and when to shut up about your faith are discussed in Session 2, and Session 5 tries to help you figure out what to say if you do decide to talk. Every adolescent has difficulty with the church, and Session 4 suggests that maybe the antidote for boredom is the rediscovery of worship. John Duckworth has done a good job in providing you real issues and honest questions, and he has created a variety of approaches to those issues and questions that should create an exciting and alive classroom experience.

The Next Step

Now the hard part. How do you teach this stuff to a real group of high school students whose attention you so desperately want when they aren't overly excited about giving it? John has given you the tools, now let me give you some philosophy.

- *What young people will remember five years from now is not the clever material and your brilliant lessons; they will remember **you.*** Who you are will have a much greater influence on that struggling high school student than your spellbinding outlines and theological dexterity. That doesn't mean you have to be Billy Graham; it doesn't mean you have to be young and cool. And it doesn't mean you have to be super-relevant and up-to-date on the latest number-one songs. It does mean, however, that your passion for the Gospel, your love of high school students, your sense of humor, and your genuine concern for each of them will be remembered. I still remember my junior church leader, Mrs. Lindsay. Mrs. Lindsay weighed close to 300 pounds, wore the same dress every Sunday, didn't have a clue about our culture . . . but she loved us. That's all she did—love us—and I have not forgotten that for 40 years.

- *High school students are not adults.* I know you have just been insulted with what seems like an obvious truth, but I am continually surprised by how many adults expect young people to act like adults. Faith at age 15 looks a great deal different than faith at 50. Some truth just can't be learned until you are 20, or 40, or 70. It is important that you allow the 15 year olds in your group to act and believe like 15 year olds. That means you recognize their short attention spans, unending questions, cynicism, idealism, and wonder. You realize that your role is not one of disciplining, but rather one of capturing attention, igniting thinking, and stimulating imagination. You want group members to experience the wild unpredictability of their adolescent faith. You are not worried when issues are not resolved, when problems are not all solved, when conclusions are not reached. The adolescent years are the searching years, and you are excited to be the one to get kids started on the search.

- *The most important thing you can do with young people is spend time with them.* Finishing the session should be very low on your priority list. How many adults do you know who decide once a week to spend an hour or more with a group of adolescents? Not too many. The power of the material is not in the material; it is in the person who teaches the material. High school students know what it costs you to spend time with them. They can sense your love and concern for them. If your kids aren't listening and the session's material isn't connecting, then drop the material, throw the kids in the car, and spend your teaching time at McDonald's over a Coke and fries. I guarantee the time you spend with them is much more significant than the content of what's said to them. Whatever time you spend with a young person will have long-term results. When I emphasize how important it is for you to spend time with a high school student, you could easily hear me saying, "You don't spend *enough* time with kids." That's not what I'm saying. What I am saying is that "something is better than nothing." If you spend 10 minutes a week with a young person, it's better than no minutes a week. If you spend one hour a month, it's better than no hours a month. Don't apologize about the time you don't spend with kids; celebrate the time you do spend with them. There is a whole church full of people who don't spend any time with kids.

- *The most frustrating part of working with young people is the seeming lack of results.* Another principle that has helped me through the years is "the significance of the insignificant." Kids don't often give us much feedback, and even if they did, much of the impact you are making on a kid's life won't be decipherable for many years to come. There are a lot of seeds planted in teaching that take years, even decades, to blossom. Much of the success of what you are doing now will never be known until eternity. Good teachers trust the truth and trust that God is at work. There are a whole lot of people sitting in the pew next to you who, during high school, no one would have predicted would be in church today. Many of them would point back to a Sunday school teacher or youth advisor who did or said something that stuck in their memory. The issue is not getting results. It is being faithful to the truth, to the Gospel, and to God.

I was lucky enough to be present at Second Baptist Church, a black church in Wheaton, Illinois, a few years ago. John Perkins was preaching from the Book of John, chapter 5, about the paralyzed man who had been lying by the healing pool for 38 years, but could never get into the pool before the others. Jesus asked him if he wanted to get well. He said yes. Jesus then healed him, and the man grabbed his bed, leaped for joy, and went running down the street, shouting and praising God. By the time John Perkins had described the man praising God, the entire church was on its feet praising God. In the midst of the shouting, John Perkins yelled out, "What a tragedy!" People were stunned by that statement and slowly began to quiet down. He yelled it out again, "What a tragedy!" The room that was just filled with shouting and dancing was now still and silent. Then John whispered into the microphone, "What a tragedy that when this man was healed he did what everyone else did when they were healed: *he left the pool!* What we need in the church today are people, who after they've been healed, *go back to the pool and help others in!*" I have thought about that sermon many times over the years. I realized that John was describing people just like you. You are one of those people who have decided to go back to the pool to help high school students be healed by the grace of God. There is no higher calling.

Mike Yaconelli was co-founder of Youth Specialties and a veteran of more than three decades in youth ministry. He authored several books on youth ministry.

The images on these two pages are designed to help you promote this course within your church and community. Feel free to photocopy anything here and adapt it to fit your publicity needs. The stuff on this page could be used as a flier that you send or hand out to kids—or as a bulletin insert. The stuff on the next page could be used to add visual interest to newsletters, calendars, bulletin boards, or other promotions. Be creative and have fun!

How "Different" Do Christians Have to Be?

Why can't Christians just blend in with the crowd?
Why do God's people have to stand apart from everyone else?
Is it possible to speak up for what's right, live a Christian life, get involved in church, and share your faith with others without being "weird"?
If you've ever asked yourself any of these these questions, join us as we begin a new series called *Going against the Flow.* You'll be glad you did.

Who:

When:

Where:

Questions? Call:

Unit Three: Going Against the Flow

What would you say?

Are your peers plotting to pressure you?

Ever feel like an alien in this world?

How Weird Do I Have to Be?

YOUR GOALS FOR THIS SESSION:
Choose one or more

☐ To help kids see that "going against the flow" at least once in a while is guaranteed when you're following Jesus.

☐ To help kids understand that some "weird" Christian beliefs and behaviors are essential, while others are optional.

☐ To help kids demonstrate that "different" doesn't always mean "weird"—by choosing a project which is both approved by God and esteemed by most non-Christians.

☐ Other:_____
_____

Your Bible Base:

1 Peter 2:7-13, 15;
   3:13-16; 4:3-5,
   15-16, 19

STEP 1

Do

And Now for Something Completely Different

(Needed: Prizes)

OPTIONS

Bring a lot of small prizes—perhaps a large bag of M&M candies. To start the meeting, have kids stand in a circle so that everyone can see everyone else. Kids should let their arms hang freely at their sides.

Say: **When I say "Go," strike a pose—any pose. You'll have three seconds to freeze in that position. If your pose is completely different from that of any other person in the circle—I'll be the judge—you'll get a prize. If your pose is too much like someone else's, neither of you gets a prize. OK? Go!** See what happens. Award prizes to those with unique poses. Play a few more rounds—as many as you have time for.

Then ask: **What did you see happening to people's poses as we got further into the game?** Chances are that kids tried to come up with stranger and stranger poses to make sure they'd be different.

Say: **Being different was the whole point of this game. You tried to be as different as possible, even if it meant looking weird. That's fine for a game, but in everyday life being different can cause problems.**

STEP 2

Too Weird!

(Needed: Copies of Repro Resource 1, pencils)

Hand out copies of "How Weird!" (Repro Resource 1) and pencils. Have kids work individually on the sheet, circling their responses. Then allow group members to share answers if they like—but don't press.

Afterward, ask: **How could some of the things on this list make us feel weird, embarrassed, out of it, or rejected?** (They make us stick out as different, since most people don't believe or do these things.)

If certain things about being a Christian make us feel too different, too weird, why not just forget those things and be like everybody else? Listen to responses, but don't evaluate them now. Simply point out that to answer that question, we have to look at the source of this "Christians must be different" idea.

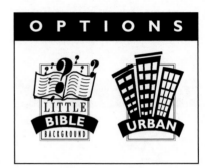

OPTIONS

LITTLE BIBLE BACKGROUND

URBAN

STEP 3

Why Stick Out?

(Needed: Copies of Repro Resource 2, pencils, prizes)

Have kids form three teams. Give each person a copy of "Aliens among Us" (Repro Resource 2). Explain: **There are at least 12 phrases in this passage that help to answer the question "Why be different just because you're a Christian?" Your team has 5 minutes to underline 3 of those phrases. The catch is that your team's phrases must be different from the ones the other teams found. So your team will have to appoint a messenger to keep the other teams updated as you go along. If all teams succeed at this, everybody gets a prize. If not, nobody gets a prize. Go!**

OPTIONS

After five minutes, award prizes (if teams succeeded) and share results. Ask: **What reason does each phrase give for being different, even when being different feels weird?**

Here are 12 key phrases, with comments to add as needed:

1. To you who believe, this stone [Christ] is precious. When someone is that special to you, you listen to Him. Jesus' teachings are full of commands to be different—from loving enemies to being everybody's servant.

2. You are a chosen people, a royal priesthood, a holy nation, a people belonging to God. If you're a Christian, God owns you. He has plans for you, no matter what other people may be planning for themselves.

3. That you may declare the praises of him who called you out of darkness into his wonderful light. Your new mission is to praise God. Most people don't have that mission, so they're bound to do different things.

4. You are the people of God; once you had not received mercy, but now you have received mercy. We are His, and we owe Him everything.

5. Aliens and strangers in the world. We won't spend much of our eternal lives here. Learning to "fit into" our future, long-term home is more important than feeling comfortable in this "overnight stay."

6. Sinful desires . . . war against your soul. We've already joined the anti-sin side in the spiritual battle. Why work for the enemy?

7. Live such good lives among the pagans that . . . they may see your good deeds and glorify God. One reason for being different is to grab people's attention and focus it on God.

8. By doing good you should silence the ignorant talk of foolish men. Christians attract enough criticism as it is. Being different in a positive way is good self-defense.

9. But in your hearts set apart Christ as Lord. If you follow Jesus only when it doesn't make you too different, how can you call Him your Lord? A lord is to be obeyed all of the time.

10. So that those who speak maliciously against your good behavior in Christ may be ashamed of their slander. This is more good self-defense.

11. You have spent enough time in the past doing what pagans choose to do. Living like those who don't know Christ is a waste of time.

12. Him who is ready to judge the living and the dead. Knowing that God will have the final say tends to make you a little more careful than those who think death is just The Big Sleep.

Ask: **Which of these reasons for being different makes the most sense to you? Which do you have the hardest time accepting?**

ll about the Red headed girls

STEP 4

The Edge of Weirdness

(Needed: Two copies of Repro Resource 3, two actors)

Say: **So we've just learned that we're supposed to be incredibly weird. Or are we?**

Give copies of "The Big Difference" (Repro Resource 3) to two volunteers. Have them act it out. After applauding your performers, ask: **What was this kid's problem?** (Being lumped in with those who do wrong or controversial things in the name of Christianity.)

Have you ever felt embarrassed by the "weirdness" of others who call themselves Christians? If so, when?

How do you know when a Christian is being *too* weird or too different?

How do you know when *you're* being too different or not different enough? If kids respond, listen without judging. Then explain that the passage you just studied has some things to say about these questions too.

STEP 5

All the Difference

(Needed: Prizes)

Call attention to Repro Resource 2 again. This time challenge each team to circle *nine* phrases that help to answer the question "How are we supposed to be different?" (There are at least 12 such phrases in the passage.) The catch this time is that all teams must have the same nine phrases circled at the end of five minutes. As in Step 3, success for everybody means prizes for everybody. Explain that some previously underlined phrases may be circled as well.

After five minutes, share results. Mention the following as needed:

1. Declare the praises of him who called you out of darkness into his wonderful light. Talk about how great God is. Most people don't.

OPTIONS

2. *Abstain from sinful desires.* You'll find lists of these in places like Galatians 5:19-21. The main thing to remember is that we can't always do as we please, even if others seem to get away with it.

3. *Live such good lives among the pagans that . . . they may see your good deeds and glorify God.* Anybody can do good deeds, but we're supposed to do them in order to make God (not ourselves) popular.

4. *Submit yourselves for the Lord's sake to every authority.* Many people break rules for fun and profit, but we're to obey those in charge—from parents to principals to police.

5. *Eager to do good.* Doing good is unusual enough. Being *eager* to do good is *really* unusual.

6. *"Do not fear what they fear; do not be frightened."* Most people are afraid to be different. We can be fearless about doing the right thing because no matter what happens, true believers end up in heaven.

7. *Set apart Christ as Lord.* If we don't do this first, all the "different-ness" in the world will be meaningless and misguided.

8. *Be prepared to give an answer to everyone who asks you to give the reason for the hope that you have . . . with gentleness and respect.* This assumes that there's something appealing about our differentness—that we're not just weird.

9. *Debauchery, lust, drunkenness, orgies, carousing and detestable idolatry. . . . Do not plunge with them into the same flood of dissipation.* Some may think we're crazy for not joining them in this stuff, but that's their problem.

10. *If you suffer, it should not be as . . . any . . . kind of criminal, or even as a meddler.* Anybody can suffer for breaking the law or for having an irritating personality. God isn't looking for *that* kind of differentness.

11. *Do not be ashamed, but praise God that you bear that name.* We should not only be known as Christians, but be happy to have that identity.

12. *Commit themselves to their faithful Creator and continue to do good.* We're supposed to be loyal to God above all, sticking with Him, making it a habit to help others in His name.

Afterward, ask: **If you followed all of these instructions, would you be (a) very different, (b) a little different, or (c) not different at all from the way you are now?**

Which instructions would be most embarrassing for you to follow?

Which instructions wouldn't be embarrassing at all?

STEP 6

The Air Out There

(Needed: Electric fans)

Set up several large electric fans at one end of your meeting place. Turn them on at their highest setting, so that they blow a sizable wind at your group.

Explain: **This wind represents the "flow" of our society—ways of thinking and acting that most people approve of. If we're Christians, sometimes we can "go with the flow"; other times we must go against it.**

Have kids stand up; clear away chairs if possible. Say: **I'm going to read a list of actions that a Christian might take. If you think an action goes "against the flow"—if you think it would seem weird or offensive to many non-Christians—walk toward the fans. If you think it goes "with the flow"—if many non-Christians would accept and even admire it—walk away from the fans.**

OPTIONS

FELLOWSHIP & WORSHIP

MOSTLY GUYS

MEDIA

EXTRA CHALLENGE

Read the following, pausing after each item to let kids determine their directions and walk a few steps.

1. **Saying in your health class that the only "safe sex" outside of marriage is abstinence.**
2. **Giving money to an organization that helps the homeless or keeps famine victims from starving.**
3. **Writing an essay that encourages kids not to take illegal drugs.**
4. **Volunteering to help a classmate who's having trouble keeping up.**
5. **Picking up litter as part of an "adopt-a-highway" program.**
6. **Trying to do more excellent work at your after-school job.**
7. **Thanking your parents for something they've done for you.**
8. **Writing an encouraging note to someone who's hurting physically or emotionally.**

After the exercise, ask: **On which of these actions did you meet "resistance" from the wind? On which could you "go with the flow"?** Answers may vary, but #1 probably is the only action that most non-Christians wouldn't approve or admire.

What does this tell you about the difficulty of being different? ("Different" doesn't always mean "weird"; doing good works is a way to obey God and make a positive impression on unbelievers; etc.)

Challenge each group member to choose one action from the exercise that allowed him or her to "go with the flow" and to take that action this week. You might want to have kids bow their heads as they consider your challenge, and keep their heads bowed to help them concentrate as you summarize.

Say: **We can walk against the wind or with it—but there's no way around it. Jesus Himself usually went against the flow, so His followers will too. But being a Christian isn't always a matter of doing the weirdest possible thing. Sometimes practically everybody agrees on what the right thing is. As Christians we can be *really* different by not just *agreeing* on what's right, but by doing it.**

Close in prayer, asking God to give group members courage to do right whether or not the right thing seems strange to others.

HOW WEIRD!

Circle the phrase that comes closest to describing the way you'd feel about each of the following if it applied to you.

1. Being the only one in biology class who believes God created the world as described in the Book of Genesis
Embarrassed Out of My Mind   No Problem, I Guess
OK—If I Could Keep It a Secret   Proud of It—and Ready to Stomp Some Pagans!

2. Feeling like the only virgin in school
Embarrassed Out of My Mind   No Problem, I Guess
OK—If I Could Keep It a Secret   Proud of It—and Ready to Stomp Some Pagans!

3. Eating lunch in the school cafeteria with your youth leader
Embarrassed Out of My Mind   No Problem, I Guess
OK—If I Could Keep It a Secret   Proud of It—and Ready to Stomp Some Pagans!

4. Eating lunch in the school cafeteria with your youth leader, who bows his or her head to thank God for the food
Embarrassed Out of My Mind   No Problem, I Guess
OK—If I Could Keep It a Secret   Proud of It—and Ready to Stomp Some Pagans!

5. Being the only one in your class who thinks hell and the devil are real
Embarrassed Out of My Mind   No Problem, I Guess
OK—If I Could Keep It a Secret   Proud of It—and Ready to Stomp Some Pagans!

6. Having to back out of starring in a school play when you discover the script is full of swearing
Embarrassed Out of My Mind   No Problem, I Guess
OK—If I Could Keep It a Secret   Proud of It—and Ready to Stomp Some Pagans!

7. Being laughed at for not understanding the punch line of a dirty joke
Embarrassed Out of My Mind   No Problem, I Guess
OK—If I Could Keep It a Secret   Proud of It—and Ready to Stomp Some Pagans!

8. Having to ask special permission to get out of a "social dancing" unit in P.E.
Embarrassed Out of My Mind   No Problem, I Guess
OK—If I Could Keep It a Secret   Proud of It—and Ready to Stomp Some Pagans!

9. Being thought of as a "religious person"
Embarrassed Out of My Mind   No Problem, I Guess
OK—If I Could Keep It a Secret   Proud of It—and Ready to Stomp Some Pagans!

10. Telling your coach you'll have to miss softball practice in order to attend a church service
Embarrassed Out of My Mind   No Problem, I Guess
OK—If I Could Keep It a Secret   Proud of It—and Ready to Stomp Some Pagans!

11. Marching in an anti-abortion picket line with others from your church
Embarrassed Out of My Mind   No Problem, I Guess
OK—If I Could Keep It a Secret   Proud of It—and Ready to Stomp Some Pagans!

12. Having to turn down a beer at a party
Embarrassed Out of My Mind   No Problem, I Guess
OK—If I Could Keep It a Secret   Proud of It—and Ready to Stomp Some Pagans!

13. Having to disagree with a friend who thinks everyone will go to heaven
Embarrassed Out of My Mind   No Problem, I Guess
OK—If I Could Keep It a Secret   Proud of It—and Ready to Stomp Some Pagans!

ALiENS AMONG US

Now to you who believe, this stone [Christ] is precious. But to those who do not believe . . . "A stone that causes men to stumble and a rock that makes them fall." They stumble because they disobey the message—which is also what they were destined for.

But you are a chosen people, a royal priesthood, a holy nation, a people belonging to God, that you may declare the praises of him who called you out of darkness into his wonderful light. Once you were not a people, but now you are the people of God; once you had not received mercy, but now you have received mercy.

Dear friends, I urge you, as aliens and strangers in the world, to abstain from sinful desires, which war against your soul. Live such good lives among the pagans that, though they accuse you of doing wrong, they may see your good deeds and glorify God on the day he visits us.

Submit yourselves for the Lord's sake to every authority instituted among men. . . . For it is God's will that by doing good you should silence the ignorant talk of foolish men.

Who is going to harm you if you are eager to do good? But even if you should suffer for what is right, you are blessed. "Do not fear what they fear; do not be frightened." But in your hearts set apart Christ as Lord. Always be prepared to give an answer to everyone who asks you to give the reason for the hope that you have. But do this with gentleness and respect, keeping a clear conscience, so that those who speak maliciously against your good behavior in Christ may be ashamed of their slander.

For you have spent enough time in the past doing what pagans choose to do—living in debauchery, lust, drunkenness, orgies, carousing and detestable idolatry. They think it strange that you do not plunge with them into the same flood of dissipation, and they heap abuse on you. But they will have to give account to him who is ready to judge the living and the dead.

If you suffer, it should not be as a murderer or thief or any other kind of criminal, or even as a meddler. However, if you suffer as a Christian, do not be ashamed, but praise God that you bear that name.

So then, those who suffer according to God's will should commit themselves to their faithful Creator and continue to do good.

—from I Peter 2:7-13, 15; 3:13-16; 4:3-5, 15, 16, 19

THE (BiG) DIFFERENCE

TEACHER: Welcome, class, to Modern Problems. Today we want to look at a very important modern problem—Christianity.

STUDENT: Uh . . . excuse me.

TEACHER: Yes?

STUDENT: Why is Christianity a problem? I mean, I'm a Christian, and—

TEACHER: Ah! Well, if you're a Christian, perhaps you can shed some light on our subject today. First, you can explain why Christians in Northern Ireland have been killing each other for so long.

STUDENT: Uh . . . I'm not that kind of Christian, I guess. I'm different.

TEACHER: Very well. Then you can tell us why TV evangelists have big, shiny hair and con people out of their money.

STUDENT: Oh, I'm not that kind of Christian, either. I'm . . . different.

TEACHER: I see. Are you the kind that handles poisonous snakes in church?

STUDENT: No. I'm different.

TEACHER: Do you bomb abortion clinics?

STUDENT: Nope. I'm—

TEACHER: Do you wear a sheet over your head, hate Jews and racial minorities, and burn crosses on people's lawns?

STUDENT: No, I'm—

TEACHER: Do you grab every non-Christian you see and tell him or her that he or she is going to hell?

STUDENT: No, no. I'm—

TEACHER: Do you ban library books, condemn AIDS victims, and believe that watching "Sesame Street" is a sin?

STUDENT (sighing)**:** No. I'm—

TEACHER (quickly)**:** Do you refuse to let sick children take medicine? Do you burn witches at the stake? Do you wear only black clothing and ride in horse-drawn wagons? Do you ruin primitive cultures by forcing them to convert to your religion? Do you believe the earth is flat? Do you believe women should not be allowed to vote? Do you think any song written after 1912 is inspired by the devil?

STUDENT (holding his head as if he has a headache)**:** No! No! I'm . . . I'm . . .

TEACHER: Yes? You're what?

STUDENT: A Buddhist. Yeah, that's it. A Buddhist!

TEACHER: Oh. Well. That's different.

STUDENT (wearily)**:** Yeah. I was hoping you'd say that.

NOTES

182

EXTRA ACTION

SMALL GROUP

LARGE GROUP

STEP 3

Instead of using teams to underline phrases, give each person a marker and a dozen stick-on name tags or labels. Each person should look for "labels" Peter gives us in the Repro Resource 2 passage ("you who believe," "chosen people," "royal priesthood," "holy nation," "people belonging to God," "people of God," "aliens," "strangers," "blessed," "Christian," etc.). Write each phrase or word on a separate label and stick it on another group member. The person wearing the most labels at the end of three minutes is the winner. Discuss what the labels mean, calling special attention to this statement from the passage: "If you suffer as a Christian, do not be ashamed, but praise God that you bear that name." Ask: **How do you feel about "bearing the name" of a Christian? Which of these labels do you like most? Which do you like least? Why?**

STEP 5

Rather than having kids look for the nine phrases on Repro Resource 2, read the phrases aloud yourself from the session plan; kids should follow along on their sheets and circle the phrases as you read them. Then have kids form pairs. Whisper one of the phrases to each pair. Each pair should act out its phrase for the rest of the group—not charades-style, but by pantomiming a way in which a person could obey the instruction in real life. See whether other group members can guess the phrases being acted out.

STEP 1

Kids in a small group may be able to strike different poses for a long time without duplication, so you might want to substitute a different opener. Explain that you're going to play a game in which the goal is to avoid being in the minority. Create a number of categories—hair color, for instance—to announce one at a time. Also create a scoring system that rewards conformity. For example, let's say that you have five group members—three brunettes, one blonde, and one redhead. The brunettes might *each* get three points. The other two people get no points. In cases of ties, such as if you have two brunettes, two blondes, and one redhead, everyone except the red-haired person would get two points. Other categories might include footwear (athletic shoes, hard soles, sandals), birth month, eye color, shoe size, school attended, and so forth. After arriving at a final score, discuss how it feels to be left out because of something you have no control over.

STEP 3

In small groups, the team activity will probably work better as an individual competition. So instead of following the instructions as written, let group members respond *verbally*. In each case, acknowledge correct answers and continue until all of the answers have been noted. Score points if you wish, but make sure that no one gets left out of the answering process.

STEP 1

If your group is too large for the "striking a pose" activity, try a different opener. Before the session, you'll need to prepare several slips of paper. On all but two of the slips, write an instruction; on the remaining two slips, write an opposite instruction. For instance, on the majority of the slips, you might write "Pretend that you're a right-handed batter swinging at pitches in a baseball game." On the two remaining slips, you might write "Pretend that you're a *left*-handed batter swinging at pitches in a baseball game." Hand out the slips, but don't allow kids to discuss their instructions. At your signal, kids should perform their assigned actions while watching what everyone else is doing. The object of the game is to find out who's doing things differently from everyone else. Use the activity to lead in to the discussion of Repro Resource 1 in Step 2.

STEP 5

Have kids form pairs. Assign one of the 12 instructions on Repro Resource 2 to each pair. Instruct each pair to come up with two practical suggestions for applying that instruction to the life of a teenager. For example, for #8, a pair might suggest (1) writing down exactly what you believe about Christ and why you believe it, and (2) committing to share your beliefs with at least two people a month. After a few minutes, have each pair share its suggestions with the rest of the group.

HEARD IT ALL BEFORE

LITTLE BIBLE BACKGROUND

FELLOWSHIP & WORSHIP

STEP 3

Kids may have heard phrases like "royal priesthood," "holy nation," and "aliens and strangers"—and found them irrelevant or threatening. Some may think, *Hey, I didn't sign up for that stuff. I just prayed to get "saved." Being weird wasn't part of the deal.* For these kids, review what happened when they became Christians and their "ownership papers" were transferred to God (read I Cor. 6:19-20). Ask: **What "price" did Jesus pay for you? How do you feel about that? If you don't want God to own you, what's the alternative?**

STEP 5

Jaded kids may be able to find and even explain the commands on Repro Resource 2, but that doesn't mean they have any interest in following those commands. Discussing the *benefits* of obedience might help. Rather than taking time to search for the phrases, read them aloud yourself from the session and have kids circle them on the sheet. Use the time you've saved to conduct a "stress test"—going over the list of phrases and asking kids which of the commands might help reduce a kid's stress at home, school, or work. For example, making up your mind to abstain from sinful desires *before* you're tempted could make it easier to resist temptation—and keep you from having to cover up a sin later. Submitting to authority could keep you out of detention or jail. Obeying the "do not fear" command would reduce inner turmoil. So would happily wearing the "Christian" label instead of feeling ashamed of it.

STEP 2

If your group members are new Christians or are unfamiliar with biblical teachings, many of the things on Repro Resource 1 (laughing at dirty jokes, swearing, drinking at parties, and so forth) may be regular behaviors for them. You can't assume that they would automatically make (or even desire to make) the "Christian" response. They might relate more directly to the pagans (who are being "stomped") than the Christian stompers. If this is the case, read the situations aloud one at a time rather than using the sheet as a handout. A verbal discussion of each situation will also allow you to more naturally talk through these issues and explain *why* Christians are expected to be different in these areas.

STEP 3

People new to Bible study may be intimidated by being asked to read a somewhat lengthy passage and find specific references. Instead, explain that you will read the passage aloud. Group members should follow along and stop you when you get to a relevant phrase. Your voice inflection (and, if necessary, long pauses) can clue members to phrases they should take note of in each case. (If you use this option, you will probably need to mark your sheet with each of the 24 key phrases to help your group members along in the discovery process.)

STEP 1

Let group members do a few poses by themselves, with each person trying to be different on his or her own. Then have kids form pairs. Instruct partners to work together to come up with new poses. Allow them a little time before each new pose to talk about what they're going to do. Afterward, ask: **Was it easier to be different by yourself or when you had a partner? Why? In which set of rounds did you feel more comfortable about being different? Why?** Point out that it's never easy to be different or to stand out in a crowd, but if we have someone who shares our "differentness," it can be easier. That's why it's so important as a Christian to spend time with other Christians. We lean on and support each other.

STEP 6

At the close of your session, refer back to the first instruction on Repro Resource 2—"Declare the praises of him who called you out of darkness into his wonderful light." Explain: **We're going to take a few minutes to praise God for His greatness through prayer**. If your group isn't familiar with "popcorn" prayer, explain that a designated person will open the prayer time and another will close; in between, people may call out their prayers as they wish. Spend a few minutes in prayer, praising God for His greatness and thanking Him for the strength He gives us to be different.

STEP 1

After having group members strike a number of different poses, change the game. Instruct group members to strike a pose that is as similar to everyone else as possible. However, group members may not discuss their poses prior to striking them. After you've done a few rounds of this, ask: **Which was easier—to be the same as everyone else or to be different?** (Your girls will probably discover that it's easier to strike a unique pose than one like everyone else.) **Why do you think that is?** (God made each of us uniquely; no one thinks exactly the same way.) Discuss the fact that God made each of us unique. To be exactly like everyone else—to go against our individual personality—is hard work.

STEP 5

Help your group members put into everyday reality what it means to be different—according to the instructions on Repro Resource 2. For each instruction on the sheet, have your girls think of a situation in which they might put their "differentness" into practice. For example, "Abstain from sinful desires" may mean that they need to shut their mouths when gossip starts to fly, or open them to say something good about the person getting slashed—even though their desire is to join in the gossiping. After you've gone through all 12 instructions (or as many as time allows), pray for your girls, asking for strength in the areas that are most difficult for them.

STEP 4

After doing the skit on Repro Resource 3 as written, using a single volunteer "student," try it again. This time, encourage group members to improvise a bit. The "teacher" should have essentially the same lines. But in this version, your guys should respond as a *group* of Christians. Encourage them to be a bit more aggressive in response to the suggestions and accusations of the teacher. Consequently, the teacher should not be nearly as effective in misrepresenting the "problem" of Christianity. This version of the skit should also help your group members see what a difference it can make to stick together and speak up for what they believe.

STEP 6

Many guys like challenges. They *want* to be different. They don't mind being considered weird. If your group contains several such individuals, try to help them channel their individuality in positive ways by challenging them to be a bit more outspoken about what they believe. One way to do so is to let them "advertise" their distinctiveness by decorating T-shirts or sweatshirts. Provide shirts and decorating supplies (available at most craft stores). Have everyone design something around the theme "I'm Different." Many guys won't be artistic geniuses or design professionals, but they'll like to "show off" what they've done. As they wear their shirts to school, games, and so forth, they will draw attention to the work you're doing and the ministry that is available to other students or teachers who may be interested.

STEP 4

Rather than merely discussing the skit on Repro Resource 3, follow it up by handing out pens and large sheets of paper to each group member. Have kids draw an example of a "Christian" individual or group that they feel is just a bit *too* weird—and to have fun with their drawings. (They might exaggerate a TV preacher's "big hair," focus on the unusual activities of a local "Christian" cult, or so forth.) Some people may want to use examples cited in the skit, but most are likely to have some personal experiences they can draw on. As group members reveal their drawings one at a time, let each person explain why he or she chose that particular individual or group. Later, discuss whether or not there's a difference between appearing "weird" and actually misinterpreting the truth of Scripture. Try to help group members see that "unfamiliar" shouldn't always mean "ungodly."

STEP 5

At the end of this step, to prepare for the fan activity in Step 6 (or to replace it if such an activity is not feasible for you), play Ping-Pong Ball Soccer. Use a table with four approximately equal sides, such as a card table. Divide into four teams and position one team at each end of the table. Team members should be side-by-side, lips level with the table top. Roll a Ping-Pong ball onto the table. The goal of each team is to prevent the ball from rolling off its side of the table. The team that allows the fewest "goals" scored against it is the winner. After playing, you can point out that sometimes we as Christians may feel blown in various directions, but we need to learn to make up our own minds and take responsibility for the direction we travel.

STEP 1

Rent the video *Pale Rider*, in which Clint Eastwood plays a mysterious clergy-man/gunfighter. Show a scene or two (after pre-screening for appropriateness) in which the bad guys assume that Eastwood's "Preacher" will be an easy mark, only to find out that he is cunning and even lethal. Then discuss, using questions like these: **What kind of behavior did the bad guys expect from "Preacher"? Did he turn out to be weirder than they expected or cooler? Do you think it's possible to be a Christian and be "cool"? Why or why not?**

STEP 6

Skip the activity in the session plan. Take time to listen to one or both of the following songs recorded by the Christian rock group Petra. Suggested discussion questions are listed after each song title.

• "Beat the System." Ask: **Why do the singers say that "going against the flow seems like such a dream"? What do you think "the System" is? What does the "assembly line" in the song represent? How can we "throw the wrench that will stop it cold"?**

• "Not of This World." Ask: **How is this song like the Scripture on Repro Resource 2? What are the advantages and disadvantages of being "not of this world"? Do you think of heaven as your "homeland"? Why or why not?**

STEP 1

Skip Step 1. In Step 2, use half of the phrases on Repro Resource 1 (1, 2, 6, 9, 10, 12, and 14). Read these aloud. As you do, have kids close their eyes and vote on whether each item would cause them "embarrassment" (signified by a raised hand) or "no problem" (two raised hands). Let kids open their eyes after each vote. Those who voted with the majority get a small prize; the rest don't. When the voting's done, discuss how it felt to be different—in the minority. Did kids try to peek, or wish they could change their votes? How do kids feel when being Christians makes them different at school or work?

STEP 3

Before the session, hide an adult volunteer in the closet. The volunteer should be very loosely bound and gagged. Instead of having kids look for phrases on Repro Resource 2, read aloud the second paragraph—the one that deals with being called out of darkness. The volunteer should start pounding on the closet door. Ignore the noise at first, but then go to the closet and "find" the volunteer. Instead of being a rescuer, criticize the noise. Close the closet and go back to leading the session. When the pounding doesn't stop, a student volunteer (with whom you've arranged this beforehand) should stand up and rescue the adult. The adult, instead of expressing gratitude to the rescuer, should thank *you* profusely and pledge to do anything for you. Ask the group: **Do you notice anything strange about this person's behavior?** Discuss how the fact that God has rescued us and owns us should lead us to obey Him—even when it costs us something.

STEP 2

Add the following scenarios to Repro Resource 1:

• Wearing a "Jesus Is Lord" T-shirt to school

• Being seen with a Christian friend at school who is talking loudly about how "sinful" rap music is

• Having your pastor walk by while you're hanging out with your friends on the street and ask you if you're coming to church on Sunday

STEP 5

Spend some time discussing specific ways that your group members might apply the 12 instructions found on Repro Resource 2. (To make sure that you have enough time for this, you might want to skip Step 4.) For instance, for #2, you might ask group members to list some of the "sinful desires" that tempt them regularly. For #3, you might ask kids to suggest ways that they can let their Christian commitment show to the people in their neighborhood.

STEP 1

If you have junior highers and high schoolers in your group, you might consider altering the opening activity. Give your high schoolers three seconds to assume a unique pose. Then give your junior highers three seconds to assume a pose that's as similar as possible to a high schooler's pose. The challenge for your high schoolers, then, will be to assume a pose that's not only unique, but also hard to imitate. After a few rounds, discuss why younger kids sometimes tend to follow the examples of older kids. Point out that a high schooler who is "going against the flow" can make it a lot easier for a junior higher who is trying to do the same thing.

STEP 5

Have kids form teams, making sure that each team has at least one high schooler and one junior higher on it. After you go through Repro Resource 2 a second time, instruct each team to choose three instructions from the sheet. For each instruction, the team should come up with an example of how a junior higher might apply that instruction to his or her everyday life and an example of how a high schooler might apply the instruction to his or her everyday life. After a few minutes, have each team share what it came up with. Pay attention to how the examples of the two age groups differ.

STEP 5

Give your group members an opportunity to offer feedback concerning the 12 instructions listed on Repro Resource 2. As you identify each of the instructions, write it on the board. Hand out paper and pencils. Instruct group members to list the instructions on their papers, ranking them from 1 to 12 according to how difficult the instructions will be to follow in their lives. Then give group members a few minutes to brainstorm some practical ways that they might apply in the coming week the 3 instructions that they ranked as most difficult. Afterward, have volunteers share some of their suggestions.

STEP 6

Rather than simply mentioning that "Jesus Himself usually went against the flow," give your group members an opportunity to study a couple of examples of this in Scripture. Among the passages you might consider using are Mark 11:15-18, in which Jesus drives out the money changers who were doing business in the temple, and Matthew 5:38-48, in which Jesus introduces some fairly radical concepts to His followers. Afterward, ask: **Do you think Jesus could have gone against the flow in less "radical" ways? Why do you suppose He chose the actions that He did? What can we learn from Jesus' example?**

DATE USED:

Approx. Time

STEP 1: *And Now for . . .* _____
❑ Small Group
❑ Large Group
❑ Fellowship & Worship
❑ Mostly Girls
❑ Media
❑ Short Meeting Time
❑ Combined Junior High/High School
Things needed:

STEP 2: *Too Weird!* _____
❑ Little Bible Background
❑ Urban
Things needed:

STEP 3: *Why Stick Out?* _____
❑ Extra Action
❑ Small Group
❑ Heard It All Before
❑ Little Bible Background
❑ Short Meeting Time
Things needed:

STEP 4: *The Edge of Weirdness* _____
❑ Mostly Guys
❑ Extra Fun
Things needed:

STEP 5: *All the Difference* _____
❑ Extra Action
❑ Large Group
❑ Heard It All Before
❑ Mostly Girls
❑ Extra Fun
❑ Urban
❑ Combined Junior High/High School
❑ Extra Challenge
Things needed:

STEP 6: *The Air Out There* _____
❑ Fellowship & Worship
❑ Mostly Guys
❑ Media
❑ Extra Challenge
Things needed:

Look What You're Missing!

☐ To help kids see that the Christian life isn't as miserable as some people claim—but it does involve self-denial.

☐ To help kids understand that giving up some enjoyable things is sometimes part of a loving relationship—in this case, a relationship with God.

☐ To help kids concentrate on the "dos" of Christian "dos and don'ts," and find pleasure in them.

☐ Other:_____
_____

Your Bible Base:

Ecclesiastes 2:1-11, 24-26;
8:11-15; 11:9; 12:13-14
Philippians 3:1, 7-21

STEP 1

Are We Having Fun Yet?

(Needed: Bibles, copies of Repro Resource 4, pencils, boring refreshments, lousy prizes)

OPTIONS

Greet the group with a little too much enthusiasm. Play the role of a leader who's trying to make a dull meeting look exciting—and who doesn't understand teenagers. Say: **Hi, guys and gals! Boy, do we have a far-out meeting today! Those non-Christians out there may think they're having a good time at their sinful movies and dances and gambling casinos, but we know better, don't we? We don't need drugs and booze to have fun! We're high on church! Let's start the fun with this off-the-wall contest! You'll split your sides with excitement!**

Hand out copies of "Zany, Fun Activities" (Repro Resource 4) and pencils. Say: **Got your Bible? OK! Ready, set, go!** During the minute that kids are supposed to be filling out the sheet, say things like **We're having some fun now!** It won't take long for kids to discover that the names in Part I aren't in the Bible, the Part II jumble is gibberish, and the words in Part III (except for "snail") are found so many times in the Book of Revelation that counting them would take forever.

After one minute, ask how many finished the sheet. Express disappointment over the fact that nobody did. Display the "fabulous" prizes kids could have won—things like empty candy wrappers, dustballs, and old bulletins you found on the church floor before the session.

Then say: **But that's OK! Let's continue the hip teen fun with some yummy refreshments!** Bring out a meager tray of snacks unlikely to appeal to your group—perhaps some prunes, a few carrots, and a couple of shredded wheat biscuits. **Don't all grab at once! There's plenty to go around, if we all have just one bite!**

When kids aren't enthused, express disappointment. Say: **I don't understand! These are Christian snacks! This is Christian fun! What's the problem, you wacky youngsters?** Let kids respond.

Then drop the act and ask: **Do you ever feel that non-Christians have more fun than Christians do? Do you ever feel like you might be missing something by spending your time in here instead of out there?**

After listening to replies, explain that you'll be looking at a problem that bothers a lot of Christians: the feeling that we're missing all of the good stuff, and that being a Christian is really a raw deal.

Have each teen. Be a recruiter & tell what kind of Church they would want - and try to recruit someone.

STEP 2

Six Degrees of Separation

(Needed: Cut-apart copy of Repro Resource 5)

Before the session, cut six cards from a copy of "Choose Your Church" (Repro Resource 5). Give the cards to six volunteers, one card per person. Explain that each person with a card is now a "recruiter" for the church whose "dos and don'ts" list appears on his or her card. The "dos" are things that members of the church are expected to do; the "don'ts" are things they must avoid.

Explain: **Each recruiter wants you to come to his or her church. He or she will try to convince you that his or her church is more fun than the others. After you've gotten acquainted with all of the churches, decide which one you want to join and line up with that recruiter. You must pick one.**

Let kids mingle for five minutes or so, finding out about the churches. Then have them choose. Congratulate the most successful recruiter. Then ask: **Recruiters, how hard was it to make your church sound fun? Why? For the rest of you—why did you choose the church you did?**

After listening to replies, ask: **What are some "dos" and "don'ts" in our church? Would you call ours a "fun" church? Do the "dos" and "don'ts" of Christianity make people miss out on things that are fun or important? Why or why not?**

Do first ✱ *If you were a recruiter what would U say to get teens to come*

OPTIONS

SMALL GROUP

LARGE GROUP

URBAN

COMBINED
JR. HIGH
HIGH SCHOOL

Tomb with a View

(Needed: Copies of Repro Resource 6, pencils, pieces of wood or sheets of cardboard, markers)

O P T I O N S

Before the session, make a blank "tombstone" for each group member. Pieces of low-grade wood or particle board should do nicely. If you can't find either of these, use tombstone-shaped sheets of cardboard.

At this point in the meeting, have kids sit on the floor, if possible. Give each person a "tombstone" and marker. Say: **Since we're talking about fun, let's make something really lighthearted—your tombstone. Put your name on it, along with any designs or sayings you'd like. Stand your tombstone against the wall, so that we'll be in the middle of our own little cemetery.**

After a few minutes, ask: **How does it feel to think about dying someday?** (Creepy, unreal, depressing, scary, etc.)

Say: **Believe it or not, thinking about death can tell us something about enjoying ourselves in this life—about who's missing out on what.**

Have kids form pairs. Give each pair a copy of "Everybody Must Get Stones" (Repro Resource 6). Have half of the pairs work on "Cemetery #1" and the other half work on "Cemetery #2," matching epitaphs with Bible passages. After a few minutes, check results. (Cemetery #1: Raul Sanchez—Eccl. 2:24-26; Jean Smith—Eccl. 12:13-14; Edith Shinn—Eccl. 11:9; Roland Barr—Eccl. 8:11-15; Vern Fleemer—Eccl. 2:1-11. Cemetery #2: Pete Moore—Phil. 3:17-21; Alice Ford—Phil. 3:1; Kay Stark—Phil. 3:12-16; Calvin Brown—Phil. 3:7-11.)

Ask kids to summarize the messages of the verses they looked up. Supplement their answers with the following information as needed.

Ecclesiastes 2:1-11—The author tried every sort of pleasure— laughter, drinking, achievement, wealth, sex, fame—and found it meaningless in itself.

Ecclesiastes 2:24-26—You can get great satisfaction from food and drink and work, as long as you also have a good relationship with God. Without God, you can't really enjoy yourself. Pleasing God brings happiness, but sin makes the life of even the wealthiest person meaningless when that life is over.

Ecclesiastes 8:11-15—People who ignore God may seem to have great lives and get away with everything, but in the end the righteous person is better off. The best approach to life is to enjoy it and remember that it comes from God.

Ecclesiastes 11:9—It's good for a young person to be happy. But if you do whatever you feel like in order to have a good time, you'll pay for it eventually.

Ecclesiastes 12:13-14—After trying every possible way to have a good time, the author concludes that the most meaningful life comes from fearing and obeying God, especially since He someday will judge everything people do.

Philippians 3:1—Be joyful, not in spite of being a Christian but because of it.

Philippians 3:7-11—The things Paul lost by being a Christian became as unimportant as garbage to him. What he really wanted was to know Christ and have eternal life.

Philippians 3:12-16—Paul put out of his mind what he'd left behind and focused on the prize ahead, which he'd get in heaven. Paul said having that attitude was a sign of growing up spiritually. He knew not everyone would have that attitude, but believed God would make the truth clear to those who didn't.

Philippians 3:17-21—Many people live only for comfort and to satisfy their appetites. They're headed for destruction. They think only about this life, but Christians should concentrate on the next life—where a great reward awaits.

Have your group members consider how Paul and the writer of Ecclesiastes might answer the following questions: **Are we missing out on anything fun or enjoyable by being Christians? Who's really better off—people who belong to God or people who don't?**

Point out that neither of these writers denies that an unbeliever might have more "fun" in the short run. But both probably would say that a believer's life is meant to be a joyful one, that pleasure isn't the most important thing in life, and that when you take eternal life into account the ones who really miss out are those who don't belong to God.

This Side of Paradise

(Needed: Toy gun, bottle of cheap cologne)

Before the session, find a volunteer to help you with this step. He or she will need to do a little acting. Also before the meeting, hide in your pocket a toy gun that makes a shooting noise.

At this point in the session, your volunteer should stand up and say in frustration, "But I'm not dead yet! I can't wait another 70 or 80 years to be happy! I want to have a good time now!"

Say: **OK! I can fix that!** Pull out the cap pistol, "shoot" your volunteer, and let him or her ham it up in a prolonged "dying" scene.

Say: **There! Welcome to eternal bliss!** Look around the room; then say threateningly: **Anybody else want to be happy now?**

After thanking your volunteer, ask: **Does it really satisfy you to know that you'll be happy in heaven even if you have to give up some fun stuff here?** If kids are honest, they'll probably express frustration over how far away heaven is and uncertainty over how much fun it will be.

Is the promise of heaven the only reason to give up some fun in this life? Listen to replies without judging them. Then suggest that a little story might help to answer this question.

Have kids form pairs. Instruct them to stand up, each pair at least arm's length from other pairs. Explain that the people in each pair are best friends. The younger person in each pair is Friend A; the older is Friend B. Pairs are to act out the story as you read it.

Say: **Once upon a time there were two best friends. They had a great time together. Then one day Friend A discovered cologne. Take out a bottle of cheap cologne.** Friend A put the cologne on. Pass around the bottle so that all "Friend A" kids can put some on. **Suddenly, Friend B began to sneeze. And cough. And sneeze some more, and cough some more. Uncontrollably. It turned out that Friend B was allergic to cologne. "That's too bad," said Friend A. "I really like cologne." So Friend A put on some more cologne.** Pass the bottle around again. **That made Friend B sneeze and cough so much that Friend B couldn't stand to be around Friend A anymore. Sneezing and coughing, Friend B walked away to a safe distance and stayed there. "Hey," said Friend A. "You're no fun. I guess I'll just stay here and use some more cologne."** Pass the bottle around again. **Friend A still claimed to be close to Friend B. But as** long as Friend A kept using that cologne, they were far apart. And except for using cologne, Friend A never seemed to have much fun anymore.

Ask: **What went wrong in this relationship?** (Friend A's refusal to give up something that bothered Friend B drove them apart.)

How is this story like what happens when a Christian refuses to give up something "fun" that "bothers" the Lord? (Insisting on doing something wrong, whether it's fun or not, drives a wedge between us and God. Even if God doesn't end the relationship, we don't experience the closeness to Him that we would otherwise.)

If Friend A had been willing to give up cologne, do you think it would have taken all the fun out of life for him or her? (Not if he or she paid attention to all the other fun things available, most of which wouldn't have bothered Friend B. And the two friends could have had more great times.)

Say: **As Friend A discovered, the more obsessed we get with things we shouldn't do, the more we miss all the things we could be doing—things that are enjoyable and that don't hurt our most important relationship.**

STEP
5

Missing Pieces

(Needed: Two jigsaw puzzles, plastic bag, pencils, two sheets of cardboard)

Before the meeting, put in a plastic bag the mixed-up pieces of a complete jigsaw puzzle. The puzzle should have at least as many pieces as kids in your group, and should be simple enough to assemble in a few minutes. Also get four or five pieces from a totally different puzzle. Write the name of a questionable "fun" activity (getting drunk, vandalizing school property, telling racial jokes, premarital sex, etc.) on the back of each of these extra pieces. Hide these extras in your pocket.

At this point in the meeting, give each person a puzzle piece from the bag. Make pencils available. Say: **We'll be putting this puzzle together in a minute. Before we do, think of one fun thing you'll try to do during the next 48 hours that doesn't involve doing anything wrong. Write that fun thing on the back of your puzzle piece.**

While kids are following your instructions, slip the extra pieces into the bag. Then collect all of the pieces and return them to the bag. Shake them up, dump them onto a sheet of cardboard that's at least as big

O P T I O N S

SMALL GROUP

HEARD IT ALL BEFORE

FELLOWSHIP & WORSHIP

EXTRA FUN

EXTRA CHALLENGE

as the puzzle, and challenge kids to put the puzzle together in three minutes. When kids are done, they should end up with one complete puzzle and several extra pieces.

Put another sheet of cardboard over the puzzle, hold the sheets together, and flip the puzzle over. Have volunteers point out which puzzle pieces are theirs and explain what they wrote.

Say: **This puzzle is like the life of a person who has a good time—but is careful not to hurt his or her relationship with God. Notice that it's complete.**

Have kids turn over the extra pieces and read what's written on them. Ask: **Were these pieces needed to make this "person's" life complete?**

Ask a volunteer to try fitting the extra pieces together. It may or may not be possible. Then say: **I leave it to you do decide which of these "lives" is missing something.**

Close by encouraging kids to remember the things they wrote on their puzzle pieces—and to enjoy doing these things during the next 48 hours.

Zany, Fun Actvities

Hey, you cool teen! Here's a groovy piece of paper with many right-on things to do! The winner will receive some keen prizes that your leader found lying around the floor at church! You have one minute! Go!

PART I: HUNT FOR INTERESTING NAMES!

Find these names in the Bible and write down where you found them! Whoopee—what a trip!

Zeraggubel _____   Chronicold _____   Shikshak _____   Phyllis _____
Thelonius _____   Moog _____   Babooney _____   Elvis _____
Al-Geezer _____   Psoriasis _____   Wilfred _____   Phlegm _____
Numbskull _____   Nacho _____   Zirconia _____

Now draw an amusing picture of your favorite Old Testament king here!

PART II: SCRAMBLED JUMBLE!

Decipher this Bible passage! Wow—it's like a neato secret code!

DHIULMBSYTQOOBRELGAMAHAHASEZWKCKWGBAUFLEYPNRN
GOIENSGOLNLKLKDOEKWBDIGYJNWLOPHJKIYHFSRFDVZCAYEIG
BZHEUGFYRJFHEOOSJJJDUWGAGPMNWIUYKGEFSGWGFHTQQSEI
SLKHGPODHVWTGUHGIRUERUHAWEJBREHOYTJNTYYYSKMJBCL
GIKNDSGWPSWYSFMNSDOWMSDOLHSDPWKDJGGOHWKWJHFHS
RUHEUGFYRJFHEOOSJJJDUWGAGPMNWIUYKGEFSGWGFHTQQSEI
DZIENSGOLNLKLKDOEKWBDIGYJNWLOPHJKIYHFSRFDVZCAYEIG
AKIULMBSYTQOOBRELGAMAHAHASEZWKCKWGBAUFLEYPNRN
ULNHGPODHVWTGUHGIRUERUHAWEJBREHOYTJNTYYYSKMJBCL

PART III: WACKY WORD COUNT!

How many times do each of the following words appear in the Book of Revelation? Ho, ho! What a goofy game!

the _____   then _____   this _____
it _____   he _____   if _____
a _____   and _____   had _____
an _____   so _____   snail _____

Now draw an amusing picture of your favorite eighteenth-century theologian here!

Now draw an amusing picture of your favorite minor prophet here!

CHOOSE YOUR CHURCH

CHURCH A

Dos

Recycling all plastic and aluminum

Witnessing to one person daily

Drinking beer

Don'ts

Drinking "hard" liquor

Playing video games

Eating cheese

CHURCH B

Dos

Picketing stores that sell *Playboy*

Wearing suits/dresses to church

Listening to contemporary Christian music

Don'ts

Smoking

Dancing

Bowling

CHURCH C

Dos

Having daily devotions

Exercising regularly

Going to live theater performances

Don'ts

Drinking anything alcoholic

Watching TV

Getting blood transfusions

CHURCH D

Dos

Giving 25% of your income to church

Going to horror movies

Attending all youth group events

Don'ts

Card playing

Swimming

Joining the military

CHURCH E

Dos

Watching MTV

Becoming a missionary

Surfing

Don'ts

Reading comic books

Playing football or hockey

Wearing jewelry

CHURCH F

Dos

Going to a Christian school

Trying to save the rain forest

Collecting baseball cards

Don'ts

Listening to rock music

Using computers

Biting your fingernails

EVERYBODY MUST GET
STONES

Can you match the tombstone inscriptions with the verses they're based on? Look up the passages in your "cemetery" and draw a line from each Bible reference to the tombstone it goes with.

CEMETERY #1

Here lies Raul Sanchez
Beneath the ground
The joys of meals and
Work he found.

She did what she wanted
Edith Shinn
And now you can see
What a fix she's in.

Here lies Vern Fleemer
Lived for pleasure
It turned out to be
A worthless treasure.

When it came to God
She knew her place
Now Jean Smith sees Him
Face to face.

He was poor but honest
That Roland Barr
He's better off now
Than the wicked are.

Ecclesiastes 2:1-11   Ecclesiastes 11:9   Ecclesiastes 2:24-26   Ecclesiastes 12:13, 14   Ecclesiastes 8:11-15

- -

CEMETERY #2

Pete Moore grabbed gusto
Every minute
Loved things of this earth
And now he's in it.

Kay Stark knew someday
She'd be dead
So she kept on pressing
For the prize ahead.

Don't cry for me
Said Alice Ford
Be happy, brothers
Rejoice in the Lord.

It was worth it all
For Calvin Brown
He's traded his troubles
For a lasting crown.

Philippians 3:1   Philippians 3:12-16   Philippians 3:17-21   Philippians 3:7-11

O P T I O N S

S E S S I O N   T W O

STEP 1

Skip Repro Resource 4. Bring two dozen cans of pop, half of which you've taped with paper labels that say "Beer." At one end of the room, stack the cans in a tower—six cans across and four cans high, mixing the pop and "beer" cans randomly. Have kids form two teams. Line them up against the wall farthest from the cans. Explain that one team is the "Christian" team; the other is the "non-Christian" team. At your signal, each person on the Christian team must run across the room, try to get a can of pop—without touching a "beer" can or knocking over the tower—and run with it back across the room. If a "beer" can is touched or the tower falls, all pop cans must be returned to the tower. After the Christian team gets its turn (allow no more than 30 seconds), the non-Christian team will try to get the "beer" cans without touching pop cans or knocking things over. Repeat the process. After three (or fewer) rounds, the team with the most cans in hand is the winner. Discuss: **Why do you think the Christian team was told to touch the pop and not the "beer"? Which team was more fun? Why? In real life, do Christians or non-Christians have more fun? Why?**

STEP 3

Instead of writing on tombstones, play "Grim Reaper." One person, chosen by you to represent death, will announce that he or she has come for a particular group member. Others may encircle the victim to protect him or her from being tagged. But the "Reaper" can change targets anytime, calling another person's name and trying to touch him or her. Anyone touched by the "Reaper" is out. Play until all or most of the group is "dead." Discuss: **Do you think you'll escape having to die someday? Why or why not? If Jesus doesn't return in the next 150 years, what will happen to you?** Afterward, go through Repro Resource 6.

STEP 2

The church recruiting activity might be a little awkward for a small group. Instead, post the dos and don'ts of each church on Repro Resource 5 (recopied in larger type, if possible) in a central location of your meeting area. Say: **Our church is disbanding, and the board has decided that we should merge with another church. These are the six options they've come up with. But we have to agree to go together to the same one. I need to report back to tell them what the young people prefer.** Let kids discuss the pros and cons of each option. After a few minutes, take a vote; see if everyone would be willing to attend the church that gets the most votes.

STEP 5

Many small groups may feel that they don't have the same opportunities and privileges of a large group. So after devoting a session to how thrilling Christian living can be, try to plan a special event. It may be a fun trip (rafting, canoeing, rock climbing, amusement park, etc.) or serious (evangelism outing, mission trip, service project, etc.). Either way, kids should see for sure that they are valued and important members of God's kingdom.

STEP 1

Rather than using Repro Resource 4, have kids form three teams for a "crazy contest." Build up the activity as being extremely wacky and fun. Then explain that the teams will be competing to see which can sing "The B-I-B-L-E" (or "Deep and Wide" or some other Christian chorus) the loudest. Ignore any negative comments about the contest; continue to act like it's the nuttiest game ever invented. After declaring a winning team (assuming that you can convince your group members to sing), use the questions at the end of Step 1 to discuss the activity.

STEP 2

With a large group, you might want to alter the recruiting activity. Rather than having individuals trying to convert everyone else in the group one at a time, make this a team activity. Have kids form six teams. Give one of the cards from Repro Resource 5 to each team. Allow five minutes for each team to come up with a "pitch" for its church—something that would make a person want to attend. After five minutes, have a spokesperson for each team present his or her team's pitch. Afterward, have the group vote on which presentation was most persuasive. Use the questions in the last two paragraphs of Step 2 to discuss the activity.

HEARD IT ALL BEFORE

LITTLE BIBLE BACKGROUND

FELLOWSHIP & WORSHIP

STEP 3

Kids may be skeptical of statements like "Without God you can't really enjoy yourself" and "Pleasing God brings happiness." As needed, encourage kids to express their doubts. Acknowledge that you can't "prove" these statements with a survey that says 100 percent of "godless" people are miserable and 100 percent of God-pleasing people feel happy. On the other hand, can kids prove that the *opposites* of the statements are true? Can they prove that people who don't know God are experiencing the greatest possible enjoyment? Can they prove that pleasing God doesn't bring happiness? Point out that the author of the Ecclesiastes passage had seen enough of life to be convinced that his statements were correct. We can choose to learn from his experience, or we can insist on repeating his mistakes by trying to find happiness apart from God.

STEP 5

If your kids aren't convinced that life can be complete without the "excitement" of sin, the puzzle activity probably won't help. Instead, have kids form teams of two or three. Instruct each team to write a half-page reaction to the session from one of the following points of view: (a) the best friend of a young movie star who's just died of a drug overdose; (b) a young person who has to pay back $75,000 for the damage he or she caused while vandalizing a school with friends; (c) an HIV-positive person who contracted the disease through sexual promiscuity; (d) a student whose drunk driving left a seven-year-old girl permanently paralyzed. After letting teams work on their reactions for a few minutes, read and discuss the results.

STEP 1

Some kids with little Bible background may still have very secular viewpoints. So after Step 1, ask: **What were your prior expectations about Christianity? What do your non-Christian friends think about "church people"? What did you think before you started coming?** Encourage complete honesty. Take plenty of time to try to get potential misconceptions out in the open. Help kids see that they are free to talk about any of their concerns in your group meetings.

STEP 4

If the concept of denying oneself is new to your group, use the "shooting" in this step in a symbolic way to signify "dying with Christ" (Rom. 6:8) rather than actual physical death. The person who is "shot" should not perform a death scene, but instead should begin to list reasons to be genuinely excited with life. Follow up by reading Romans 6:1-14 and introducing the concepts described there: dying to sin, living in Christ, living under grace rather than the law, and so forth. Explain that as God's grace is realized in our lives, the joy of "here and now" Christianity increases.

STEP 1

Have kids form pairs. Instruct the members of each pair to brainstorm a list of things that they really enjoy doing—things that they consider to be fun. Their goal is to come up with as long a list as possible. After a few minutes, collect the lists and write on the board a composite list for the entire group. Then, as a group, go through the list, identifying which activities kids consider OK for Christians to do and which they consider taboo. Ask: **Do you ever have the feeling that non-Christians have more fun than Christians do? Do you ever feel like you might be missing something by spending your time in here instead of out there?**

STEP 5

Give group members a few minutes to refer back to the list of fun things you created earlier (see "Fellowship & Worship" option for Step 1). Have each person choose two or three things from the list that he or she specifically wants to thank God for today. Spend a few minutes in prayer, thanking God for creating pleasure and for giving us fun things to do so that we may enjoy life.

MOSTLY GIRLS

MOSTLY GUYS

EXTRA FUN

STEP 3

Point out that both Ecclesiastes and Philippians were probably written by men. Then ask your girls: **Do you think these verses would read any differently if they were written by women?** Have group members form pairs. Assign each pair one of the passages on Repro Resource 6. Instruct the pair to rewrite the passage from a female perspective. Group members will probably find this to be quite difficult. After they've had some time to think about their passages, say: **Even though these words were written by men thousands of years ago, they can still speak to you—teenage girls—centuries later without many changes needed. Why do you think that is?** (Because the words came from God, and He knows the needs of everyone of every age.)

STEP 4

Before moving on to the skit, ask your girls to share some things that they struggle with "giving up" or things that they feel they may be missing out on because they're Christians. If your group is made up of all girls, you may get some deeper openness and sharing than you would with a mixed group. If your girls are open and willing to talk, you may wish to skip the skit entirely and spend some time talking with them about their struggles and feelings.

STEP 1

Replace the opening activity and Repro Resource 4 with a skit. Ask your guys to roleplay a situation in which they are a group of tough guys who are skeptical, antagonistic, and even hostile toward Christianity (and Christians). They should discuss church habits, "fun" activities, youth group meetings, and so forth. While this is an impromptu skit, pay attention to the comments. You're likely to hear a few statements that express honest opinions of group members. Other comments may reflect the actual opinions of some of their friends. After having some fun with the roleplay, discuss how your group can combat some of the actual misconceptions people have about Christians and Christianity.

STEP 3

Sometimes guys have big dreams and perhaps unrealistic expectations. Between making tombstones and doing the Bible study, let guys speculate on the lifestyles they would pursue "if money and parents were no object." Let them envision wild and affluent options. Then, as you get into the Bible study, explain that Solomon (the author of Ecclesiastes) had everything he could envision and more. Yet he found that such things could do nothing to add meaning to life. Challenge your guys to be careful not to spend a lifetime pursuing something that won't benefit them even if they obtain it.

STEP 3

Rather than making tombstones, give your kids a few minutes to prepare one-minute eulogies to deliver for themselves. What do they want said about them at their funerals? What accomplishments do they want to be remembered for? What personal characteristics do they wish to develop? Which relationships will mean the most to them? After everyone has delivered his or her own eulogy, point out that if kids want their deaths to be so "successful," they need to begin now by making their lives that way.

STEP 5

You opened with a spoof of wild and wacky activities. Close by announcing an actual event that will be zanier than anything the group has done in the recent past. It should be something that literally thrills your kids. No one knows your group like you do, so you should spend a lot of time coming up with something unique and tailor-made for them. Point out that while self-denial is part of the Christian lifestyle, that doesn't mean we can't have all of the *appropriate* fun and excitement we want along the way.

MEDIA

STEP 1

Rather than using Repro Resource 4, play a couple of upbeat songs about having fun. Some older examples you might consider using are "Fun, Fun, Fun" (The Beach Boys), "Girls Just Want to Have Fun" (Cyndi Lauper), "Everybody Have Fun Tonight" (Wang Chung), "Dancing on the Ceiling" (Lionel Richie), and "Footloose" (Kenny Loggins). As you play the songs, however, bring in a couple of adult volunteers to act as the "Fun Police." Their job is to patrol the room as the songs are played, making sure that kids aren't moving to the rhythm, smiling, or enjoying themselves in any way. Anyone who seems to be enjoying himself or herself gets tossed into "Spiritual Confinement" (a corner of your choosing). About halfway through the second song, your "Fun Police" should get fed up, "confiscate" your tape or CD player, and leave. Then move into a discussion of the questions at the end of Step 1.

STEP 3

Instead of having kids make tombstones, introduce the subject of death by showing one or more of the following video excerpts (which you've pre-screened for appropriateness):

• A scene from the last part of *My Girl*, in which Anna Chlumsky's character discovers that her friend (played by Macauley Culkin) has died.

• The opening title sequence from *The Big Chill*, in which a dead body is dressed carefully in preparation for enclosure in a coffin.

• The scene near the end of *Amadeus*, in which the corpse of the young man Mozart is dumped into a pauper's grave.

After the excerpt(s), ask: **What did this scene have to say about death? How do you feel when you think about dying?**

SHORT MEETING TIME

STEP 1

Replace Steps 1 and 2 with a shorter opener. Bring a bunch of unrelated equipment from sports and board games (bat, bowling pin, football, golf club, volleyball, boomerang, racquet, chess piece, timer, etc.) and pile it in the middle of the room. Have kids form teams. At your signal, each team will run to the pile, take three items, and return to its place. Then say: **Your job is to create the ideal game for Christians to play—using the equipment you took. But here are the rules: Since your game is for Christians, it must not be exciting. It can't involve noise—especially laughter—violence, prizes, or physical contact between players. The most "Christian" game will win. You have two minutes. Go!** After two minutes, have teams demonstrate their games. Ask: **Do you think there could be an "ideal Christian game"? Why or why not?** Discuss the questions about Christians and fun at the end of Step 1. Then move to Step 3.

STEP 3

Make kids' "tombstones" yourself before the session (with or without epitaphs). Hand them out at this point so that kids can place them against the wall. From Repro Resource 6, use either Cemetery #1 (the Ecclesiastes passages) or Cemetery #2 (the Philippians passages), but not both. In Step 4, don't take time to pass around a cologne bottle; simply have pairs act out the story as you tell it. In Step 5, skip the puzzle activity. Instead, bring two copies of a local newspaper entertainment section that includes a community events calendar, as well as TV listings and movie ads. Split the group in half and give one copy of the paper to each half. Have kids spend three minutes circling activities they think Jesus would approve their participation in. Then share results; affirm the most wholesome choices.

URBAN

STEP 1

If you don't think your group members will enjoy the exaggerated humor on Repro Resource 4, try another opening activity. On the board, list several activities that your kids consider to be fun. Depending on the interests of your group, you might list things like playing basketball, hanging out with friends, cruising, going to parties, going to dance clubs, watching sports on TV, and playing video or computer games. Go through the list one activity at a time, asking kids to vote on whether each activity is "Christian fun" or "non-Christian fun." Their responses should give you an idea as to whether your group members consider "Christian fun" to be an oxymoron.

STEP 2

Replace the information on "Church E" on Repro Resource 5 with the following: *Dos*—Watching MTV; Working at a fast-food restaurant; Going to summer school; *Don'ts*—Joining a gang; Buying new clothes; Talking on the phone.

STEP 2

Ask your group members to brainstorm a list of "fun" things that their friends do that they as Christians don't do—the don'ts of Christianity. (Examples might include drinking, swearing, gossiping, and going to wild parties.) Write group members' responses on the board in a column labeled "Fun." When you have a good-sized list, talk about the results of each of these activities. (For example, drinking kills brain cells, can become addictive, and changes your personality. Swearing is offensive to others and to God, and makes you look like you have no class. Gossiping hurts feelings, destroys another's self-image, and breaks up friendships.) Write the list of results next to the "fun" list. Ask: **By missing out on these things, do you think we're really missing out on fun? Why or why not?**

STEP 3

Your junior highers may have a difficult time with the tombstone activity. If so, divide your group into teams of three or four, getting a balance of junior and senior highers on each team. Assign each team one of the passages listed on Repro Resource 6. Instruct the members of each team to look up their passage and rewrite it in their own words. (Help them as needed by using the summaries provided in the session.) Then have each team come up with a short skit based on its passage in which each team member has a part. After a few minutes, have each team present its skit to the rest of the group. Afterward, discuss the activity, using the questions at the end of Step 3.

STEP 1

After you "drop the act" from the Repro Resource 4 activity, have kids form pairs. Say: **Let's say that you're walking down the hall at school when a couple of your classmates start teasing you about being a Christian. "No sex, no drugs, no drinking, no cussing, no partying. What do you Christians do for fun?" they ask. How would you respond?** Give the pairs two minutes to come up with a response; then have each pair share what it came up with.

STEP 5

As you wrap up the session, refer back to the recruiting activity in Step 2. As a group, come up with three "dos" (things church members are expected to do) and three "don'ts" (things church members must avoid) for your church. Then have volunteers take turns being recruiters for your church, giving brief presentations to the group, explaining why your church is fun or interesting. Afterward, have group members critique each presentation, sharing whether they'd be likely to visit your church based on what the presenter said. As you close, encourage your group members use some of the principles they picked up in this activity to invite their non-Christian friends to church or to a youth group meeting.

DATE USED:

Approx. Time

STEP 1: *Are We Having Fun Yet?* _____
❑ Extra Action
❑ Large Group
❑ Little Bible Background
❑ Fellowship & Worship
❑ Mostly Guys
❑ Media
❑ Short Meeting Time
❑ Urban
❑ Extra Challenge
Things needed:

STEP 2: *Six Degrees of Separation* _____
❑ Small Group
❑ Large Group
❑ Urban
❑ Combined Junior High/High School
Things needed:

STEP 3: *Tomb with a View* _____
❑ Extra Action
❑ Heard It All Before
❑ Mostly Girls
❑ Mostly Guys
❑ Extra Fun
❑ Media
❑ Short Meeting Time
❑ Combined Junior High/High School
Things needed:

STEP 4: *This Side of Paradise* _____
❑ Little Bible Background
❑ Mostly Girls
Things needed:

STEP 5: *Missing Pieces* _____
❑ Small Group
❑ Heard It All Before
❑ Fellowship & Worship
❑ Extra Fun
❑ Extra Challenge
Things needed:

The Truth about Peer Pressure

YOUR GOALS FOR THIS SESSION:

Choose one or more

☐ To help kids see that even though adults may sometimes overstress the dangers of teenage peer pressure, it's a problem worth watching out for.

☐ To help kids understand that with God's help, they have more power to influence non-Christians than non-Christians have to influence them.

☐ To help kids target people on whom to exert a positive influence.

☐ Other:_____
_____

Your Bible Base:

Daniel 1; 3; 6
1 John 4:4

STEP 1

It Ain't Heavy, Brother

(Needed: Suitcase, paper bricks, paper, pencil, prizes)

Before the session, cut 15 brick shapes from construction paper. Put them in a large suitcase. Close the suitcase and put it against a wall in your meeting place, out of the way so that kids won't be tempted to pick it up before you start the meeting.

To begin the session, say: **This suitcase contains 15 bricks. Do you think you could lift it over your head in one try?** Don't let anyone touch the suitcase yet. Ask each person to predict whether he or she will be able to perform this weightlifting feat. Write down kids' predictions. Explain that group members who predict correctly will win a prize.

One at a time, let kids try to lift the suitcase over their head. Then show them the "bricks" that were inside. Give a prize to each person whose prediction was correct.

Then ask: **Why did you make the prediction you made?**

Can you think of another time in your life when the job you had to do turned out to be easier than you expected? What happened?

Can you think of a time in your life when you turned out to have more strength or power than you expected? What happened?

Explain that you'll be talking about a contest in which most of us have more power than we think we do—a contest that's a lot more important than lifting bricks.

STEP 2

The Paranoids Are After Us!

(Needed: Four copies of Repro Resource 7, four actors)

Hand out copies of "The Conspiracy" (Repro Resource 7) to four volunteer actors. Have the actors perform the skit for the whole group.

Afterward, ask: **What do you think of when you hear the words "peer pressure"?** (The influence people sometimes feel to act or think as those around them do.)

Do you think parents and youth leaders exaggerate the dangers of peer pressure? Why or why not?

Does this skit show how peer pressure really works? If not, how does it work?

Can you think of a case in which it would be harmful for a Christian to go along with what everybody else seems to be doing?

Can you think of a case in which it wouldn't hurt anybody?

O P T I O N S

EXTRA ACTION

LITTLE BIBLE BACKGROUND

MOSTLY GUYS

EXTRA CHALLENGE

STEP 3

Babylon Three

(Needed: Bibles, copies of Repro Resource 8, pencils)

Hand out copies of "Tales of the Resistance" (Repro Resource 8) and pencils. Have kids form three teams. Instruct each team to read one of the stories from the sheet as well as its counterpart in the Book of Daniel.

Afterward, ask Team 1: **How was your story like the one in Daniel 1?** (In both stories, four young believers were uprooted from a place they were used to and taken to a strange place where they knew no one. They were given insulting names [those given to the Israelites honored false gods of Babylon]. They were pressured to put something in their bodies that they believed was wrong to eat or use [the royal food and drink would have "defiled" the Israelites because a portion of

it had been offered to false gods, the meat was from ceremonially unclean animals, and biblical rules about preparing the food had not been followed]. The four Israelites and four brothers convinced an assistant to the "head guy" to let them demonstrate that they could succeed without sinning. Their tests worked, and they went on to receive special honors.)

Ask Team II: **How was your story like the one in Daniel 3?** (A corrupt and powerful leader demanded that everyone "bow down" to him, and one or more of God's people resisted. The leader's henchmen brought this news to their boss, who tried to kill the resister[s]—and failed due to God's direct action. The leader was so impressed that he reversed himself and promised punishment to anyone who messed with the one[s] who had resisted.)

Ask Team III: **How was your story like the one in Daniel 6?** (Enemies of a believer used a government rule to get the believer in trouble—even though the person enforcing the rule didn't want to do it. When the believer refused to go along with the misguided authorities, things got worse—and the believer was locked up. God protected the believer and used the incident as a springboard for new rules which resulted in less harassment for believers.)

Ask the whole group: **In your incident from the Book of Daniel, why did the unbelievers pressure God's people to do wrong?** (The unbelievers thought their way of doing things was best; they felt threatened; they wanted to keep others looking up to them; they feared punishment from higher-ups; they carried personal grudges; they would have been embarrassed to publicly change their minds.)

From what you've seen at school and elsewhere, why might a non-Christian pressure a Christian to do wrong? Answers will vary, but may echo the suggested answers to the previous question. It's important to note, however, that kids often feel pressured by their own fears of not fitting in—whether or not other people are trying to pressure them.

In your incident from the Book of Daniel, why was it important to resist the pressure? As needed, point out that in each case the believers were showing respect for God by obeying His rules and maintaining their relationship with Him. The rules were important, but only because God had given them. To give in would have been like telling God, "You're important to us, but not quite as important as things like safety and popularity." God isn't interested in being somewhere on our top 10 list. He wants only the number one spot.

What might happen if we never resisted the urge to be like everybody else? (We'd be like everybody else—or we'd keep changing to be like whomever we felt most pressured to imitate at the moment. We'd be demonstrating that other people, not God, had first place in our lives.)

Each incident from the Book of Daniel involved a miracle. Is it fair to expect you to resist peer pressure without the help of a miracle? Answers will vary. But point out that in each case, the miracle came *after* the believers had decided to resist the pressure and had acted on their choices. There was no guarantee that God would prevent painful consequences of those choices (see Dan. 3:17-18). The Bible is full of examples of people who suffered because they did the right thing.

STEP 4

Split Decision

(Needed: Cut-apart copy of Repro Resource 9, index cards, markers, name tags, prize [optional])

Before the meeting, cut the five situation descriptions from a copy of "Olympic Pressure" (Repro Resource 9). At this point in the session, give five kids the situations (one per person). Each person with a situation should gather a small group around him or her to help in deciding what to do. Be sure everyone finds his or her way into a small group. If your group is small, let kids consider the situations individually or use fewer situations.

Ask kids to consider these questions: **What would I really want to do in this situation? What would be the right thing to do? What would doing the right thing cost me?**

After a couple of minutes, have the five kids who received situations prepare to act out their decisions. Appoint five other kids to be "Olympic judges." Give each judge five index cards and a marker. Using name tags, identify the judges as "Conscience," "Best Friends," "Other Kids," "Parents," and "Adults at Church." Each judge, playing the role indicated on his or her name tag, will be rating the decision-makers' performances. Judges will mark their ratings Olympics-style (0.0 to 6.0, with 6.0 being perfect) on the index cards, then hold them up for everyone to see.

Let the decision-makers act out their decisions; then let the judges do their thing. If you like, award a prize to the performer with the highest average score. Give participants a chance to explain why they decided and judged as they did.

Then ask the group: **When you're deciding what to do in real life, which of these judges should you be trying to please?**

OPTIONS

HEARD IT ALL BEFORE

MOSTLY GIRLS

EXTRA FUN

URBAN

JR. HIGH / HIGH SCHOOL COMBINED

Why? After hearing replies, point out that the only Judge who really counts is God. All five judges could be right, but only to the degree that they reflect God's view. There may be good reasons to give some judges' ratings more weight (parents because we're supposed to honor them, best friends because they know us better, etc.). But unlike Olympic athletes, we can't just average the scores to get the answer. God is the only reliable Judge, because only He is perfect.

So how can you know what God's view is? Kids may say "read the Bible" or "pray," and both are true. But point out that Bible reading, prayer, advice from other Christians, etc., are not just steps to take when you face a big decision. They're ways to keep training your conscience, day in and day out, so that it better reflects God's perspective. We can't do much to turn other people into better judges, but we can train our consciences to help us make the right choices when we're under pressure.

STEP 5

Another Brick in the Wall

(Needed: Paper bricks from Step 1, markers)

Say: **Think back to your stories from the Book of Daniel. Who won each of those contests?** (God did. The believers survived, and at least some of the unbelievers gained new respect for God.)

Do you think it's possible for a Christian kid to influence non-Christians in a positive way? Encourage kids to share even "minor" examples, if they know of some. Have an example of your own ready, if possible.

What are some reasons a Christian kid might give for not trying to influence others to respect God? (It's too hard; I don't know how; nobody would listen; I'd be embarrassed; etc.)

Point to the suitcase you used in Step 1. Say: **Some of you predicted you wouldn't be able to lift that suitcase full of bricks. But you had more power than you thought—and the bricks were lighter than you thought.**

Open the suitcase and take out the paper bricks. (You'll need one per group member; so if you have more than 15 kids, you'll want to make more bricks before the session and add them now. Give each person a brick and a marker.

OPTIONS

Read I John 4:4. Then say: **Maybe you know someone who needs to be influenced by a follower of Jesus. Maybe it's somebody who has no respect for God—or for anyone who believes in Him. Maybe it's somebody who just has a lot of questions. On the brick I gave you, please write the initials of a person like that.** Give kids a few minutes to do this.

You may have thought you could never influence that person—that it would be too hard. But if you're a Christian, God lives in you. And the One who is in you is more powerful than anyone else. That's the truth about peer pressure. It may be hard to believe, but with God's help you have more power to influence non-Christians than they have to influence you. But only if you want it that way.

If time allows, close in silent prayer for those whose initials kids wrote on the bricks. Encourage kids to take their bricks with them as reminders of the power they have to influence others

THE CONSPIRACY

CHAIRMAN: This meeting of the Society of Nasty, Obnoxious Teenagers will now come to order. Will the secretary please read the minutes?

SECRETARY *(with an evil chuckle):* At the last meeting, we decided to put more peer pressure on those goody-goody Christians at school. We want to force them to be like us, to make them do awful, sinful things.

MEMBER 1: Yeah! We're sick of those Christians. Let's make them evil, like us!

MEMBER 2: Make them go along with the crowd!

CHAIRMAN: They must conform! *(ALL applaud and snicker.)*

SECRETARY: We also decided to change our name. When you think about it, the initials of the Society of Nasty, Obnoxious Teenagers are a little gross. *(Pause to let audience think about it.)*

CHAIRMAN: Right. Now, back to those Christian kids. How are we going to force them to be like us?

MEMBER 1: Well, everybody knows we evil teens have a mysterious power over good kids. All we have to say is "What are you, chicken?" and they do whatever we tell them.

MEMBER 2: Or "What are you, a baby?" Or "What are you, a religious fanatic?" Or "What are you, a pork chop?"

SECRETARY: Hmm. I've never used that last one before.

MEMBER 1: It works for me.

CHAIRMAN: We need to step up our vast, invisible conspiracy to turn Christian kids into foul-mouthed, alcoholic drug addicts who think premarital sex is OK. How can we do that?

MEMBER 2: We could disguise ourselves as good kids and sneak into their homes and churches.

CHAIRMAN: No, that would never work. Their courageous parents and youth leaders would see through that!

MEMBER 1: We could multiply our influence. Instead of working one-on-one, we could roam around in big groups, catching unsuspecting victims alone and squashing them with our combined peer pressure until they give in!

CHAIRMAN: That's it! And before we know it, every Christian teen in the world will be ours! *(ALL applaud and snicker.)* Now, is there any new business?

SECRETARY: About changing the name of our organization—I'd like to suggest Peers United to Kill Excellence.

CHAIRMAN: Hmm. Peers United to Kill Excellence. What do those initials spell? *(Pause to let audience think about it.)* Uh, no.

MEMBER 1: Nope.

MEMBER 2: No way.

CHAIRMAN: Let's keep working on that. For now, let's go crush some Christians! Meeting adjourned! *(Cheering, ALL exit.)*

NOTES

TALES of the
RESISTANCE

I. The Training Table

When they were in high school, four brothers named Steve, Chad, Tom, and Mike had to move from Bozeman, Montana to a Chicago suburb because their father was changing jobs. When they got to Chicago, it was as if they'd entered another world.

Kids at their affluent new school gave the four "farm boys" insulting nicknames—Bozo, Clodhopper, Geek, and Dorkman. But the four made the football team, an honored place to be since the school had won every state championship for the last eight years.

Soon the brothers discovered the secret of the school's success. The coach, an aggressive and demanding man, routinely encouraged players to increase their muscle mass by taking steroids. The four boys knew that taking the drugs was dangerous as well as illegal. As Christians, they decided they had to refuse.

When they told the assistant coach of their decision, he shook his head. "Look, guys," he said. "I like you. But if you don't take steroids, you won't look as strong as the other players. If the coach finds out that I said you didn't have to take the stuff, he'll fire me."

Steve, the oldest brother, had an idea. "Give us a test," he said. "Let us work out and eat right, with no steroids, for the first month of the season. Then compare us with the players who are taking the drugs. Treat us according to what you see." The assistant coach agreed.

At the end of the test period, the four brothers looked and played better than any of the guys who were taking steroids. So the assistant coach let them continue playing without drugs.

The brothers were such outstanding players, in fact, that each received a college football scholarship at graduation. And all of them were drafted by the National Football League, where they all played in the Super Bowl.

Now compare this story with the one in Daniel 1. How is it similar?

II. Cool and the Gang

Joining a gang seemed to be the only way to survive in Maurice's neighborhood. He'd seen what happened to those who opposed the Dragon Lords, the gang that controlled his part of town.

Saying no to the Dragon Lords meant angering the head of the gang—a merciless killer known only as Iceman. Anyone who wouldn't bow down to the Iceman risked sudden death, usually in a drive-by shooting. But Maurice, a Christian, would bow down only to God— and said so to some of the Iceman's henchmen.

Soon those henchmen went to their leader. "Iceman," one said. "You are lord of this territory. But one dude, Maurice, refuses to give you respect. We warned him to join up, but he paid no attention to us."

Furious, the Iceman vowed to kill Maurice. Grabbing an assault rifle, he ordered seven times the usual number of gang members to follow him to Maurice's house.

TALES of the
RESISTANCE

As the gang members' cars pulled up to their destination, Iceman could see Maurice through the front window of the house. He seemed to be the only one home. Guns were drawn. "Fire!" Iceman shouted, and the bullets began to fly.

Windows shattered. Bullets pierced the siding. But to the amazement of Iceman and his thugs, Maurice didn't fall. Even more incredibly, a shining figure appeared next to Maurice, as if protecting him.

"Cease fire!" yelled Iceman. "Maurice, come out!"

Maurice, unharmed, walked out of the bullet-riddled house. "Listen up!" shouted Iceman to the rest of the Dragon Lords. "This dude has some kind of connection to God! So anybody who lays a hand on him or his family from now on will answer to me! You dig?"

They dug.

Now compare this story with the one in Daniel 3. How is it similar?

III. Danielle in the Principal's Den

Danielle Lyons, a junior at Ben Franklin High, was pretty popular as well as being a Christian. But she'd made some enemies—especially three girls who mistakenly thought "super-straight" Danielle had turned them in for having drugs in their lockers. "We've got to get back at her," they said.

One day they got their chance. The school district announced a new policy based on a Supreme Court ruling: No student could hold a Bible study on the school grounds. After one of Danielle's enemies spotted Danielle and a friend reading Bibles on a bench in front of the school, the three enemies went straight to the principal.

"Sir," one of the girls said, "Danielle Lyons is breaking the rule about Bible studies. We know you wouldn't want to get in trouble with the school district, not to mention the Supreme Court. So we're sure you'll enforce the rule."

The principal groaned. He knew what the three girls were up to, but couldn't undo the rule. Reluctantly he suspended Danielle from school.

Some people at church urged Danielle to challenge the rule by going back to school. She did—and was expelled. She continued to challenge the rule, and finally was thrown in jail for contempt of court.

The judge refused to let Danielle out of jail unless she promised not to read her Bible at school anymore. She said she couldn't promise that. She ended up spending most of the year in jail—until another Supreme Court decision set her free.

Danielle had to take her junior year again, but otherwise she was fine. The school board, however, was voted out of office—and the new board fired the principal.

Now compare this story with the one in Daniel 6. How is it similar?

OLYMPIC PRESSURE

1. You and your boyfriend, both Christians, knew premarital sex was wrong. But that didn't seem to matter when you were so in love and marriage was so far away. Now you're five weeks pregnant. You used to think abortion was a sin, but now it seems like a solution. Your boyfriend says it's up to you, but you get the impression he'd really like you to end the pregnancy so things can get back to normal. Neither of you has told your parents yet, and legally you don't have to. You can just imagine how hurt your parents would feel about what you've done, and how some people at church would want you to disappear if you showed up pregnant. After deciding what to do, act out for the judges how you'll reveal your decision to your boyfriend.

2. Kids whose athletic shoes don't pump up or light up are considered subhuman right now at your school. But shoes like those cost megabucks, and you're not rich. You could save up the money, but you can also think of better ways to spend it. You keep thinking about a film you saw at church about people starving in Africa and wonder how you could buy expensive shoes when some people don't have food. On the other hand, you don't feel too excited about saving up money for hunger relief. You decide to save up enough money for shoes, then decide what to do with it. Act out for the judges what you'll do when you've saved up the money.

3. In your part of the country, it's considered every guy's patriotic duty to serve in the military. The few young men in your town who have never done so are thought to be cowards or homosexuals. As a guy who's turning eighteen, you have to register in case there's a military draft. After studying the Gospels, you believe you shouldn't fight—and that you should register as a conscientious objector. If you do, practically everyone you know (including your church leaders) will disagree with you. You might even have to go to jail for refusing to fight. Act out for the judges what happens when you walk into your local post office to register.

4. You'd rather eat rat poison than be seen with your parents at the mall. But there seems to be no way to avoid it today; it's your mom's birthday, and she wants you to help her spend the money Dad gave her. You, Mom, and Dad are coming out of a store when six of your friends walk up. Act out for the judges the way you greet your friends.

5. You're in an unfamiliar town for a speech tournament, where your team has just taken first place in debate. Other members of your team have found a bar where nobody ever checks a high schooler's I.D. All of the kids are going to the bar, having told the team advisor that they're going to a pizza place. If you don't go, you'll have nothing to do but stay in the motel room and watch TV. You really feel like going out and celebrating. You wouldn't even have to drink if you went to the bar. You'd only have to lie about the whole thing later. Act out for the judges what you do when the other team members say, "Let's go!"

EXTRA **ACTION**

SMALL GROUP

LARGE GROUP

STEP 2

Before (or in place of) the skit, stage a "Greased Balloon Squash." You'll need an inflated balloon for every two kids, plus a can of vegetable-oil cooking spray. Have kids form pairs. Give each pair a balloon which you've coated with the oily spray. At your signal, each person must face his or her partner, reach out one hand, palm toward the partner, and try to squash the balloon between his or her palm and the partner's palm. The first two pairs to accomplish this win a prize. (You'll want to try this outside or over a floor that's easily cleaned. Provide soap and water so that kids can wash their hands afterward too.) After awarding prizes, ask: **Is this what peer pressure is like? Why or why not? Is it possible to "slip away" from peer pressure, or are we bound to get squashed by it? Explain.**

STEP 3

Skip the third story on Repro Resource 8. Choose either "The Training Table" or "Cool and the Gang" for the whole group to act out as a narrator reads it aloud. Assign the main roles. The rest of the group will act as either steroid-using football players or gang members, depending on which skit you're using. Encourage kids to get into their roles. Then discuss similarities between the skit and the corresponding Daniel passage.

STEP 3

Depending on the capabilities of your group members, the extent of reading and comparing required for Repro Resource 8 might be somewhat intimidating. If you think this might put too much pressure on some of your group members, work through the stories as a single group. It won't take too long in a small group in which you as leader (or some of the more mature members) do most of the reading. Then make the most of your small group benefits by encouraging *everyone* to interact, respond to one another, express opinions, and share personal experiences.

STEP 5

In addition to feeling peer pressure as *individuals*, small-group members may feel second-rate *as a group*. Ask: **What can we as a group do to influence and affect our friends in a positive way? What are some of the "lame" things we do that we can eliminate? Do you think God might significantly increase our numbers if we showed faith and began to try to meet the needs of our peers?** You might want to consider nonthreatening ways to get new people to attend and "check out" the group (lock-ins, retreats, etc.).

STEP 1

Ask for six volunteers; divide them into two teams (three per team). Announce that your group members will be competing in a contest (don't reveal what the contest is)—and that they will be allowed to choose their own teams. Then have your two sets of volunteers start trying to recruit teammates from among the rest of the group. They may use whatever tactics they like—threats, peer pressure, bribes—to recruit players. Don't tell your group members, but the actual contest is to see which team can get the most players to join. After everyone has chosen a team, discuss what role peer pressure played in group members' decisions. Then move on to the paper brick activity.

STEP 3

After assigning teams the stories on Repro Resource 8, instruct each team to perform its story for the rest of the group, with one person narrating and other team members acting out the events. After each team has performed its story, discuss as a group the story's similarities to events in the Book of Daniel.

STEP 4

Kids may nod their heads out of habit at the assertion that only God's opinion really counts. Deep down, though, they're probably more worried about the short-term price of alienating peers than they are about the long-term cost of offending God. Acknowledge that it really does hurt when doing the right thing puts us at odds with people who mean a lot to us. But people don't own us, and God does. People make mistakes, and God doesn't. People can embarrass us and punish us and even kill us, but only God can give us eternal life. People can withdraw their friendship, but God never withdraws His. He also can see to it that we find other friends—ones who don't reject us for following Him.

STEP 5

Kids may be used to "responding" superficially, going along with instructions to write down a friend's initials and take them home—and then tossing the paper and forgetting the initials at the first opportunity. You can't force kids to respond sincerely, but you can prod their memories during the week. As kids write on their "bricks," ask them to write initials on a sheet of paper for you too. Then call kids during the week to remind them of the initials they wrote down. Don't demand a progress report; just remind them and let them know that you're thinking about the pressures they face.

STEP 2

The skit on Repro Resource 7 assumes that group members are established Christians. If this is not necessarily the case in your group, don't use the skit as written. Instead, let kids work in pairs to create impromptu skits. In each case, let one person in the pair suppose that he or she is being paid to persuade a good kid to do bad things. The other person in the pair is the "good kid." Let kids see who is best at applying negative peer pressure, and who is best at resisting it. Then ask: **How do you recognize times like these in real life when other people are trying to convince you to do things you really shouldn't do? How do you usually respond in *real life*?**

STEP 3

If your group isn't accustomed to covering a lot of Bible material individually, you might want to focus on only one of the three stories from Daniel and devote more time to covering it in detail. (Since almost everyone is somewhat familiar with the account of Daniel in the lions' den, you might want to emphasize one of the other two.) Use Repro Resource 8 as a take-home sheet. Encourage kids to read the other two stories sometime during the week. In fact, you might want to take this approach each week, if your group members are willing. Rather than dealing with large "chunks" of the Bible in group meetings, keep introducing "bite-sized" amounts of Scripture while providing related weekly assignments to help your group members become familiar with biblical teachings on their own.

STEP 1

Have kids form teams. Give each team some markers, crayons, and a large piece of poster board on which kids can draw graffiti. Before the session, you'll need to write the following Scripture references on each "graffiti wall" (or piece of poster board): Joshua 1:7-9; John 14:25-27; Romans 6:6-7; Romans 12:1-2; 2 Timothy 1:7. Give the members of each team several minutes to write or draw on their "graffiti wall" words or pictures depicting the struggles they face and the things they feel pressured to do. After everyone is finished, have the teams display their work. Note the similarities and differences in the situations depicted by different teams. Briefly discuss how the passages that are listed on the "graffiti walls" can help with the struggles that were identified.

STEP 5

Have kids reassemble into the teams they formed for the "graffiti wall" activity (see "Fellowship & Worship" option for Step 1). Instruct the teams to read the passages listed on the "graffiti wall." Afterward, say: **We face some strong pressures every day, but as we can see from these passages and many others throughout the Bible, God doesn't expect us to face these pressures alone. He's gone before us, defeated the enemy, and now offers to walk with us and help us in our battles.** Spend a few minutes in prayer, thanking God for His strength and guidance and asking for His help for each struggle identified on the "graffiti walls."

STEP 3

Replace the first scenario on Repro Resource 8 with the following story:

• *Modeling School.* Four sisters—Chris, Pam, Jill, and Sandy—are sent by their parents to modeling school, where the girls are encouraged by the owner of the school to take diet pills and laxatives and to starve themselves in order to maintain their "model weight." They talk to their coach, who reluctantly agrees to let them work out a plan of healthy diet and exercise—on trial for a month. At the end of the month, the girls look far healthier than their emaciated counterparts, and each lands a big contract with Cover Girl.

STEP 4

Replace Situation 3 on Repro Resource 9 with the following scenario:

• In your part of the country, it's considered every female's role to get married and start having babies right out of high school. "The woman's place is in the home" has been preached from many a pulpit. Those who don't get married are considered worldly and wicked. You want to go on to college, however, and possibly to law school. You know you'll be the talk of the town, but it's time to send out those college applications. Act out for the judges what happens when you walk into the post office to mail your first round of college application forms.

STEP 1

Most guys would never turn down a lift-a-suitcase-of-bricks-over-your-head challenge—not unless they were already worn out. So begin with a shot-put competition using actual bricks. (This is definitely an outside, in-the-grass activity.) Warn the guys against trying to throw the bricks as they would throw a baseball. To prevent potential injury, the brick must be held against the chest, under the chin, and tossed with a single outward thrust. Begin by giving each person three attempts with his "good" arm (whether right-handed or left-handed). The farthest distance should be marked and the winner determined. Then try three rounds with "opposite arms" (left for right-handers, right for lefties). When guys begin to tire, *then* introduce the lifting exercise and move ahead with the session from there.

STEP 2

The words "peer pressure" may never pass the lips of most guys, so you'll need to "translate" for them. Try speaking their own unique language to see what happens. So rather than asking the questions in this step as written, ask: **What's the dumbest thing you've ever done because some said . . .**

• **"I dare you!"**

• **"What are you, *chicken?*"**

• **"A *real* man would do it."**

• **"I will if you will."**

Let guys provide other hard-to-resist challenges and stories that accompany them.

STEP 1

If cutting out bricks is a bit too time-consuming for you, bring a package of construction paper (assorted colors) instead. Have kids form three or four teams. Instruct each team to line up in a different corner of the room. Give the first person on each team four sheets of different-colored paper. (All teams should have the same four colors.) This person should be positioned so that he or she cannot see the other teams. At your signal, the first person on each team should hold up one of the four sheets of paper. If two or more players choose the same color, they must stay where they are. But if a player chooses a color that is different from all of the others, that person goes to the back of his or her team's line; the next person in line then takes his or her place. The first team to rotate all the way around (by being unique and different from all of the others) is the winner. In Step 5, let kids use the construction paper instead of the cut-out bricks to record the initials of the people they think of.

STEP 4

Give kids an opportunity to express which peer pressures have the greatest effect on them—but try to do so in a fun and non-threatening way. Most of your kids have probably seen the anti-drug ad that features a dad roleplaying a situation as a drug dealer to help his young son learn how to say no if he ever experiences the reality of that situation. Similarly, have kids form groups for "drinking," "sex," "cheating," or any other peer pressure situations that your group members bring up. Let kids join the group that most pertains to them to create anti-peer-pressure ads directed toward that activity. Give them the opportunity to respond in proper ways here in the group. Then challenge them, when faced again with the actual problem, to respond in the same way.

STEP 3

At your local Christian bookstore, rent or buy the video *Where's God When I'm Scared?* from the "Veggie Tales" series (Word). Though designed as a children's video, this production's high-quality computer animation and wry humor can appeal to any age. The second segment on the tape, "Daniel and the Lion's Den," is a retelling of Daniel 6—an opera featuring talking vegetables as Daniel, the king, and the conniving wise men. Play this segment instead of using Repro Resource 8; then discuss the real story in Daniel 6 and the questions in the session.

STEP 5

Augment your discussion of positive peer pressure by playing contemporary Christian songs that encourage kids to stand firm and to influence others. Here are some examples: "I Know" (Michael W. Smith), "Who to Listen To" (Amy Grant), "You Can Go" (David Meece), "We Are the Light" (Servant), "Rock Solid" (Russ Taff), and "I Want to Make a Difference" (Michele Pillar). After each song, ask: **Does this song have more to say about what to do or what not to do? Why? How could the song's message be boiled down to three words? Where and when might you need to remember those words this week? Why?**

STEP 1

Skip Step 1. Before the session, get a few group members to help decorate your meeting place with overly dramatic signs about the dangers of peer pressure. Here are some examples of what your signs might say: "Beware! Peer Pressure Is Out to Get You!" "Don't Go Along with the Crowd!" "If Your Friends Jumped Off a Cliff, Would You Do It Too?" "Warning: Your Peers Are Plotting to Destroy You!" If you can make the sign lettering look "scary" and glue on some old-fashioned magazine pictures of teenagers, so much the better. Use these posters to set the tone as you melodramatically introduce the "true, behind-the-scenes story of peer pressure" presented in the Step 2 skit.

STEP 3

Use just the Daniel 1 and 3 passages and the two corresponding stories on Repro Resource 8. In Step 4, use just situations 3, 4, and 5 from Repro Resource 9. Instead of acting out decisions and judging them Olympics-style, have the small groups discuss what each "judge" might want the people involved to do. Then share results. In Step 5, skip the paper bricks activity and simply ask each group member to think of a person who needs his or her influence. Close with the comments from the next-to-last paragraph of the session.

STEP 4

Replace Situation 3 on Repro Resource 9 with the following scenario:

• Your church youth group is planning to march in a "Take Back the Street" demonstration designed to protest crime in your neighborhood. Some of your friends are planning to disrupt the march by shooting fireworks at the protesters. Your friends have even asked you to buy some of the fireworks. Act out what happens when you approach your friends to tell them what you plan to do.

STEP 5

After completing the paper-brick activity in Step 5, give your group members an opportunity to come up with their own applications for this material on peer pressure. Have kids form teams. Instruct each team to create a verse for a rap song that deals with resisting peer pressure. Each verse should describe a specific way for kids to resist the negative influences of others. You might want to choose a popular rap song to use as a model so that the teams' verses all have a similar rhythm pattern. After a few minutes, have each team perform its verse for the rest of the group.

STEP 4

Substitute the following scenarios for the corresponding ones on Repro Resource 9:

• 1. It's the beginning of the school year, and the new cliques are beginning to form. Your best friend is sliding right into a group that you really don't feel comfortable with. These kids are a bit rough. They don't watch their language, they smoke, and they're way into gossip and tearing others apart. If you don't follow into the group, though, you're left by yourself. After deciding what to do, act out for the judges what you'll say to your best friend.

• 3. The student council—of which you are a member—is having a fundraiser to support a local crisis shelter for pregnant women. You know that this shelter often encourages women to have an abortion. Everyone on the council must participate in the fundraiser—it's the big event of the year. Act out for the judges what you tell the student council advisor.

STEP 5

Hand out paper and pencils. Encourage each group member to write down an example of peer pressure that he or she is currently facing—something that he or she is really struggling with right now. Don't have group members write their names on their papers. After a few minutes, collect the sheets in two containers—one for junior highers and one for high schoolers. Then redistribute the sheets, making sure that a junior higher gets a high schooler's paper and vice versa. Encourage kids to pray for the situation throughout the week. Remind them that though they don't know the name of the person they're praying for, God knows whose struggle it is.

STEP 2

For a biblical illustration of the negative effects of giving in to peer pressure, have group members read Exodus 32:1-6, in which Aaron gives in to the pressure of the Israelites and builds a golden calf for them to worship. Ask: **What do you think might have happened to Aaron if he'd refused the people's request?** (Most likely, the people would have done nothing more than grumbled against him and whined. If they'd tried to physically harm him, it's likely that God would have protected him.) **So why do you think Aaron went along with the people's plan?** (Perhaps he wanted to look good in the eyes of the people.) Summarize the results of Aaron's actions (found in Exod. 32:6-35). Then ask: **If Aaron had it to do over again, how do you think he would respond to the people's pressure?**

STEP 5

As you wrap up the session, you might want to list some Scripture passages on the board that tell of Bible characters who resisted negative peer pressure. Among the passages you might use are Numbers 13–14 (in which Joshua and Caleb resist the pressure to give a negative report about the promised land) and 1 Samuel 24 (in which David resists the pressure from his men to kill Saul). Ask your group members to choose one of the passages (or find another one on their own) to study in the coming week. At your next meeting, group members should be prepared to summarize the passages, explaining what kind of pressure each character faced and how he or she resisted or dealt with the pressure.

Date Used:

Approx. Time

STEP 1: *It Ain't Heavy, Brother* _____
❑ Large Group
❑ Fellowship & Worship
❑ Mostly Guys
❑ Extra Fun
❑ Short Meeting Time
Things needed:

STEP 2: *The Paranoids Are After Us!* _____
❑ Extra Action
❑ Little Bible Background
❑ Mostly Guys
❑ Extra Challenge
Things needed:

STEP 3: *Babylon Three* _____
❑ Extra Action
❑ Small Group
❑ Large Group
❑ Little Bible Background
❑ Mostly Girls
❑ Media
❑ Short Meeting Time
Things needed:

STEP 4: *Spit Decision* _____
❑ Heard It All Before
❑ Mostly Girls
❑ Extra Fun
❑ Urban
❑ Combined Junior High/High School
Things needed:

STEP 5: *Another Brick in the Wall* _____
❑ Small Group
❑ Heard It All Before
❑ Fellowship & Worship
❑ Media
❑ Urban
❑ Combined Junior High/High School
❑ Extra Challenge
Things needed:

Join the Club!

CHRISTIANS WELCOME!

YOUR GOALS FOR THIS SESSION:
C h o o s e   o n e   o r   m o r e

☐ To help kids see that most Christians feel isolated at times because of their faith, and that joining forces can go a long way toward solving that problem.

☐ To help kids understand how to break the ice and form partnerships with Christian peers.

☐ To help kids start building support networks to encourage them as they seek to live for Christ at school and elsewhere.

☐ Other:_____
_____

Your Bible Base:

Ecclesiastes 4:7-12
Acts 2:42-47
Ephesians 4:11-16

They Call Him Flipper

(Needed: Frozen pancakes, spatulas, paper plates, team prize)

Begin the session with a pancake-flipping relay race. Bring two boxes of frozen pancakes, four paper plates, and four spatulas.

Have kids form two teams. Place a paper plate on the floor in front of the first person on each team, with a stack of unwrapped frozen pancakes on each plate. Place another plate on the floor at least 10 feet across the room from each team. Give a spatula to the first and second members of each team.

At your signal, the first person on each team will run to a spot halfway between the team's two plates and stand there. The second person on each team will use his or her spatula to scoop a pancake from the nearby plate and toss it to the first person—who will try to catch it with his or her spatula and toss it onto the second plate. Once this process is tried, successfully or not, the second person will take the first person's place between the plates; the first person will hand off his or her spatula to the third person and go to the end of the team's line.

After all of the pancakes have been tossed, the team with the most pancakes on the second plate (and the fewest on the floor) wins. Award a prize to the winning team.

Then ask: **How do you think this race would have gone with just one pancake flipper on each team?** (It would have been harder to get the pancakes from one plate to another, for one thing.)

What are some other times when it's good to have two people working together instead of working alone? (Studying for a test, learning lines for a play, learning to drive, exploring a cave, mountain climbing, etc.)

How about when you're trying to live like a Christian at school? Do most of us tend to go it alone, or do we get help? Someone may point out that God helps us, but explain that you're talking about support from human friends.

Say: **It's hard enough to "go against the flow" when you have help. When you try to do it alone, it's like trying to flip these pancakes across the room by yourself—it's tougher, and not nearly so much fun.**

Daily Affirmation

(Needed: Copies of Repro Resource 10, pencils)

Hand out copies of "Heard Any Good Ones Lately?" (Repro Resource 10) and pencils. Say: **Let's find out how much help you're getting from the people around you—at least as far as your faith is concerned. In a typical day, how often do you see or hear things that make you feel good about being a Christian? Circle the answers on this sheet that come closest to being correct.**

Tell kids to ignore statements that don't apply—if they have fewer than six classes or don't have an after-school job, for instance. Give kids a couple of minutes to mark their answers. Then discuss as much as kids are willing.

Chances are that your group members are getting little affirmation of their faith outside of church activities, especially if they don't attend Christian schools or don't have deep conversations with strong Christian parents.

Ask: **What kinds of things might you hear from these sources that could make you feel bad about being a Christian?** (A non-Christian parent might criticize spending time at church; a teacher might imply that "religious" people are too sheltered; a friend might laugh at someone who refuses to cheat; a TV show or textbook might portray religious people as backward or unstable; etc.)

What happens when you're excited about something, but people around you couldn't care less? What happens if they put you down for being excited? Answers will vary. Point out that some people may be able to stay excited on their own for a while, but most of us tend to cool off when nobody shares our excitement. And when others think our commitment to Jesus is stupid, we may eventually start to believe them—especially if they're the only ones we spend time with.

STEP 3

Soapbox Speakers

(Needed: Bibles, cut-apart copy of Repro Resource 11, paper, pencils, two envelopes, three chairs or stepstools)

OPTIONS

SMALL GROUP

HEARD IT ALL BEFORE

LITTLE BIBLE BACKGROUND

MOSTLY GIRLS

SHORT MEETING TIME

JR. HIGH HIGH SCHOOL COMBINED

EXTRA CHALLENGE

Before the session, cut apart a copy of "Seekers and Speakers" (Repro Resource 11). You'll need one slip per person; so if you have more than nine kids in your group, you'll need to make and cut more copies. Put the "Seeker" slips in one envelope and the "Speaker" slips in another.

At this point in the meeting, give each person one of the slips. Be sure to hand out all three Speaker slips; try to give these to your better readers. Give a sheet of paper and a pencil to each Seeker, along with a Seeker slip. If your group is small, don't pass out all of the Seeker slips.

Have each Speaker stand on a "soapbox" (a chair or stepstool) and read his or her passage aloud, over and over. Seekers should go from Speaker to Speaker, listening and taking notes on how the passages might apply to the situations described on their slips.

After all Seekers have had a chance to hear all Speakers, regather the group. Discuss the activity, using the following questions. As needed, supplement answers with the information that follows each question.

What did you get from listening to Speaker A (Eccl. 4:7-12)**?**

Seeker 1—Trying to do anything alone can seem meaningless. If this person could find even one other Christian somewhere, he or she probably wouldn't get so discouraged.

Seeker 2—Youth group meetings aren't enough. This person needs to find Christians at school, or at least stay in touch with youth group members during the week.

Seeker 3—Everybody needs the kind of support this person has. He or she should reach out to help someone else in the group.

Seeker 4—This person needs to find a Christian or two to help him or her through this conflict.

Seeker 5—This person needs to find one other Christian in the group or outside of it who's willing to listen.

Seeker 6—Being busy doesn't mean this person doesn't need help; it means he or she needs *more* help. And somebody in the group probably needs this person, no matter how big the group is.

What did you get from listening to Speaker B (Acts 2:42-47)**?**

Seeker 1—This person may be the only Christian at school, but probably not at church. Finding a supportive friend at church—even if he or she is older—might be a place to start.

Seeker 2—Christian togetherness wasn't meant to be a once-a-week thing. Besides checking in with Christians at school, how about in each other's homes and on the telephone?

Seeker 3—Those who follow Jesus are supposed to be concerned about meeting each other's needs, not just their own. If people in the group lack support, it *is* this person's problem.

Seeker 4—Maybe kids from the youth group could spend time with this person's parents—helping with a project around the house or having dinner at a restaurant—so the parents could see that the group's not a cult. Many unbelievers who saw the early Christians close up were won over.

Seeker 5—This person's youth group isn't doing what Christians were meant to do. The person needs to be willing to share his or her feelings with the group or at least with the leader to see what can be changed.

Seeker 6—Following Jesus is meant to be a shared experience. Everybody needs to be part of it, giving as well as receiving.

What did you get from listening to Speaker C (Eph. 4:11-16)**?**

Seeker 1—God has equipped someone to help this person, whether or not the helper goes to the person's school.

Seeker 2—This person won't be prepared for a whole week of challenges just by going to a youth group meeting. Maturity and strength come partly from frequent contact with other Christians who build us up.

Seeker 3—This "part" of the body isn't doing his or her work. Everybody needs help from everybody else to reach maturity.

Seeker 4—New Christians especially need help from the rest of us to grow strong in the faith.

Seeker 5—If this person's group really is uncaring, he or she should try "speaking the truth in love" and asking for change. But if the person is expecting everyone to reach out with no effort from him or her, then the person isn't doing his or her part.

Seeker 6—This "supporting ligament" isn't doing anything to hold the body together. Is he or she really taking orders from the Head?

Ask: **If our group worked as well as the church did in the Acts passage, and as well as it's told to work in the Ephesians passage, would you find living as a Christian during the week any easier? Why or why not?**

Network

(Needed: Badges cut from Repro Resource 12, tape, refreshments, recorded music and player)

OPTIONS

It's party time! Play some upbeat music. Bring on the refreshments. Give kids a chance to talk with each other about what it's like to be a Christian outside your meeting place. Explain: **People who want to give their careers a boost sometimes go to parties to "network." They try to make connections with others who could help them later on. We're going to have a "networking party" right now so that you can find people who could help support you as a Christian during the week.**

To help kids mingle and to keep conversation focused, give each person a badge cut from "Party Favors" (Repro Resource 12). Kids should tape these badges on their shirts, blouses, or sweaters. Say: **Our party will last about 10 minutes. During that time, talk with at least 3 different people and follow the instructions on their badges.**

After 10 minutes (or longer if you have time), wrap up the conversation. Ask volunteers to tell you what they learned about the following:

- other Christians at area schools
- Christian teachers
- how group members could do a better job of supporting each other during the week.

Then ask: **Are you used to talking about things like this when you see each other at church? At school? Why or why not?**

How could we do a better job of telling each other what kinds of support we need to "go against the flow"? Do we need a special time during our meetings for that?

What could the leaders of our group do to make sure no one goes without support? Listen carefully to any suggestions; if possible, consider them next time your leadership group gets together.

Never Alone

(Needed: List of group members, paper, pencils)

Before the session, go over a list of kids you think will attend. Divide the list by schools, grade levels, or neighborhoods—whatever will give you some fairly equal small groups. At this point in the meeting, divide the group accordingly and have the small groups sit in different parts of your meeting place. Give each person a piece of paper and a pencil. Instruct each person to do the following:

- Write down the names, addresses, and phone numbers of others in your group.
- Write down a day and hour of the week when each person in your group could use some prayer—maybe because of a hard class or after-school job.
- Give one person in your group permission to call or talk to you during the week to ask you how your efforts to follow Jesus are going.

If kids are used to praying together in your group, close the meeting by having members of small groups pray for each other. Whether or not kids pray, ask them to take their small group notes with them as reminders to pray for and call each other this week.

Heard Any Good Ones Lately?

1. During breakfast, your family members say something positive about being a Christian.

   Frequently   Sometimes   Seldom   Never

2. During your trip to school, the kids on the bus, the driver of the car, or your walking companions say(s) something positive about being a Christian.

   Frequently   Sometimes   Seldom   Never

3. During your first class, your teacher or classmates say(s) something positive about being a Christian.

   Frequently   Sometimes   Seldom   Never

4. During your second class, your teacher or classmates say(s) something positive about being a Christian.

   Frequently   Sometimes   Seldom   Never

5. During your third class, your teacher or classmates say(s) something positive about being a Christian.

   Frequently   Sometimes   Seldom   Never

6. During lunch, the people you eat with say something positive about being a Christian.

   Frequently   Sometimes   Seldom   Never

Heard Any Good Ones Lately?

7. During your fourth class, your teacher or classmates say(s) something positive about being a Christian.

   Frequently   Sometimes   Seldom   Never

8. During your fifth class, your teacher or classmates say(s) something positive about being a Christian.

   Frequently   Sometimes   Seldom   Never

9. During your sixth class, your teacher or classmates say(s) something positive about being a Christian.

   Frequently   Sometimes   Seldom   Never

10. During an extracurricular activity, your coach, teammates, or others say(s) something positive about being a Christian.

    Frequently   Sometimes   Seldom   Never

11. During your after-school job, your boss or coworkers say(s) something positive about being a Christian.

    Frequently   Sometimes   Seldom   Never

12. During your trip home, the kids on the bus, driver of the car, or walking companions say(s) something positive about being a Christian.

    Frequently   Sometimes   Seldom   Never

13. During dinner, your family members say something positive about being a Christian.

    Frequently   Sometimes   Seldom   Never

14. During your homework time, your textbooks or study partners say something positive about being a Christian.

    Frequently   Sometimes   Seldom   Never

15. During your TV watching time, your favorite shows and characters say something positive about being a Christian.

    Frequently   Sometimes   Seldom   Never

16. During your youth group activities, your youth leader or other group members say(s) something positive about being a Christian.

    Frequently   Sometimes   Seldom   Never

SEEKERS AND SPEAKERS

SEEKERS

Seeker 1: You feel like the only Christian in your whole school. Sometimes going it alone doesn't seem worth it.

Seeker 2: Youth group meetings are usually OK, but they don't help you a bit when you're on your own at school during the week.

Seeker 3: You have two good friends from youth group who happen to go to your school. They give you all the support you need. If others in the group don't have friends like that—well, it's not your problem.

Seeker 4: You decided to receive Christ as your Savior a few months ago, and your parents don't understand at all. They think you've joined some kind of cult.

Seeker 5: You don't get much out of youth group events. Nobody really seems to care about you or what you're going through. The only time you see kids from the group is at the meetings.

Seeker 6: You're too busy to go to many youth group events. That doesn't bother you. It's a big group, and you figure they don't really need you.

SPEAKERS

Speaker A: Ecclesiastes 4:7-12

Speaker B: Acts 2:42-47

Speaker C: Ephesians 4:11-16

DO ME A FAVOR...
TELL ME WHAT IT'S LIKE TO BE A CHRISTIAN AT YOUR SCHOOL OR JOB.

DO ME A FAVOR...
TELL ME ABOUT A TIME WHEN IT WOULD HAVE BEEN NICE TO HAVE ANOTHER CHRISTIAN IN A CLASS.

DO ME A FAVOR...
IF YOU KNOW OF ANY OTHER CHRISTIANS IN MY SCHOOL, TELL ME WHO THEY ARE.

DO ME A FAVOR...
IF YOU KNOW OF ANY CHRISTIAN TEACHERS IN OUR DISTRICT, TELL ME WHO THEY ARE.

DO ME A FAVOR...
TELL ME HOW I SHOULD PRAY FOR YOU THIS WEEK.

DO ME A FAVOR...
TELL ME ONE WAY THAT OUR GROUP COULD DO A BETTER JOB OF HELPING YOU FEEL SUPPORTED DURING THE WEEK.

DO ME A FAVOR...
TELL ME ABOUT ONE PERSON AT YOUR SCHOOL OR IN YOUR HOME WHO NEEDS TO HEAR ABOUT JESUS, AND HOW OUR GROUP MIGHT HELP THAT HAPPEN.

DO ME A FAVOR...
TELL ME WHAT HAPPENED THE LAST TIME YOU TRIED TO ACT ON YOUR FAITH AT SCHOOL OR WORK—AND WHAT YOU WANTED TO HAPPEN.

STEP 2

Instead of handing out Repro Resource 10, try another option. During the week before the session, find a volunteer (student or adult) who doesn't mind getting wet. At this point in the session, have the person sit in a child's empty wading pool at the front of your meeting place. (You won't need the pool if you meet outside.) Next to the pool, place a few loaded squirt guns and a few bowls of small candies. Have group members stand in front of the pool. Read the items from Repro Resource 10 aloud, one at a time. As you do, kids should demonstrate their answers as follows: "Frequently"—Give the person in the pool two candies; "Sometimes"—Give the person one candy; "Seldom"—Squirt the person once; "Never"—Squirt the person twice. After working your way through the list, ask: **What happens to your faith when people "feed" you positive comments about Christianity? What happens when they "throw cold water on you" with negative comments?** Be sure to thank your volunteer before discussing the kinds of comments about faith that kids typically hear.

STEP 5

Instead of having kids sit in small groups, give each person paper and a pen. Send each group member hunting for three others who go to the same school, are in the same grade, live in the same part of town, or have some other common interest. Kids should write down the names, addresses, phone numbers, and prayer concerns of the three people they find.

STEP 1

Members of a small group may feel isolated much of the time. So you may want to try to intensify those feelings with a roleplay. When group members arrive, meet them at the door using hushed tones and implying a sense of urgency. Usher them to a dark, secluded area—perhaps a closet. Explain that every other Christian in the country has been arrested and imprisoned. The people listening to your voice are the only remaining free people. Ask: **Where do we go from here? Do we disband and attempt to protect ourselves? Do we continue to meet secretly? Should we try to tell our closest friends that we're meeting, and try to build up a bigger group, or should we keep our mouths shut?** Afterward, explain that we don't actually face such dangers. The only things that prevent us from telling other people about Jesus are our personal fears. Then continue the session as written.

STEP 3

Rather than using Repro Resource 11 as written, try a simpler option for your small group. Ask volunteers to read aloud the three Scripture passages on the sheet—Ecclesiastes 4:7-12; Acts 2:42-47; and Ephesians 4:11-16. Then discuss as a group how different people might respond to these passages. Ask: **For what kinds of situations might these passages be especially helpful? Why?** Use the information on the "Seeker" slips on Repro Resource 11 to supplement your discussion.

STEP 1

With a large group, you might want to try a different opening game. Have kids form two teams. Give each team a bucket of golf balls. Place two wastebaskets (one for each team) at one end of the room. The object of the game is for a team to get all of its golf balls in its wastebasket. One team will line up relay-style. Each member will run a golf ball across the room, drop it in the wastebasket, and run back to tag the next person in line (who will do the same thing). The other team will line up "fireman style," with its members spaced evenly from one side of the room to the other. Team members will pass golf balls from person to person as quickly as possible. See which team finishes first. Afterward, ask: **What are some other times when it's good to have more than one person working together on something?** Get a few responses, then go through the last two paragraphs of Step 1.

STEP 5

As a group, plan a "Fellowship Night." Assign group members to different planning committees for the event. Put one committee in charge of getting a speaker for the event. Put another committee in charge of special music. Put another committee in charge of games and activities. Put another committee in charge of setup and cleanup. Put another committee in charge of refreshments. Make sure that everyone is involved in the planning process. If your event is successful, it could do wonders in setting the tone of fellowship for your group.

HEARD IT ALL BEFORE

LITTLE BIBLE BACKGROUND

FELLOWSHIP & WORSHIP

STEP 3

Many kids have heard that Christians should be close and supportive, but have never experienced such relationships themselves. As a result, they may feel a support network of Christian friends can exist only in Bible verses and curriculum plans. If at all possible, share a personal example of how having Christian friends in high school or college made it easier for you to hold onto your faith. If you can't come up with an example, try to find someone else—a group member or an adult in your church—who can. Interview that person, asking questions like these: **How did you find your Christian friend(s)? How did you spend your time together? How did that help you? What might have happened to your faith if you hadn't found Christian friend(s)?**

STEP 5

Kids may be cynical about the long-term significance of this brief sharing of information. They may think, *Why bother? Next week we'll go right back to being totally disinterested in each other.* If that's the case, you may need to start small and build relationships slowly and steadily over the weeks and months ahead. Start with just names, addresses, and phone numbers in this meeting. In future weeks, consider bringing group members together by using some of the sessions in *When Kids Aren't Close,* a resource in the First Aid for Youth Groups series from David C. Cook.

STEP 3

If your group members don't have much Bible background, it's good to let them interact with Scripture as much as possible during your meetings. So restructure the seeker/speaker activity a bit. You should play the role of the seeker. Divide members into three groups, assigning each group one of the "speaker" passages. Read one of the seeker situations at a time, and let each group give you advice from its assigned Bible passage. Groups will be able to interact with one reasonably short passage of Scripture, yet will make six different applications.

STEP 4

Some group members without a lot of Bible background may feel a bit awkward asking and answering the "Do me a favor" questions from Repro Resource 12. If you think this might be a problem for some of your kids, have them go back through Repro Resource 10 instead. This time, have each person record all of the ways that he or she might become a positive Christian influence in the course of an average day. Can group members think of anyone during first period that they could invite to youth group? Can they eat lunch with a loner and invite her to church? Kids may be surprised at the number of opportunities that come to mind.

STEP 1

Have kids form teams. Give each team a deck of cards to use in building a house of cards. Let the teams know that a prize will be awarded for the house with the most stories. Kids will soon discover that their task is much easier when they work together. After the contest, ask the winning team: **Do you think it would have been possible for any of you to build this house by yourself—getting help from no one? Why or why not?** (It was much easier to build when ideas were shared, when there were more hands to support the building, and when they worked together as a team.) Use this activity to introduce the idea that "going against the flow" is a lot easier when you have others helping you.

STEP 5

To continue the party theme begun in Step 4, say: **God doesn't demand that all of our worship time be somber and slow. He calls us to rejoice with a harp, lyre, and clanging symbol, to praise Him with song, to celebrate our faith.** Play an upbeat tape of Christian music that your group members will enjoy. Wrap up your session with a time of worship to God, celebrating His goodness and thanking Him for giving us other Christians for support and strength.

MOSTLY GIRLS

MOSTLY GUYS

EXTRA FUN

STEP 3

Give your group members a chance to discuss some of the things they struggle with because they don't have Christian friends or family supporting them. If they're shy about opening up, you may wish to hand out paper and pencils for them to write down their struggles. Or you might have them share how they would feel if they were in the situation of one of the seekers on Repro Resource 11. When you hear some of the struggles your girls face, just listen. Don't try to offer solutions at this point; just encourage them to share their feelings and frustrations and allow them to get emotional support from the group. Encourage others to share how they feel upon hearing some of the struggles their peers are facing. Then say: **How did it feel to just be heard? To have someone share your hurts and frustrations? We don't always have the answers to each other's problems, but God created community so we can support each other as we did just now. Feels pretty good, huh?**

STEP 4

If the girls in your group are like most high school girls, they're very used to talking to their friends. They may not be used to talking to their friends about their Christianity, however. Make a statement to that effect. Then ask: **Is that true in your case? If so, why do you think that is?** (Some girls may say that their friends wouldn't understand. Others may say that they'd be embarrassed. Others may say that it's not a "normal" thing to do.) The first step in getting group members to talk with others about their faith is helping them understand why they don't. Take just a minute to pray for your girls and their reasons for not sharing; then move on to Step 5.

STEP 1

Many guys prefer activities that are messier than flipping frozen pancakes. If time and space permit, go outside and conduct an egg toss. First, have kids compete in the traditional way, with two-man teams seeing who can toss an egg the farthest distance without breaking the shell. After determining the winner in the two-man event, mark the distance covered by the winning team. Then have group members form three-person teams for which a double toss is required. (Person A tosses to Person B, who then relays the egg to Person C.) Again, determine the winning team and mark off the distance. Compare the distance covered by the two-person team with the distance that three people were able to cover. (The three-man teams should cover considerably more ground.) Point out that sometimes we limit ourselves by not including more people in our lives. This can be especially true when it comes to spiritual matters.

STEP 5

Rather than trying to establish spiritual intimacy by having the guys in your group pull inward, you may do better by challenging them to *reach out*. If they don't want to feel alone, many guys will be willing to go out and bring some more people in. Spend some time having group members plan some church-sponsored "guy things" that they can invite friends to. These activities can be as simple as Saturday morning touch football on the church lawn (check your church insurance policy) or as exotic as weekend camping or skydiving. Sometimes Christianity seems unappealing because it is perceived as being too wimpy. Challenge your guys to do what they can to change that misconception.

STEP 1

Begin the session with Hug Tag, a game in which the object is not to be caught alone. Explain that you will shout out a number; when you do, kids should form clusters with that number of people in each cluster. Anyone not in a cluster with the appropriate number of people is out. Continue calling out numbers until only two people remain. Afterward, point out that getting caught alone in trying to live a Christian life can also be a problem.

STEP 5

Assign each person the name of a different fruit, announcing each person's "fruit name" to the rest of the group. Have kids sit in a circle with one person standing in the center. One of the seated people (let's say it's "Apple") should begin by saying, "Apple loves Pear" (or any other "fruit" present, other than the one in the center). The center person, who is holding a rolled-up newspaper, should try to remember who Pear is and attempt to whack him or her before the person says, "Pear loves Banana" (or whomever). The seated "fruits" should try to keep from being whacked. If the center person succeeds in whacking one of them before he or she can name one of the other fruits, the center person exchanges places with the whacked person. Play until everyone is familiar with each other's "fruit" names. Then challenge kids to try to encourage each other during the week—using each other's secret fruit identities. The encouragements can take the form of phone calls, notes, cards, flowers, balloons, personal comments, or anything else kids can think of. If kids can infuse some of the fun of their youth group meetings into their school lives, they are a lot less likely to feel alone throughout the week.

STEP 1

Instead of flipping pancakes, rent one of the following videos. Show a scene as noted (after pre-screening it for appropriateness).

• *The Three Musketeers*. Play a scene in which the Musketeers display their friendship and defense of each other. Ask: **Apart from the swordplay, do you have any friendships like this? How could a "support group" like this help at school? Do you think Christian kids are more likely or less likely to have such a group than non-Christians are? Why?**

• *My Bodyguard*. Show a scene in which high school student Clifford is protected by Linderman, his hired bodyguard and fellow student. Ask: **When could you most use a bodyguard at school? What would you want your bodyguard to do? Do you ever feel you're "going it alone" at school? If so, when? Do you ever feel especially alone because you're a Christian? Explain.**

• *Robin Hood: Prince of Thieves*. Play a scene showing the camaraderie of Robin and his "merry men." Ask: **How would your life be different if our group were more like this group of friends? What would you expect from other members of the group? What could they expect from you?**

STEP 4

During Steps 4 and 5, while group members are "networking," play recorded songs in the background that encourage kids to think of themselves as belonging to each other as well as to God. Some examples might include "We Will Stand" (Russ Taff), "Friends" and "The Race Is On" (Michael W. Smith), "Where Do You Hide Your Heart?" and "On and On (Love Song)" (Amy Grant), "Undivided" (First Call), "Find a Hurt and Heal It" (Debby Boone), and "Help Me Love My Brother" (Tanya Goodman).

STEP 1

Bring in an Etch-a-Sketch drawing screen. Post one volunteer at one knob and another at the other knob. Explain that the two people are going to work together to draw something. The rest of the group will then try to guess what it is. But when you whisper to your volunteers what they're to draw, tell one to draw a fire hydrant; tell the other to draw a dog. Volunteers may not communicate in any way while they're drawing. See what happens. After a frustrating minute or two, call a halt to the drawing and explain what was going on. Use this as an illustration of what happens when we don't work together. In Step 2, save time by condensing Repro Resource 10 statements 3-9 into "At school, your teachers or classmates say something positive about being a Christian." You may want to read the statements aloud and let kids respond with voice votes rather than using the sheet as a read-and-circle exercise.

STEP 3

To reduce discussion time, use only the Seeker 1 and Seeker 5 slips. Instead of having Seekers roam and Speakers read verses continuously, have half the group at a time listen to each Speaker. To save more time, use either Step 4 or Step 5, but not both.

STEP 2

Add the following situations to Repro Resource 10:

• During the time you spend at an after-school club or organization, the staff people say something positive about being a Christian.

• During the time you spend just hanging out, your friends say something positive about being a Christian.

STEP 4

In the tradition of "Meteor Man" and "Blankman," create a superhero called "Fellowship Man." As a group, brainstorm some things that Fellowship Man might do in your kids' neighborhoods to promote fellowship among Christians. For instance, he might deliver at supersonic speed encouraging messages from one Christian to another. Or he might singlehandedly renovate an abandoned building to be used as a meeting place for a Christian Bible study. Afterward, discuss how your group members might accomplish some of the things they brainstormed for Fellowship Man.

STEP 1

To further illustrate the point that it's harder to stand up for something when you don't have support, divide your group into teams of three or four. Provide each group with the game Jenga. (If you can't find Jenga, building blocks from the church nursery will suffice nicely.) Instruct each group to remove parts of the tower one at a time until the tower collapses. You may wish to award prizes to the team with the fewest number of pieces remaining in its still-standing tower. Afterward, say: **As the support system of your tower was removed, it was gradually weakened until it collapsed. We're going to take a look today at how the same thing can happen to our faith.**

STEP 3

If you have very young junior highers who might find the soapbox step intimidating or a good target for junior high humor, make three audiotapes prior to each session on which you record a reading of each of the Speaker's passages repeated many times. When it's time for this activity, hand out only the Seeker slips. Have kids move from tape recorder to tape recorder, listening to the Speakers' messages.

STEP 3

After the Repro Resource 11 activity, have someone read aloud Hebrews 10:24, 25. Then spend a few minutes brainstorming as a group what might happen if Christians were to "give up meeting together." For instance, without others around to correct and challenge misguided ideas, some people might begin to follow cultish teachers. Without the support of fellow Christians, people who are facing tough times may be more likely to deal with their trying circumstances in negative ways.

STEP 5

As you wrap up the session, spend a few minutes as a group discussing the similarities and differences between the fellowship of first-century Christians and the fellowship of Christians today. Have group members read Acts 2:42-47; 4:32-37. Then ask: **Which practices of the first-century Christians have carried over to today? Which first-century practices have been dropped or changed? Why do you think those things haven't carried over to today? How do you think our society would be different today if Christians were more like their first-century counterparts? If you had your choice, would you rather be a first-century Christian or a Christian today? Why?**

DATE USED:

Approx. Time

STEP 1: *They Call Him Flipper* _____
- ❏ Small Group
- ❏ Large Group
- ❏ Fellowship & Worship
- ❏ Mostly Guys
- ❏ Extra Fun
- ❏ Media
- ❏ Short Meeting Time
- ❏ Combined Junior High/High School

Things needed:

STEP 2: *Daily Affirmation* _____
- ❏ Extra Action
- ❏ Urban

Things needed:

STEP 3: *Soapbox Speakers* _____
- ❏ Small Group
- ❏ Heard It All Before
- ❏ Little Bible Background
- ❏ Mostly Girls
- ❏ Short Meeting Time
- ❏ Combined Junior High/High School
- ❏ Extra Challenge

Things needed:

STEP 4: *Network* _____
- ❏ Little Bible Background
- ❏ Mostly Girls
- ❏ Media
- ❏ Urban

Things needed:

STEP 5: *Never Alone* _____
- ❏ Extra Action
- ❏ Large Group
- ❏ Heard It All Before
- ❏ Fellowship & Worship
- ❏ Mostly Guys
- ❏ Extra Challenge

Things needed:

SESSION 5

A Time to Zap, a Time to Zip

YOUR GOALS FOR THIS SESSION:

Choose one or more

☐ To help kids see that every conversation with an unbeliever can be important, and that we need to speak wisely.

☐ To help kids understand that God expects us to be honest and loving in our contacts with non-Christians, but that He doesn't expect us to always know what to say or to convince everyone.

☐ To help kids find their unique "voices" as witnesses for Christ and think about what they might say in specific situations.

☐ Other:_____
_____

Your Bible Base:

John 4:1-30, 39-42;
18:28—19:22

All the Answers

(Needed: Cut-apart copy of Repro Resource 13, table, prizes)

Before the session, cut the question cards from a copy of "Nothing but Questions" (Repro Resource 13). Place the cards facedown on a table at the front of your meeting place. Keep the answer card for yourself.

To start the meeting, have kids form two teams. The first person on Team A will come to the front of the room and pick a question card. The first person on Team B will also come to the front of the room and wait while the Team A player decides whether to try to answer the question and run to the back of the room, or just run to the back of the room without answering.

If the Team A player runs without answering, the Team B player must try to tag him or her before the person reaches the back of the room. If the Team A player answers and the Team B player thinks the answer is wrong, the Team B player should try to tag him or her.

Team A gets a point if its representative tries to answer and does so correctly—or if he or she doesn't answer and runs to the back of the room without being tagged. Team A gets an *extra* point if the Team B player tags an answerer whose answer was correct. Team B gets a point if the Team A member doesn't answer and is tagged, or if he or she gives a wrong answer and is tagged. If an answer is wrong and the answerer isn't tagged, nobody gets a point.

Repeat the process until you've used up the question cards. Give a prize to the team with the most points.

Then ask: **Team A members, did you feel like answering, bluffing, or running when it was your turn? Why?**

Team B members, what clues did you watch for that might tell you whether your opponent was about to run or was bluffing?

After hearing replies, point out that when it comes to talking with non-Christians about God, some Christians feel like Team A. They think non-Christians are just waiting to get them for not knowing the answer to every question.

Ask: **How do you feel about talking to non-Christians about God? Does the idea make you want to run? Bluff your way through? Or do you feel confident? Why?** Listen to volunteered replies, if there are any—but don't pressure anyone to answer.

STEP 2

Double-Oh-Heaven

(Needed: Three copies of Repro Resource 14)

OPTIONS

MOSTLY GIRLS

URBAN

Say: **There's another way to relate to non-Christians, of course. Let's find out what it is**.

Give copies of "For Our Guys Only" (Repro Resource 14) to three volunteer actors, with whom you've rehearsed beforehand (if possible). Have them perform the skit.

Afterward, ask: **What were the attitudes of James Bomb and "K" toward non-Christians?** (Non-Christians are scary, dangerous; we need to fight them even though we're supposed to witness to them too.)

Why might some Christians fear or even hate unbelievers? (The Christians may feel inferior, threatened, ridiculed; the sins of some unbelievers may be offensive; some Christians may feel frustrated when unbelievers don't respond to the Good News about Jesus.)

What was the problem with the approach James Bomb and "K" took? (It kept them from carrying out their real mission, which was to tell others about Jesus.)

In the skit, "K" said, "If you're going to be around non-Christians, James, you'd better be prepared." Is that true? If so, how do we need to prepare? Listen to answers without evaluating them. Then explain that studying the way Jesus talked with unbelievers is one good way to be prepared.

STEP **3**

Word Balloons

(Needed: Bibles, balloons, markers)

Have kids reassemble the two teams from Step 1. Give Team A at least 20 uninflated balloons. Give Team B at least 15. Each team will need a few broad-tipped markers too.

Say: **You know those word balloons that show what people are saying in comic strips? We're going to make some real word balloons today.**

Have Team A read John 4:1-30, 39-42—the story of Jesus' conversation with the Samaritan woman at the well. Have Team B read John 18:28–19:22—the story of Jesus' conversation with Pilate.

After a few minutes, say: **As a team, boil down the conversation you've just read about. Team A should take each line spoken by Jesus or the Samaritan woman or the townspeople, condense that line to no more than three words, and write those three words on a blown-up balloon. You'll need 16 balloons to record the whole conversation.**

Team B should take each line spoken by Jesus or Pilate, condense it to no more than three words, and write those three words on a blown-up balloon. You'll need 10 balloons to cover the whole conversation. [NOTE: Team B should record only the lines spoken in John 18:33-38; 19:8-11 rather than in its whole passage.]

After several minutes, ask: **What was tough about this exercise?** (Boiling each part of the conversation down to three words or less; writing on the balloons without breaking them.)

Say: **In this exercise, you had to choose your words carefully. You also had to be gentle. The same is true of our conversations with people who don't know Jesus.**

Have Team A hold up its balloons in order and use them to describe its conversation to Team B. The condensation could take many forms, but here's one possible version.

John 4:1-30, 39-42
Jesus: "A drink, please?"
Woman: "We can't talk."
Jesus: "Want living water?"
Woman: "What living water?"
Jesus: "Drink, never thirst."
Woman: "I'll take it!"

Jesus: "Get your husband."
Woman: "I have none."
Jesus: "You've had five."
Woman: "We worship differently."
Jesus: "Soon you'll learn."
Woman: "Messiah is coming."
Jesus: "I am he."
Woman: "I found Christ!"
Woman: "He knows everything!"
People: "He's the Savior!"

Ask Team A: **From the passage you read, what can we learn about how to talk to someone who doesn't know Jesus but is open to learning about Him?** Answers will vary. As needed, supplement replies with the following points.

1. *You don't have to jump right to the "big message."* Jesus started by asking for a drink.

2. *Don't let your differences stand in the way.* Jews and Samaritans, men and women didn't talk much. Jesus talked to the woman anyway.

3. *Talk about things the other person understands and is interested in.* Jesus talked about water and the woman's husbands.

4. *Respect the other person's beliefs, but explain yours too.* Jesus didn't ridicule Samaritan worship, but made it clear that salvation was from the Jews and would be available to Samaritans too.

5. *Be willing to say clearly who Jesus is and what He wants from us.* Jesus came right out and said He was the Messiah, even though the woman could have responded by laughing at him.

6. *Spend as much time as it takes.* Instead of just talking once with the woman, Jesus stayed in town for two days so that everyone could get to know Him.

Then have Team B hold up its balloons in order and use them to describe its conversation to Team A. Here's one possible condensation.

John 18:33-38; 19:8-11
Pilate: "You're the king?"
Jesus: "You think so?"
Pilate: "What's your crime?"
Jesus: "My kingdom's elsewhere."
Pilate: "You're a king."
Jesus: "King of truth."
Pilate: "What is truth?"
Pilate: "He is innocent."
Pilate: "Speak or die!"
Jesus: "God's in charge."

Ask Team B: **From the passage you read, what can we learn about how to talk to someone who's skeptical about God or even hostile toward Him?** Answers will vary. As needed, supplement replies with the following points.

1. *Don't be afraid.* Pilate could have had Jesus killed at any moment, but Jesus spoke honestly and without fear.

2. *Find out what the person believes and why.* Jesus first asked what Pilate really believed about Him and how Pilate had come to that conclusion.

3. *Answer questions when you can, but you don't have to answer everything.* Jesus answered most of Pilate's questions, but not all of them.

4. *Speak politely, even if the other person doesn't.* Pilate lost his temper, but Jesus kept giving thoughtful replies.

5. *When possible, keep bringing the conversation back to the main subject—God.* Pilate wanted to solve a legal problem, not discuss religion. Jesus had more important things in mind. Without ignoring Pilate, Jesus managed to keep talking about His kingdom, truth, and the fact that Pilate had power only because God allowed it.

6. *Don't expect visible results.* Pilate was impressed with Jesus' innocence, but still okayed His crucifixion. We may not see positive results for a long time, if ever.

STEP 4

Zap or Zip?

(Needed: Copies of Repro Resource 15)

Say: **Every encounter Jesus had with people was different. Sometimes He zapped them—as He did with the self-righteous Pharisees. Sometimes He "zipped" up and didn't say a thing—as He did with Pilate. Sometimes He did something else—as with the Samaritan woman.**

If you're talking with someone who doesn't know Jesus, when should you zap? When should you zip? When should you do something else? Listen to a couple of replies, if there are any. Then explain that looking at some hypothetical situations might help your group sort its zips from its zaps.

Distribute copies of "Open-and-Shut Cases" (Repro Resource 15). Have kids form three groups. Assign one situation to each group. Give kids a few minutes to discuss their situations and to come up with ideas on what they might say. Then have them share results. Don't be surprised if kids disagree with each other over what should be said. Affirm as many answers as you can and avoid branding any as wrong. Instead,

OPTIONS

EXTRA ACTION

SMALL GROUP

LARGE GROUP

MOSTLY GIRLS

EXTRA FUN

URBAN

JR. HIGH / HIGH SCHOOL COMBINED

EXTRA CHALLENGE

ask kids how their answers square with the principles you've already talked about in this session. Encourage kids to wrestle with the situations and to be open with you about how they'd feel in each case.

Pay special attention to kids' replies to the "d" questions for each case. It's likely that many of your kids feel the confusion and doubt reflected in these questions, though they may be reluctant to say so. Rather than berating those who feel this way or trying to deal with their doubts in this meeting, simply acknowledge that we won't have much to say to unbelievers if we're not sure about our own beliefs.

If the "d" questions bring doubts to the surface in your group, plan to deal with these in a future meeting. Such resource series as the *Custom Discipleship* series or other books in this series, both from Cook Communications Ministries., can help you address those issues.

Have It Your Way

(Needed: Paper, pencils)

Give each person a piece of paper and a pencil. Have kids move their chairs as far apart as possible. Say: **I can't tell you what you should say about your faith to the non-Christians you know. What you say should come from who you are, from what you really believe, from your own experience with Jesus. It doesn't have to sound like anybody else. It should sound like you. I'm going to read some sentence starters. Your job is to complete each sentence on your paper. I'm not going to collect your papers, so feel free to write what you really think and feel.**

Read as many of the following sentence starters as you have time for, pausing after each to let kids think and write.

The thing that appeals to me about Jesus is . . .
I used to think God was . . .
I first heard about Jesus when . . .
The thing that caught my attention was . . .
I was confused about . . .
What helped me understand was . . .
I wasn't sure about . . .
But I knew I wanted . . .

OPTIONS

EXTRA ACTION

HEARD IT ALL BEFORE

LITTLE BIBLE BACKGROUND

FELLOWSHIP & WORSHIP

EXTRA FUN

MEDIA

EXTRA CHALLENGE

I finally decided when . . .
I decided to . . .
One person who helped me was . . .
I went ahead and . . .
I felt . . .
It took me a while to . . .
Now I think God is . . .
I still have trouble with . . .
I recommend Jesus because . . .

When kids are done, encourage them to keep their papers and to look at the first and last sentence completions during the week as reminders of what Jesus has done for them personally.

Close in prayer, thanking God that each person in your group is different, and that each person has something special to share with others about Him. Encourage kids to talk with you later if they aren't sure about their relationship with Christ or if they have questions that keep them from sharing their faith.

NOTES

N?THING B?

QUESTI?NS

? 1. How many miles from the sun is the planet Mercury? ?

? 2. What makes Mexican jumping beans jump?

? 3. Is pine a hardwood or a softwood? ?

4. Which has more people in it—Portland, Maine, or Portland, Oregon? ?

? 5. What does "Eureka," the motto of the state of California, mean?

? 6. In what country was the inventor of the telephone born?

7. What is Occam's Razor? ?

? 8. How many lines is a sonnet supposed to contain? ?

? 9. Which is worse: a first-degree burn or a third-degree burn? ?

? 10. In the manual alphabet, what letter is represented by holding up the index finger, the middle finger, and the ring finger at the same time? ?

? 11. What word could mean "harpoons," "golf clubs," or "handcuffs"? ?

? 12. In what year was Abraham Lincoln born? ?

ANSWER CARD (for leader only)
1. 36 million
2. The movement of a moth larva inside
3. Softwood
4. Portland, Oregon
5. "I have found it"
6. Alexander Graham Bell was born in Scotland.
7. A scientific rule that entities should not be multiplied unnecessarily
8. 14
9. Third-degree
10. W
11. Irons
12. 1809

For Our Guys Only

PENNYCANDY: Oh, there you are, James. "K" has been waiting for you in the top-secret laboratory.

BOMB (striking a macho pose)**:** The name is Bomb. James Bomb.

PENNYCANDY: Yes, I know. You're James Bomb, Christian secret agent. You don't have to keep reminding me.

BOMB: Very well, Miss Hennypenny.

PENNYCANDY: That's Pennycandy. (She exits.)

BOMB: Right. (He opens an imaginary door and sees "K," who is pouring imaginary chemicals from one imaginary test tube to another.)

K: Ah, Double-oh-Heaven. You've arrived at last.

BOMB (striking a macho pose)**:** The name is Bomb. James Bomb.

K: Yes, yes, I know. You're James Bomb, Christian secret agent Double-oh-Heaven. You needn't remind me all the time.

BOMB: Very well, "T."

K: That's "K."

BOMB: Right. What have you got for me today?

K: As you know, James, it's a frightening world out there. It's full of . . . non-Christians!

BOMB: I know, "K." But that's why we have you, eh?

K: Exactly. If you're going to be around non-Christians, James, you'd better be prepared. So I've come up with a few items to help when you get into tight situations.

BOMB: Such as?

K: Let's say you're in biology class. The teacher is promoting the theory of evolution. You're wearing this specially designed cuff link (holds up imaginary cuff link and puts it on BOMB's sleeve), which contains a tiny heat-seeking missile. You simply raise your hand and blow that atheistic teacher to kingdom come.

BOMB: I like it. Subtle, yet effective.

K: Now, let's say you're in the locker room. One of those non-Christian students starts to tell a dirty joke. What do you do?

BOMB: Shoot him with my cuff links?

K: No, Double-oh-Heaven—you're not wearing cuff links. You're in the locker room! You take this specially designed towel (holds up imaginary towel), which has been impregnated with sulfuric acid, and fling it over the joke-teller's head. His filthy laughter turns to screams as the acid dissolves his flesh—right down to the skull.

BOMB: I like it. Quick, yet unobtrusive.

K: Precisely. Now, let's assume your school day is over. You are approached by a group of non-Christians who want you to go to a party. You know what that means.

BOMB: Of course. Drinking, drugs, loud music—even young men without ties.

K: Disgusting, but true. What do you do?

BOMB: Hmm. Cuff links and towels won't do the trick.

K: Correct. You need this ballpoint pen. (Holds up imaginary pen.) Just push the button, and you detonate a nuclear device that wipes out every living thing within a radius of ten miles.

BOMB: But aren't I a living thing? Wouldn't I be wiped out too?

K: Not to worry, Double-oh-Heaven. Your pocket protector will surround you with an electromagnetic force field.

BOMB: So I'll be shaken, not stirred?

K: You might say that. And once you've destroyed everyone around you, you can complete your mission.

BOMB: Which is?

K: To share your faith with those around you.

BOMB: But won't they all be dead?

K: Blast it, James, whose side are you on? Every invention is bound to have a few bugs in it! I can't help it if the plan isn't absolutely perfect!

BOMB: Sorry, "K." It's a wonderful plan. You've done it again.

K: That's better. Try not to forget yourself again, eh, Double-oh-Heaven? (He exits.)

BOMB: Oh, I haven't forgotten myself. (Strikes macho pose.) I'm Bomb. James Bomb. Right, "Z"?

K (from offstage)**:** That's "K"!

BOMB: Just testing. (He exits.)

OPEN-AND- SHUT CASES

1. Eric, a non-Christian, is a friend of yours. Last night, his long-time girl-friend said she didn't want to go out with him anymore. Today at school, Eric looked so tense you thought he might try to put his fist through a wall. After school, in the parking lot, he suddenly tells you, "From now on, my life is [expletive], I just know it." What should you say if . . .

    (a) you and Eric have never talked about anything really serious before?
    (b) Eric knows you're a Christian, and once said he wished he could feel as peaceful about life as you seem to?
    (c) you tried to tell Eric about Jesus once, and he didn't seem interested?
    (d) you'd like Eric to become a Christian, but doubt that being a Christian would solve his girlfriend problems?

2. During the sex education unit in your health class, a guest speaker says, "Homosexuality used to be considered abnormal. Today we know it's simply an alternative, neither right nor wrong in itself." What should you say if . . .

    (a) the teacher says afterward, "Some of you may disagree with the views expressed by our speaker; feel free to comment on what she said"?
    (b) the teacher asks for comments, and you know that the student sitting in front of you is struggling with what seem to be homosexual tendencies?
    (c) the teacher doesn't ask for comments, but the guest speaker asks whether there are any questions?
    (d) you know the Bible opposes homosexuality, but aren't sure why?

3. Hariko is a Japanese exchange student you've come to know fairly well. You invite her to a church youth group party, where she seems to have a good time. Afterward, you ask what she thought about it. She says, "It was fun. The part at the end where they talked about the Bible was strange to me, but my family is Shinto." What should you say if . . .

    (a) you know Hariko's family doesn't take its religion very seriously, and she's curious about this thing called Christianity?
    (b) you know Hariko's parents are serious about their religion, and would be extremely offended if Hariko became a Christian?
    (c) Hariko is returning to Japan tomorrow, and you may never get to talk with her again?
    (d) you can't see how God would keep a nice person like Hariko out of heaven, even if she's not a Christian?

NOTES

STEP 4

Skip the case studies on Repro Resource 15. Plan to make one point: our decisions to "zap" or "zip" should be based on which action is more likely to bring others closer to God. Introduce this idea with the following activity. Designate one spot in your meeting place as "where God is." As you call out the following statements, pausing after each, kids should move closer to or farther away from the spot to show whether they think the statements attract people to God or drive them away. Here are the statements: (a) **Your religion is really dumb.** (b) **I'd like to hear more about your beliefs if you'll let me tell you about mine too.** (c) **Hey, it's fine with me if you're a homosexual; who am I to judge?** (d) **God says homosexual behavior is wrong, but He loves homosexuals.** (e) **I've had doubts about the Bible too; I don't have all the answers.** (f) **Quit asking all these questions; you just have to believe, that's all.** (g) **Jesus will solve all of your problems.** (h) **I don't know quite how to say it, but I want to tell you about God because I care about you.** After discussing kids' responses, point out that it may be better to stay silent than to insult someone (a), water down the truth (c), try to pressure people to believe (f), or make false promises (g). But it's better to speak up if we can do it with respect, honesty, and care.

STEP 5

Instead of having kids complete sentences, have them express their feelings about Jesus by finding an object in or around your meeting place that somehow reminds them of Him or their relationship with Him. Let volunteers explain their choices.

STEP 3

Assembling the word balloon conversations may be a lot of trouble for a small group. If so, let group members simply act out the stories. They can still paraphrase the conversations in their own words, and the same points can be made without so much effort. Each of the stories has two main characters. If your group has more than four people, one person can serve as narrator for each story. Give your performers a few minutes to plan how they want to present their story and to familiarize themselves with the speaking parts. Then have each group perform its story.

STEP 4

Don't have kids form groups to discuss the situations on Repro Resource 15. Let kids act out the situations as roleplays instead. (A small group should zip through all three of them fairly quickly.) Group members should take turns acting out what they would (or wouldn't) say in each situation. With roleplays, characters (Eric, the guest speaker, and Hariko) are allowed to "talk back," which prevents group members from coming up with any "easy answers." It's one thing to express what you might say in a situation. It's quite another thing to be placed in that situation while other people witness your words and actions.

STEP 1

With a large group, you might want to try a different opening activity. One at a time, have each group member stand up and give a trivia question—one that he or she knows the answer to—to everyone else in the group. If the person successfully stumps everyone else in the group (including you)—if no one else can answer the question correctly—he or she gets a point. The person with the most points after three or four rounds is the winner. Afterward, introduce the topic of the session by pointing out that all of us know things that other people don't. In the case of Christians, we should be sharing the things we know about Christ that others don't know.

STEP 4

With a large group, you have the opportunity to expand the Repro Resource 15 activity. Ask for volunteers to act out the scenarios on the sheet. After each scenario has been performed, go through the four variables (a, b, c, and d), asking group members to suggest responses for each situation. Then have your volunteers continue their roleplays, using group members' suggested responses to see how the scenario plays out.

STEP 3

Kids may know perfectly well that Jesus knew how and when to talk about faith, but don't see the need to follow His example. Before looking at the stories of the Samaritan woman and Jesus' meeting with Pilate, take time to read Philippians 2:3-8. Ask: **What is it about Jesus that Paul wants us to imitate? If we care only about our own interests, will we tend to talk about our faith or not? Why? If we look out for others' needs, will we tend to tell them about Jesus or not? Why?** Kids may be used to seeing faith-sharing as their awful burden, not as an expression of love to someone else. Encourage them to think of "witnessing" as one of many ways in which they can serve others, meeting people's real needs. In other words, it's supposed to be something we do *for* people, not *to* them. In Step 4, if kids seem to feel the situations on Repro Resource 15 are hokey or implausible, invite them to rewrite the first paragraph of each situation to make it more "realistic."

STEP 5

If you think the sentence starters will encourage kids to write insincere, clichéd completions, try the following starters instead: (a) **My biggest question about Jesus is . . .** (b) **You might not like being a Christian because . . .** (c) **I wish somebody else from my church could talk to you about this because . . .** (d) **I hope you won't think that because I'm a Christian I . . .** (e) **In spite of everything, believing in God makes sense to me because . . .** (f) **If you wanted to know more about Jesus, the best thing to do would be . . .**

STEP 3

If the Bible is new to your group members, the issue of witnessing is likely to be a novel concept as well. During this step, you probably shouldn't assume that group members know they are *supposed* to go around telling other people about Jesus. Introduce the story of the Samaritan woman at the well as an example of what can happen when people *do* tell others about Jesus. You might also want to have kids look at Matthew 5:13-16; Acts 1:8; 1 Timothy 4:12-16; and 1 Peter 3:15-17. Read each of these passages and discuss the importance (and potential results) of Christians telling other people about Jesus and the truths of God's Word.

STEP 5

Rather than having group members silently write out the completion of the sentences in this step, ask them instead to describe to the others in the group how they found out about God (or Jesus), how they got involved with church, and so forth. Perhaps the importance of evangelism will become obvious from their personal stories. In addition to helping kids see what they may have in common, this option will also help them begin talking about spiritual things in a safe environment. If you can help them become comfortable conversing openly in your group, it should be more natural for them to do so in secular settings.

STEP 1

Have your kids form small groups. Give each group several markers and a piece of poster board or a large sheet of paper. Instruct the members of each group to share with each other—and write on their poster—their response to this sentence starter: **When I think about talking to a non-Christian about Jesus, I . . .** Give kids several minutes to think about their answers. Encourage them to be honest in their responses. After everyone is finished, set aside the posters to use later in the session.

STEP 5

After you've discussed how Jesus responded to non-believers and after you've considered some of the wonderful things He's done, refer back to the posters your kids created earlier (see the "Fellowship & Worship" option for Step 1). As a group, discuss the responses listed on the posters. Based on what they've learned in this session, group members should brainstorm some things that they can do about the negative responses listed on the posters. Close the session in prayer, asking God to help your group members deal with the fears and concerns they have about sharing their faith.

STEP 2

The skit "For Our Guys Only" (Repro Resource 14) should work pretty well as written, but you may wish to change "James Bomb" to "Jane Bomb." After the skit, ask: **Does the fact that we're female change in any way our responsibility to talk to non-Christians about Jesus?** (No. Though the ministry as a profession has been and continues to be dominated by males, females have just as much right and responsibility to share the Gospel.) **Is Jesus restricted from working through someone by gender, age, height, or hair color?** (Of course not. There are many examples in the Bible of women—young and old—who did great things for God.) Say: **The fact that we are female in no way excuses us from a life that is glorifying to God and that reaches out to non-Christians in a loving and Christ-like way.**

STEP 4

Change the scenarios on Repro Resource 15 as follows:

• 1. Change Eric to Erica, who just lost her boyfriend. She's terribly depressed, has been crying all day, and comes to you saying, "My life is over. I'm a failure in life. Nobody can love me." (The options remain the same.)

• 2. During the sex education unit in your health class, a guest speaker says, "When abortions were illegal, they were a risky procedure. Now that they're legal, there's no reason a woman shouldn't be able to obtain one if she desires." What should you say if . . .

(b) the teacher asks for comments, and you know the student sitting in front of you recently had an abortion?

(d) you know that the Bible opposes abortion, but aren't sure where it actually says that? (Options "a" and "c" remain the same.)

STEP 1

If some of your guys might think a tag game is a bit silly, try a lying game instead. Expand the quiz (using an almanac or a similar resource); focus on open-ended questions that no one is likely to know the answers to. Ask for three volunteers at a time; give each of the three a slip of paper. On one of the slips should be the correct answer to the question you will ask. The other two slips should be blank. When you ask the question, the two guys with the blank slips should try to fake an answer. The person with the correct answer should, of course, read it without being obvious that he has been given the answer. After each of the three volunteers has provided an answer, let the rest of the group members vote for the person that they think is correct. Score one point per vote. Rotate trios of volunteers until everyone has had an equal opportunity to answer a question; then tally the votes. See if any of the "bluffers" in the group were more convincing than those who told the truth. Afterward, make applications to evangelism, challenging your guys to be honest in their own expressions of faith and to watch out for others who might deceive them with clever bluffing.

STEP 3

The account of the Samaritan woman at the well is a classic Bible story. But if you're looking for more of a "guy thing" to discuss, you might consider substituting or adding Jesus' interactions with Nicodemus (John 3:1-21) and Zacchaeus (Luke 19:1-9). Both of these passages record conversations that Jesus had with males who were seeking truth.

STEP 4

At the end of this step, give kids one of the balloons that they went to the trouble of blowing up. Have kids stand in a circle. Ask each person to name a reason that he or she is occasionally reluctant to tell others about Jesus. Kids should be honest and should list as many reasons as they can possibly think of. For each reason that's mentioned, a balloon should be tossed into the center of the circle. When kids can think of nothing else, have a volunteer read Luke 12:4-12. Assure your group members that God will be with them, no matter what happens. But then suggest that it is also important for kids to be there for each other. To demonstrate, have group members gradually tighten the circle, keeping the balloons in front of them at all times. As kids keep getting closer together, have them "crush their fears" (by popping the balloons with their feet) as they go. Kids will probably have to physically lean on each other in order to do so. Explain that if they continue to draw closer to one another and to God, their fears will not seem nearly as severe.

STEP 5

No matter what you say or do, some kids are likely to remain reluctant to talk about Jesus with other people face-to-face. Try not to make them feel guilty about such feelings. Instead, close with a positive reinforcement that there are many ways to express one's faith besides verbal interaction. Provide an opportunity for kids to express their feelings about Jesus in other ways—such as writing a song, creating a poem for the school newspaper, painting or drawing, creating a jingle for a top-40 radio station, and so on. Ask all of your kids to select a creative way to express their faith in God and demonstrate it for others in the group.

STEP 3

Instead of using the balloon activity, rent or purchase the animated video *The Easter Story* (from Turner Home Entertainment's "The Greatest Adventure: Stories from the Bible" series). Play the section in which Jesus is tried before the religious leaders (starting with the high priest's words "Speak! Speak!") and Peter denies Jesus (ending with Peter sobbing and running away). Afterward, say: **In these scenes, Jesus was reluctant to speak. So was Peter. How were their motivations different?** (Jesus chose not to defend Himself; He was on His way to the cross for our sake. He did reveal His identity, which only got Him in more trouble. Peter, in contrast, was afraid to be identified with Jesus. He tried to protect himself by not telling the truth.) **What can we learn from this about when to speak up as Christians and when to stay silent?** (We need to tell the truth, even when it's risky; we should be careful about getting defensive; being afraid isn't a good reason to remain silent; sometimes we might need to be silent for another's sake.) Then, as a group, look at the story of the Samaritan woman (John 4) as a model of how to speak up.

STEP 5

Play one or more songs that encourage kids to tell others about Jesus. Some examples you might use include "Asleep in the Light" (Steve Camp), "Can You Reach My Friend?" (Debby Boone), "In His Name" (White Heart), "How Can They Live Without Jesus?" (Keith Green), and "People Need the Lord" (Steve Green).

STEP 1

Try a shorter opener. Bring a bag of assorted small, edible items—a gummy worm, a lima bean, a chocolate-covered peanut, a brussels sprout, etc. About half of the items should be "yummy" and half should be "yucky." As soon as kids are seated, take an item out of the bag and hide it in your hand. Without revealing what the item is, offer it to a group member. He or she must decide in five seconds whether to open his or her mouth. If the mouth opens, you get to pop the item in. The person must eat it. If not, you reveal the item, put it aside, and repeat the process with another item and the next person. Do this until everyone's had to choose, or until two minutes elapses, whichever comes first. Then ask: **How did you decide whether to open your mouth?** Chances are that fear played a major role in many of the decisions. Point out that you're going to be discussing when Christians should open their mouths and when they should close their mouths—and the role fear sometimes plays in that decision.

STEP 3

Skip the balloon activity and the conversation condensations. Simply have the teams read their passages and go directly to the two discussion questions in the session (each of which begins with **From the passage you read, what can we learn . . .**). In Step 4, use only situations 1 and 2; discuss them as a whole group instead of splitting up, rejoining, and sharing results. In Step 5, use just one sentence starter: **Five words that I think best describe Jesus are . . .**

STEP 2

Rather than using Repro Resource 14, give your group members an opportunity to use their creativity as well as their performing skills. Have kids form pairs or small groups. Instruct each group to come up with a brief (30-45 seconds) skit that illustrates how *not* to tell others about Jesus. The skits should be humorous, but should not be offensive. After a few minutes, have each group perform its skit. Afterward, ask: **Why might some Christians fear or dislike non-Christians? How might Christians prepare to talk to non-Christians?** Then move on to Step 3.

STEP 4

Replace Situation 2 on Repro Resource 15 with the following:

• During the sex education unit in your health class, a guest speaker says, "Being sexually active is OK, as long as you're ready for it and you practice safe sex." What should you say if . . .

(a) the teacher says afterward, "Some of you may disagree with the views expressed by our speaker; feel free to comment on what she said"?

(b) the teacher asks for comments, and you know that the student sitting in front of you has a reputation for being quite sexually active?

(c) the guest speaker asks whether there are any questions?

(d) you know that the Bible says to save sex for marriage, but you're not quite sure that you agree?

STEP 3

Junior highers may not be able to condense the conversations between Jesus and the Samaritan woman and Jesus and Pilate. So you may want to write the condensed statements on the balloons prior to the session. Then instruct kids to put the statements in order. (Be ready to assist with this, if necessary.) After the balloons are blown up and in order, ask Team A: **From the passage you read, what can we learn about how to talk to someone who doesn't know Jesus but is open to learning about Him?** Continue with Step 3 as written.

STEP 4

Replace Situation 1 on Repro Resource 15 with the following:

• Eric, a non-Christian, is a friend of yours. Last night, after another fight, his dad walked out on his mom and the family. Today at school, Eric looked so tense that you thought he might put his fist through a wall. After school, in the gym, he suddenly tells you, "My life is over. I just know it." What should you say if . . .

(a) you and Eric have never talked about anything really serious before?

(b) Eric knows you're a Christian, and once said he wished he could feel as peaceful about life as you seem to?

(c) you tried to tell Eric about Jesus once, and he didn't seem interested?

(d) you'd like Eric to become a Christian, but doubt that being a Christian would solve his family problems?

STEP 4

After you've worked through Repro Resource 15, have someone read aloud 1 Peter 3:15 ("Always be prepared to give an answer to everyone who asks you to give the reason for the hope that you have"). Then give your group members an opportunity to test their ability to carry out this instruction. One at a time, ask for volunteers to sit in a "hot seat" at the front of the room. The rest of the group members will then fire questions at the volunteer that a non-Christian might ask a Christian. For instance, they might ask, "How do you know the Bible is true?" "Do you think that being a Christian makes you better than non-Christians?" and "How could a loving God send anyone to hell?" If a volunteer struggles in answering a question, brainstorm as a group some responses that he or she might give.

STEP 5

As you wrap up the session, give your group members an opportunity to study the "Gospel-sharing techniques" of some other people in Scripture: Peter (in Acts 2:1-41), Philip (in Acts 8:26-40), and Paul (in 2 Cor. 11:16–12:10). If you don't have time to study these passages during the session, assign them as homework. Ask kids to make a list of the principles they find in these passages that they might apply to their own lives as they share the Gospel with others.

DATE USED:

Approx. Time

STEP 1: *All the Answers* _____
❏ Large Group
❏ Fellowship & Worship
❏ Mostly Guys
❏ Short Meeting Time
Things needed:

STEP 2: *Double-Oh-Heaven* _____
❏ Mostly Girls
❏ Urban
Things needed:

STEP 3: *Word Balloons* _____
❏ Small Group
❏ Heard It All Before
❏ Little Bible Background
❏ Mostly Guys
❏ Media
❏ Short Meeting Time
❏ Combined Junior High/High School
Things needed:

STEP 4: *Zap or Zip?* _____
❏ Extra Action
❏ Small Group
❏ Large Group
❏ Mostly Girls
❏ Extra Fun
❏ Urban
❏ Combined Junior High/High School
❏ Extra Challenge
Things needed:

STEP 5: *Have It Your Way* _____
❏ Extra Action
❏ Heard It All Before
❏ Little Bible Background
❏ Fellowship & Worship
❏ Extra Fun
❏ Media
❏ Extra Challenge
Things needed: